Government and Society in Nineteenth Century Britain
Commentaries on British Parliamentary Papers

CRIME AND LAW
in Nineteenth Century Britain

Government and Society in Nineteenth Century Britain
Commentaries on British Parliamentary Papers

CRIME AND LAW
in Nineteenth Century Britain

W. R. Cornish   Jenifer Hart
A. H. Manchester   J. Stevenson

Introduction by P. and G. Ford

IRISH UNIVERSITY PRESS

IRISH UNIVERSITY PRESS

Irish University Press British Parliamentary Papers Series
CHIEF EDITORIAL ADVISERS
P. Ford
Professor Emeritus, Southampton University
Mrs. G. Ford

All forms of micro-publishing
© Irish Academic Press

ISBN 0 7165 2213 6

Published by IRISH ACADEMIC PRESS LTD
46 Kildare Street, Dublin 2, Ireland

Printed in Great Britain by offset lithography by
Billing & Sons Ltd, Guildford, London and Worcester

Contents

Abbreviations

BM Add. Mss.	British Museum Additional Manuscripts		
C., Cd., Cmd.	Command Paper	mins. of ev.	minutes of evidence
Ch.	Chairman	PRO	Public Record Office
ev.	evidence	q. (qq.)	question(s)
HC	House of Commons	R. Com.	Royal Commission
HL	House of Lords	Rep.	Report
		Sel. Cttee.	Select Committee

Citations

The form used for House and Command papers is:

> session/paper no./volume no./volume page no.

Example:

> 1845(602)xii,331

If the title has not been given in the text, the form should be preceded by the title and description:

> title and description/session/paper no./volume no./volume page no.

Examples:

> Game Law. Sel. Cttee. Rep.; 1845(602)xii,331
> London Squares. R.Com. Rep.; 1928-29 Cmd. 3196,viii,111

References are to the *House of Commons* bound sets, *except* where the paper is in the House of Lords set only. From this it follows:

a. Where the paper is the report of a Lords select committee (communicated to the Commons) it must be marked HL to indicate this and to distinguish it from a Commons select committee:

Example:

> Sale of Beer. Sel.Cttee.HL.Rep.; 1850(398)xviii,438.

b. Where the paper is in the Lords papers only, HL should be added to the paper number. This can be done in the form HL(259) or (HL.259).

c. For a reference to a statement on a particular page of a paper, the title and description should be followed by the *printed* page number of the paper:

> title etc./printed page no./session/paper no./volume no./vol. page no.

Example:

> Finance and Industry. Cttee.Rep.p.134;1930-31 Cmd.3897,xiii,219

Where the reference is to the Irish University Press the citation is:

> IUP/subject/title/volume no.

Example:

> IUP Monetary Policy: General 4.

Introduction to Parliamentary Papers

P. and G. Ford

A fully comprehensive definition of parliamentary papers would include all those which form part of the necessary machinery of parliamentary government, even those concerned with the procedures of the day-to-day business. But from the point of view of the researcher three groups are of primary importance. The first group, the Journals, record the things done in parliament. The second group, the Debates, record the things said in parliament (the publication of the House of Commons Debates became known as Hansard throughout the world and was at first not an official but a private venture receiving public subsidy). The third group, Papers arising in or presented to parliament deal with the formulation, development and execution of its policy. It is to this third group, for many years known as 'Blue Books' because of the blue paper with which most of them were covered, that the name Parliamentary Papers became particularly attached.

After 1801 the papers were gathered together and bound in two separate sessional sets, one for the House of Commons and the other for the House of Lords. These volumes include reports of select committees, composed of a limited number of members of either House appointed to examine particular problems, and reports of royal commissions and committees of enquiry appointed in form by the Crown though on the advice of ministers or by ministers themselves. These latter have the double advantage of comprising persons from outside the House thought to be experts on the subjects in hand, persons prominent in public affairs or representative of some body of opinion, experience or interest, and of not being limited in their work to the length of a parliamentary session. All these bodies reported the results of their enquiries together with the evidence taken to the authority which appointed them. The reports of select committees and the papers which departments were required by Act to send to parliament, because they originated *in* the House were grouped into a numbered series as House Papers. Royal commissions reported formally to the Crown — even submitting massive volumes of evidence for it to read — and committees reported to the minister concerned. Because these were the work of bodies *outside* the House, the papers were brought to the House and incorporated in the Sessional Papers through the use of an historic formula which embodies much of the development of constitutional monarchy, 'Presented by Command'.

It was these committees and commissions which uncovered the evils of the work of children in factories and mines, the evils of bad housing and sanitation and of inadequate water supply in the new sprawling towns created by the Industrial Revolution, as well as the difficulties relating to monetary policy and the new phenomenon of recurrent trade depressions. The witnesses brought before the enquiring bodies included the victims of the new industrial conditions — little children who had worked in factories and mines, the exploited immigrants in the sweated trades, and the leaders of the early efforts to unionize workmen, such as John Gast in 1815, John Doherty in 1838 and the whole of the top leadership of the great trade unions in 1867-69. What is more remarkable is that the oral evidence was printed verbatim. Even Marx was impressed by the commissions' plenary powers for getting at the truth, the competence and freedom from partisanship and respect of persons displayed by the English Factory Inspectors, the Medical Officers reporting on public health and the Commissioners of Enquiry into the exploitation of women and children, into housing and food. There is no parallel in the world for such a series of searching and detailed enquiries covering so long a span of years and embracing every phase of the transition from a rural aristocratic society to an industrialized democracy. It is the most significant of these reports on a century of investigation, the 'policy papers', that are embodied in the Irish University Press series.

The method of personal examination of witnesses had occasionally to be modified when central hearings were not practicable. Before the Benthamite conception of a unified central and local government machine had been realized in practice, the central authorities often knew little of what was going on in the localities. The many thousands of parishes administered the poor laws in their own ways so that the *Royal Commission on the Poor Laws* (1834) had to send round assistant commissioners to carry out and report on a detailed standardized plan of enquiry. The *Royal Commission on Municipal Corporations* (1835) had to make district enquiries on how the boroughs and 'places claiming to be boroughs' conducted their affairs. The effect of adverse forces on agriculture could be country-wide: the *Royal Commission on the Depressed Condition of the Agricultural Interests* (1881-82), on *Agricultural Depression* (1894-97) and the *Labour Commission* (1892-94) looking into agricultural labour, each made use of assistant commissioners to find out what was common and what was different in the problems of the various districts. These papers are a mine of information.

There are also the various famous reports by great civil servants, such as Horner's on the enforcement of factory legislation, Tremenheere's on the state of the mining districts, bound in the sets under the heading of commissioners' reports, and Southwood Smith's on the *Physical Causes of Sickness and Mortality to which the Poor are Exposed,* tucked away in an appendix to an annual report.

Two aspects of these investigations — the membership of the committees and the importance of British constitutional procedure — are worthy of note. The fullness and considerable integrity of these penetrating investigations were remarkable in that in the first half of the century the members of the committees and commissions which made them were not, as they would be today, drawn from or representative of the great bodies of the working classes. On the contrary, they were from the wealthy and ruling groups, for the composition of the House of Commons reflected the fact that even after the Reform Act of 1832 the number of voters was still but a tiny fraction of the adult population. The Northcote-Trevelyan proposals for the reform of the civil service by replacing recruitment by patronage with open competition, were approved by a cabinet all of whom, said Gladstone, who was a member of it, were more aristocratic than himself. No doubt they had their blind sides. For most of the century they assumed the existing class structure without much question; and there were fields in which their approach to problems and the conclusions they drew were influenced not only by the prevalent social philosophies, but class ideals and interests, as in the investigations into trade unions, game laws, etc. No matter how experienced or impartial they may be, members of a committee come to the task of inquiry with patterns of ideas related to their time. The report is not just summarized evidence, but evidence as interpreted by the committee. In weighing a report, therefore, a distinction must be made between the evidence upon which it is based and what the members have contributed to it. But the facts elicited in the examination of witnesses were not covered up or hidden — because apart from pressure by reforming groups, the constitutional procedure was that reports and evidence should be submitted and printed verbatim (see P. G. Ford, *A Guide to Parliamentary Papers*, 3rd ed., IUP, 1972).

Further groups of papers are those which arose from the expansion of Britain overseas to control widely scattered colonial possessions and the development of areas of white settlement, Canada, Australia, and New Zealand. At the outset both kinds of territories were in some degree controlled from Whitehall. On the latter, beside formal committees of enquiry, there was a mass of despatches to and correspondence with colonial governors on the opening and sales of land for settlement, taxation, the administration of justice and the slow replacement of central control by primitive local representative bodies which eventually become the parliaments of self-governing dominions. In the case of the colonial possessions, after the Act abolishing slavery had been passed, the most striking feature was the immense body of papers which offer unique insight into the problem of enforcing this new political principle in widely scattered territories, differing in climate, crop conditions, land tenure, in the character and importance of slavery and in social structure. These are revealed in an immense volume of despatches, correspondence and instructions issued by the Colonial Office and the Foreign Office to colonial governors and their little Assemblies, which offered varying degrees of co-operation and resistance, and by the

Admiralty in orders to commanders of naval vessels engaged all over the world in efforts to suppress the slave trade.

The great body of material for the nineteenth century occupies some 7,000 official folio volumes. At the outset the problem of making it available had to be met by the Printer to the House of Commons, Luke Hansard, who kept it in stock and numbered the House papers. He was frequently asked by M.P.s and others for sets of existing papers on particular questions then under discussion in the House or by the public. This led him to take two steps. He made special collections of papers arranged in subject order, and prepared a series of indexes to the papers, some in subject and some in alphabetical order. But the passage of a century has enlarged the number of papers to be handled and the scale of the problems; and at the same time we now have to meet the demand not only of the politician concerned with the problems of his time, but those of professional historians and researchers ranging over the whole century.

To deal with the papers on Home Affairs the Fords' *Select List of British Parliamentary Papers 1833-99* includes 4,000 policy papers arranged in subject order, so that researchers can follow the development lines of policy easily through any collection of papers. But complete collections are few and far between and even ample ones not common. The Irish University Press Parliamentary Papers series supplies this deficiency first by reprinting all the major policy papers, conveniently brought together in subject sets, e.g. 32 volumes on Agriculture, 44 volumes on Industrial Relations, 15 volumes on Children's Employment, 55 volumes on Education, and so on. Secondly, it has retained what was the great virtue of the original enquiries by reprinting with the reports all the volumes of evidence. Thirdly, in those fields where despatches, correspondence and instructions are vital as in the case of the papers on slavery, Canada, Australia, New Zealand, as far as possible all the papers on these matters found in the British Parliamentary series have been reprinted, e.g. 95 volumes on Slavery, 36 on Canada, 34 on Australia.

The series includes the most commonly used official general alphabetical indexes from which researchers can trace papers referred to in the footnotes of scholarly works and in the references in parliamentary reports themselves. In addition to the official indexes, a special index[1] to the 1,000 volumes has been prepared which will also provide cross references, so that the official indexes can be used either with the official sessional sets or with the IUP reprints. Finally, indexes to subjects, persons and places (some of which are already published[2]) are being compiled for the papers in the IUP series.

1 *Checklist of British Parliamentary Papers in the Irish University Press 1000-Volume Series 1801-1899* (Shannon: 1972).

2 *Index to British Parliamentary Papers on Children's Employment* (IUP, 1973)
Index to British Parliamentary Papers on Canada and Canadian Boundary, 1800-1899 (IUP 1974).
Index to British Parliamentary Papers on Australia and New Zealand, 1800-1899, 2 vols. (IUP 1974).

Criminal Justice and Punishment

W. R. Cornish

Commentary

The machine of criminal justice has three principal components: detection, trial and punishment. The first of these forms part of the subject-matter of other sections of this *Commentary*. The other two are treated in this chapter. The number of important questions is considerable and they will be discussed in an order which emphasises their relative significance. In the early nineteenth century there was one issue that dominated all others: the question of capital punishment. Beccaria had challenged the whole of Europe to replace harsh cruelty in dealing with criminals by enlightened moderation. This novel penal philosophy had implications for every part of the criminal process. But in relation to English practice, it required, first and foremost, the abandonment of the great range of capital offences for crimes against property. The active stages of the campaign for abolition run from 1808 to 1840; in the parliamentary papers the question is particularly prominent in the report of the Select Committee on the Criminal Law relating to Capital Punishments in 1819[1] and one of the Reports of the Criminal Law Commissioners.[2] This debate is reviewed in the first section of the chapter.

If offenders were not to be executed, how were they to be dealt with? The problems of transportation abroad and imprisonment at home became the subject of constant debate. These 'secondary' punishments are covered in three subject sets of parliamentary papers in the Irish University Press series — *Transportation, Penal Servitude* and *Prisons*. The special problems posed by the large numbers of young offenders were also a long-standing preoccupation as is witnessed by the papers collected under a fourth title, *Juvenile Offenders*. Of course, the different forms of punishment were not always considered separately from one another. Particularly in the early nineteenth century, there were a number of official inquiries too broad in scope to be neatly classified under these separate headings. The second section of this chapter, in reviewing the shift in opinion about the different forms of secondary punishment, will offer some guidance through the maze of this material.

The lifting of capital punishment was accompanied by pressure for more adequate policing. The growth of modern police forces, while not here our direct concern, had an important effect on the process of trial, just as the abandonment of the death penalty made it feasible to consider reforming the substantive criminal law. The parliamentary papers contain important material on the two great attempts to codify the substantive criminal law and criminal procedure: the Reports of the succession of Criminal Law Commissions of 1833-1849 and the Report of the Commissioners who in 1878-79

1   1819 (585), VIII; IUP Criminal Law 1.
2   Second Report, 1836 (343), XXXVI; IUP Criminal Law 3.

revised FitzJames Stephen's Criminal Code. These are included in the subject set, *Criminal Law,* and are discussed in the final sections of the chapter.

The fifty-one volumes of parliamentary papers under review highlight some features of the criminal process and obscure others. Before we turn to details, let us view the scene in general perspective. This may make clear both the limitations of the material and the emphasis that is in consequence acquired by a commentary upon it.

The official character of the papers means that they are largely preoccupied with the views of administrators upon practical problems. Among the 'administrators' we may include all those who carried through the process of trial and punishment — not only the lawyers and the growing number of police and prison officials, but also many lay representatives of the established classes, participating as constables, prosecutors, justices of the peace and jurymen, grand and petty. People who had reason to feel how easily the fabric of social order could be rent were ready enough to play their part in conserving and strengthening it. Their view of criminal behaviour largely determined the content of the substantive law. Their desire for deterrence, in one form or another, contributed to the revisions of the old penal system in the name of efficacy. They devoted great energy to such practical considerations in punishment as labour, diet, moral contamination and discipline for the refractory. But they also asked larger questions about the aims and effects of the process. For such punishment is an assertion of governmental power that demands justification, and so has a special place in the intellectual history of the age.

Beccaria had begun the debate on capital punishment in philosophical terms and he became one of the earliest influences upon Jeremy Bentham. Throughout his life Bentham took a deep interest in every aspect of criminal justice: the substantive law, policing, the process of trial and the punishment that followed it.[3] The principle of utility had an evident application to these practical questions of government through law. Followers of Bentham, close and more remote, took up many of his ideas for reform of the criminal law both during his life and after his death. They were particularly active in the campaigns to replace the death penalty and transportation with imprisonment, in the plan for a code of criminal law and procedure, and in schemes to rid the courts of archaic fetters upon the trial process.

Many reformers, however, were moved not by a calculated balance of pain against pleasure but by a revulsion of feeling against the cruelty and indifference which characterised eighteenth-century penal administration. In the earlier nineteenth century, evangelical humanitarianism is frequently the mainspring of action, particularly in the reform of punishments. Christian

3   For a general discussion of Bentham as a penal reformer, see Coleman Phillipson, *Three Criminal Law Reformers* (1923) Part II, Chs. 3-5; Margery Fry in G. Keeton and G. Schwarzenberger (eds.) *Jeremy Bentham and the Law* (1948) Ch. 2.

conscience impelled wealthy amateurs such as Elizabeth Fry and her circle, and equally it moved the first 'professionals', the prison inspectors appointed under the Act of 1835.[4] We can also observe how, as the penal system is remodelled, there grows a pragmatism born of hard experience. The phenomenon that administrative historians have recently done so much to demonstrate — the independent momentum of established bureaucracies — is particularly well-illustrated by the history of the prison authorities.

Utilitarians and Christian moralists shared one assumption — that, save in exceptional cases such as mental disorder, criminals were to be treated as personally responsible for their behaviour. The Benthamite assumed that an individual calculated the balance of pleasure against pain, the Christian that a person might be dissuaded from an action by a sense of its wrongfulness. Explanations of criminal behaviour as the product of social conditions or of individual physical and psychological characteristics, and therefore not the subject of blame, were not entirely unknown. The social foundations of criminal behaviour, first studied in France by Quételet and Guerry,[5] sparked off a certain interest in England in the collection of statistics and evidence about the background and mode of life of criminals.[6] Rather more sustained was the interest shown in the manner in which youngsters were drawn into a life of crime; but this concern was not inimical to notions of individual responsibility, since juveniles were thought to be specially suited to moral redemption. The writings of Darwin and Spencer pointed generally in the direction of physical inheritance as an explanation of criminal behaviour. But Cesare Lombroso, who worked out the implications of this in a theory that criminality was determined by physical type, did not quickly attract adherents in Britain.[7] Whatever comfort it might offer the respectable to be told that criminals were biological anomalies recurring from an earlier stage of human development, the theory adopted an uncompromisingly deterministic position and thus required a wholesale reassessment of the methods of dealing with criminals. It could no longer be the business of criminal justice to measure the moral guilt of an offender, though there might be justification in taking 'measures of social defence calculated, having regard to his personality and circumstances, to restrain him from committing further crimes'.[8] But if those who influenced British thinking on penological

---

4 For the early inspectors, see D. Roberts, *Victorian Origins of the Welfare State* (1960) esp. 172 ff.

5 See, e.g., L. Radzinowicz, *Ideology and Crime* (1966) Ch. 2.

6 See Terence Morris, *The Criminal Area* (1957) Ch. 3.

7 The English prison doctor, Charles Goring, was among the first to refute the Lombrosian theory of criminal atavism, preferring the view that criminals tend to be drawn from the mentally and physically weak of all classes and occupations: *The English Convict* (officially published by the Home Office, 1913).

8 Radzinowicz, *Ideology and Crime*, p. 53.

matters were by the end of the nineteenth century increasingly pragmatic in their approach, they were nonetheless coming to admit that *some* criminals must be dealt with on the assumption that dissuasion from wrong was a fruitless exercise. This is manifest in the growing concern over persistent offenders and it becomes an accepted view with the creation of the separate offence of 'habitual criminality' in 1908.[9]

In the parliamentary papers the *ipsissima verba* of people actually subjected to trial and punishment are infrequent and accordingly striking. But then the bulk of criminals were convicted of 'ordinary' crimes against property — ordinary, that is, in the sense that the crime was motivated only by a personal desire for material gain at another's expense and did not apparently express wider criticism of the existing political order or of social conditions.[10] These 'ordinary' criminals were mostly drawn from the lowest strata of society — people who would speak to official investigators only when an account of their experiences was demanded of them. This did not often happen, for criminals were commonly thought of as a class apart, with whom (at least in the case of adults) there could be no useful communication.[11] In particular, there was a tendency to distinguish the honest labouring classes from the criminal class, which drew its recruits, in Mary Carpenter's phrase, from the 'perishing and dangerous classes'.[12] Certainly, as Tobias has shown,[13] contemporaries in the first half of the century could easily enough find evidence of the distinct institutions of those who lived by crime: the 'rookeries' where they sheltered, the 'flash-houses' where they met and disposed of stolen goods, the brothels that provided employment for their women and easy victims for their depredations.

While most offenders were convicted of 'ordinary' property crimes, the system of criminal justice had a wider role to fulfil. It was used against those who committed injuries to person or property with some motive that, in at least a broad sense, was political; those who disturbed the civil peace by their

9 For this and the later history of the treatment of recidivists, see Norval Morris, *The Habitual Criminal* (1951) Ch. 2.

10 As the amount of urban crime grows, it is easy to assume that it was 'ordinary' in this sense. But our knowledge of the matter is still shallow and vague. Recent investigations of eighteenth-century crime, most of it rural, suggest that the laws against smuggling, wrecking and the taking of game were used, sometimes with remarkable ruthlessness, to resolve important social conflicts in favour of the law enforcers: see E. P. Thompson, *Whigs and Hunters* (1975); Douglas Hay and others, *Albion's Fatal Tree* (1975). As yet there is only sporadic evidence of the degree to which the same can be said of the succeeding century.

11 Views on 'the criminal class' and the extent of their responsibility for 'ordinary' crime are investigated by J. J. Tobias, *Crime and Industrial Society in the 19th Century* (1967) Part II.

12 *Reformatory Schools for the Children of the Perishing and Dangerous Classes* (1851).

13 See n. 10 above.

demands for food or higher wages, those who broke up the new machines, those who rioted for the Reform Bill were all dealt with by prosecution. So equally those who did no more than incite others to dissidence, insurrection or anti-religious views might be guilty of such overtly political offences as treason, sedition or blasphemy. In the long years of civil unrest that stretch from the wars with France to the end of militant Chartism there were many prosecutions of both kinds. The trials could easily inflame public feeling and so create their own disorders. But it had been part of the constitutional settlement of the seventeenth century that, save when habeas corpus was suspended by Parliament, those detained would be tried for a prescribed offence against the law and that they would have the ordinary advantages of the 'liberal' English criminal procedure — most notably a jury to decide the question of guilt.[14] The government by no means always won these contests.

While the problems of public order and political dissidence have a central role in the development of the 'new' police, there was little feeling amongst the respectable classes that the criminal law under which 'political' defendants were charged, the trial process to which they were subjected or the punishments imposed upon them needed special reform. The offenders themselves, so far as they took an interest in such matters, used their talents to mount highly indignant and sometimes effective campaigns against the general conditions of punishment.[15] Their articulateness only serves to underline the dumb subjection with which the 'ordinary' transportee and prisoner accepted his lot. But their numbers were small, their protests accordingly isolated. Those who administered the system could conceive it as designed principally for the robber, burglar or thief, with a fringe of murderers, assaulters and rapists, almost all coming from the lowest depths of society.

Despite the fact that crime was commonly considered to be an activity of the 'dangerous classes', a system of criminal law based upon individual responsibility survived with great tenacity. Those whose voices are heard in the parliamentary papers rarely felt that this presented any paradox, and the papers themselves suggest why this was so. We have already noted that, with the exception of juveniles (who raised special considerations), interest in specific social causes of crime was sporadic and not very penetrating.[16] As

14 Indeed, defendants charged with treason had, as a result of their special character, acquired certain advantages, such as the right to advance notice of the charges and a full right to counsel, well before these were conceded to persons charged with felonies: see below, p. 56.

15 Examples which forced official inquiries upon the authorities included Finnerty's case against the keeper of Lincoln Castle prison (1812-13 (4) V; IUP Prisons 7) and Hunt's against the keeper of Ilchester (1822 (7, 54, 30, 70) XI; IUP Prisons 9), Lovett and Collins' complaints about Warwick gaol (1839 (462), XXXVIII; IUP Prisons 11) and the various charges levied by the Fenians (collected in IUP Prisons 21).

16 Above, p. 9.

one would expect, where a paper does touch upon the causes of crime, there is considerable emphasis on factors that demonstrated moral degeneration. Tobias suggests that, while in the period after Waterloo poverty was considered to drive people to crime, in the Victorian years it was common to suppose that criminals deliberately chose their life for its ease, allowing them to indulge a pronounced distaste for work. He considers that the Report of the Constabulary Commissioners in 1839, with its abundant detail of how the predatory classes lived, crystallised this change of attitude.[17] Equally drink was regarded as a major cause of crime— both as a stimulant and as a craving: neither the breakdown of established social patterns among the growing numbers crowded into the cities, nor the squalid, fetid conditions in which they lived, could explain, let alone excuse, particular criminal acts.

Contemporary opinion may be one thing and reality quite another. The extent of crime and its causes, and the effectiveness of policies designed to reduce crime, are difficult enough issues today, for all our relative sophistication in information-gathering. As one looks back in time, they become increasingly difficult to investigate. In the nineteenth century there was at least some attempt to keep statistical records concerning crime and these have become the source of an interesting debate.

From 1805 onwards returns were made of the numbers committed for trial on an indictable offence.[18] To these were later added returns of the numbers committed to prison,[19] the numbers of persons summarily tried and the numbers of indictable offences known to the police.[20] There were also important reorganisations affecting the manner in which the figures were collated. These have been carefully described by Gattrell and Hadden,[21] who demonstrate how they may usefully be read in conjunction with one another and with other statistical material, such as that on the size of police forces. Their suggestive analysis cannot be adequately summarised here, though some of their conclusions may be touched upon. They note the impossibility of ever determining the quantity of crime, but suggest that the long term national and regional trends to be observed in some of the returns (notably offences known to the police) have a value that cannot be ignored. The statistics for instance confirm the view commonly (but not uniformly) held[22] in the later nineteenth century that the overall volume of crime was declining.

On the other hand, when it comes to the causes of crime, the statistics do

17   *Op. cit.*, n. 11, Ch. 8.

18   Published under the headings Judicial Proceedings or Criminal Offenders.

19   Published from 1836 onwards under the title Gaols and Prisons.

20   Both published from 1857 in the Police Returns.

21   V.A.C. Gattrell and T. B. Hadden, 'Criminal Statistics and their Interpretation' in E. A. Wrigley (ed.), *Nineteenth Century Society* (1972) ch. 8.

22   See below, p.61.

not so easily bear out the comfortable aphorisms of the day. Gattrell and Hadden show an interesting correlation between the troughs in the business cycle and increases in crimes against property, at the same time pointing to a somewhat less exact correlation between crests in the business cycle and increases in crimes of violence and drunkenness. The phenomenon of 'prosperity-based crime' in relation to property offences, they suggest, emerged a good deal later than is claimed in Tobias' literary sources. Whatever the moralists might assert, economic necessity did produce more crime in times of special hardship, and it can be inferred that in other years as well, sheer want remained a significant explanation of property crime. Tobias rejects any such case *au fond*, by claiming the collation of the statistics to have been so unsatisfactory that 'when they point to a conclusion opposed to that based on contemporary description, they can perhaps be disregarded without much anxiety'.[23] It is hard to see, however, that the repeated correlations demonstrated by Gattrell and Hadden can be explained away as the chance medley of incompetent record-keepers.

In truth we are only beginning to explore evidence that may lead to a three-dimensional view of the social significance of nineteenth-century crime. Recent work, such as that of the Centre for the Study of Social History at Warwick University upon aspects of crime in the eighteenth century,[24] suggests the variety of material, official and unofficial, that may be incorporated into the reconstruction. In the nineteenth century, reference to court and other local archives, to newspapers and to private documents acquires the added importance, that, if it is not undertaken, the voluminous, accessible and relatively cogent evidence provided in blue book inquiries will acquire an authenticity that may be quite unwarranted.

To this should be related a point recently emphasised by Noel McLachlan, in the context of prison history.[25] Criminal justice was, most of the time, a neglected cause, in which reform proceeded snail-like, starved of funds and blighted by the expedience of the moment. Enthusiasts there were, and official inquiries offered them a special opportunity to have their principles and their plans minuted for posterity. What is less graphically recorded is the smallness of their number and the indifference and the parsimony with which their projects were often treated.

---

23 *Op. cit.*, n. 11, p. 235. And see his Ch. 2 and Appendix.

24 E. P. Thompson, *Whigs and Hunters* (1975); D. Hay and others, *Albion's Fatal Tree* (1975).

25 'Penal Reform and Penal History: Some Reflections' in L. Blom-Cooper (ed.) *Progress in Penal Reform* (1974) Ch. 1.

The Penalty of Death

During the first forty years of the nineteenth century, capital punishment was the issue around which every other aspect of the penal system turned. The indifference with which eighteenth-century Parliaments added to the pile of capital statutes is a familiar story, the details of which are traced in Radzinowicz's exhaustive survey.[26] In the earliest years of the nineteenth century, Parliament was still creating new 'felonies without benefit of clergy' (i.e. capital offences in which the penalty would be commuted to transportation on the first occasion that the offender claimed the benefit).[27] In 1803, for instance, Lord Ellenborough, Chief Justice of the King's Bench and a prominent opponent of any relaxation of the capital laws, was responsible for an Act making a variety of aggravated wounding offences capital 'without benefit'.[28] In 1812, the outbreaks of Luddite machine-breaking provoked a capital statute and, though the penalty of death for the new offence was lifted two years later, it was reimposed in 1817 after further disturbances.[29] Other instances of new capital offences were numerous enough, particularly revenue violations, commercial forgeries and misappropriations by agents and servants.[30]

In 1764 Beccaria, in *Dei Delitti e delle Pene*, had developed certain ideas of Montesquieu into a sustained critique of the ferocious penal codes of the European states. He couched his arguments in contractualist terms, denying that there was any natural right to surrender one's life, and asserting that therefore the social contract could not embrace a surrender of the power of life and death by the individual to his sovereign. Accordingly he opposed the imposition of capital punishment for any offence whatsoever. But the practical efficacy of the criminal law was his principal concern and many who did not take so extreme a position were attracted by his arguments in favour of certain, prompt and moderate punishment. In England he found followers not

---

26 *A History of English Criminal Law*, I *passim* and IV, Ch. 8 (cited as 'Radzinowicz *History*').

27 'Benefit of clergy', as Blackstone was pleased to demonstrate (*Commentaries* IV, pp. 365-74), had proved an adaptable institution of the law; it had grown out of the ecclesiastical jurisdiction over ordained clerks, into a privilege against ordinary punishment that was open at first to laymen who could read, later to women and illiterates. By the eighteenth century it was available to all offenders, but it could be claimed only once. See Holdsworth, *History of English Law*, III, pp. 294-302.

28 43 Geo. III, c. 58.

29 See 52 Geo. III, c. 16, s. 1; 54 Geo. III, c. 42; 57 Geo. III, c. 126. Radzinowicz *History* I, 521.

30 The capital laws amassed up to this period are outlined by Radzinowicz *History* I, App. 1. For the place of this demand for justice beside ideas of liberty and equality in eighteenth-century thought, see Radzinowicz, *Ideology and Crime* (1966) pp. 7-14.

only in Eden, Romilly and Bentham but also in Blackstone. The progress that these ideas made in the period before the wars with France is marked in various ways,[31] perhaps most significantly by the successful opposition in the Commons in 1788 to a proposal to make the destruction of stocking frames a non-clergyable offence.[32]

By the first decade of the new century, however, Parliament had withdrawn to a position of retrenchment, and when Samuel Romilly began the first real campaign to reduce capital punishment he was met by steely opposition.[33] The popular exponent of contemporary orthodoxy was Archdeacon Paley.[34] His thesis was that criminals would be deterred from committing a wide range of offences only if death was the punishment. But he believed that this effect would be achieved even if the sentence was carried out only in cases where there were aggravating circumstances. In such utilitarian terms did Ellenborough join with the Lord Chancellor, Eldon, the Archbishop of Canterbury and six bishops in opposing Romilly during the great debates of 1810.[35] Ellenborough purported both to rely upon a convention that measures of law reform should have the approval of the judges and to speak for the entire bench in opposing Romilly's Bills.[36] This became the best-remembered instance of judicial antagonism to change in penal matters, but it was symptomatic of a continuing phenomenon.[37]

Romilly's campaign in Parliament consisted of attempts to remove the death penalty from the offences where its imposition was least defensible.[38] His suicide in 1818 left the abolitionist cause in the hands of Mackintosh and Fowell Buxton. It was Mackintosh who moved for the Criminal Law Com-

---

31   See Radzinowicz *History* I, Chs. 13-15.

32   *Ib.* 479-84; cf. the creation of the capital offence of machine-breaking in 1812, above, n. 29.

33   Romilly recorded in his journal for 1808: 'If any person be desirous of having an adequate idea of the mischievous effects which have been produced in this country by the French Revolution and all its attendant horrors, he should attempt some legislative reform on humane and liberal principles. He will then find, not only what a stupid dread of innovation, but what a savage spirit, it has infused in the minds of many of his countrymen.' (Patrick Medd, *Romilly* (1968) p. 215).

34   *Principles of Moral and Political Philosophy* (1785) Ch. 9.

35   The occasion was the first of Romilly's repeated attempts to have the death penalty removed from three minor property offences: shoplifting to the value of 5s., and stealing from dwellings and from vessels to the value of 40s.

36   Radzinowicz *History* I, pp. 507-11.

37   G. Gardiner and N. Curtis-Raleigh, 'The Judicial Attitude to Penal Reform' (1949) 65 L.Q.R. 196.

38   He succeeded twice only, in respect of pickpocketing (48 Geo. III, c. 129) and stealing from bleaching grounds (51 Geo. III, cs. 39 and 41). In the latter case he was assisted by petitions from the owners of bleaching grounds complaining of the unenforceability of the law as it stood, a phenomenon which was to be repeated over and over again as the reform campaign burgeoned.

mittee of 1818 and was appointed its chairman. The Report is the first sustained discussion of the case against the capital laws to appear in the parliamentary papers.[39] It was an early example of those official reports that were so effectively to be used by radicals to state a case for reform, and it recapitulates the lines of argument that Romilly had taught his followers. When the elders of the church and the law had insisted that if crime was to be prevented there must be no reduction in the cases to which the death penalty applied, Romilly had responded by demonstrating how ineffective the existing administration of the law was rendered by the threat of execution for so many offences. The Committee's Report was able to add to Romilly's statistical evidence of the rapid increase in the number of prosecutions for capital property crimes and the declining frequency of executions.[40]

While the Committee avoided consulting any of the judges apart from the retired Chief Baron, Macdonald, it heard much evidence from merchants, bankers and manufacturers, the very people whose protection had chiefly been intended by some of the most recent capital laws.[41] They spoke of the hazards involved in securing enforcement of the law at every stage of criminal procedure. In particular, victims were reluctant to institute prosecutions where death might be the consequence of some quite minor transgression; likewise the grand jury might refuse to find a 'true bill';[42] counsel, or even the judge, might ensure that the indictment covered only a non-capital offence, or might induce the accused to plead guilty to such a count in return for an abstention from proceeding on a capital count; the trial jury (sometimes encouraged from the bench) might acquit or by 'pious perjury' find the value of the property in question to be less than that necessary to make the offence capital. It was even said that some defendants preferred trial for a capital offence because their chance of acquittal was so much better.

The progress of arguments about the efficacy of capital punishment is closely linked with changing ideas on secondary punishments and police. Part of the argument made against Romilly in the second decade of the century stemmed from the growing doubt whether transportation to Australia was sufficiently fearful to act as a deterrent.[43] Thereafter came attempts to make transportation and penal servitude more severe; the search had begun for a deterrent of comparable harshness to death, which the courts would nonetheless be willing to impose on offenders.

39   1819 (585), VIII; IUP Criminal Law 1.

40   This was the first historical collation of criminal statistics. In 1805, 68 of the 350 convicts sentenced to death were executed (19.5%); by 1817 only 115 of 1302 (8.8%) suffered the penalty. See further, Radzinowicz *History* I, 536-39.

41   Before the Committee was appointed petitions to Parliament in favour of reform had grown substantially in number: Radzinowicz *History* I, 526-28.

42   For this procedural step, see below, p. 60.

43   See below, p. 24.

Likewise the governing-class fear of a professional police, with its French overtones of government spying, remained strong for many years after 1815. Yet before the beginning of the century Colquhoun, and with him Bentham, had argued that an effective system of criminal justice could exist only if the agencies of detection were strengthened and penalties were moderated. Sir Robert Peel saw matters in Colquhoun's terms. His arrival at the Home Office in 1822 provided the political weight necessary to begin removing the death penalty where the 1819 Committee found it to be least justified. In 1823 Peel succeeded in respect of shoplifting to the value of 40s. and stealing from ships to the same amount — both offences which had been the subject of unsuccessful campaigns by Romilly. Many lesser property, quarantine and revenue offences were soon treated in similar fashion.[44] But Peel was not prepared to go beyond those cases where the capital sentence was so much more severe than the crime that public opinion prevented its enforcement. Much of the 1819 Committee's evidence had been concerned with the difficulty of securing prosecutions and convictions of capital forgery, but Peel wanted to retain the penalty for many of the more important types of forged document, including bank notes and negotiable securities. By 1830, he was using statistics of convictions to argue that offences from which capital punishment had been removed were being more frequently *committed*. In the Commons Mackintosh successfully moved an amendment substituting non-capital punishments for most forgeries, and though the Lords restored Peel's clause, it was evident that the commercial community and other sectors of opinion still strongly favoured further reductions of capital punishment.[45] In 1832, all forgeries, save of wills and certain powers of attorney, became non-capital, as did horse and cattle stealing, larceny from dwelling houses and even housebreaking with larceny.[46]

Lord John Russell had early taken the reform of capital punishment as one of the radical platforms that he supported and when he became Home Secretary in 1835 he at once referred the issue to the Criminal Law Commis-

---

44 For details, see Radzinowicz *History* I, 578-87. Hand-in-hand with these revisions of penalties went the long-needed work of consolidating together the statutes relating to crimes of the same nature. In four great acts, covering larceny, malicious damage to property, offences against the person and forgery, the provisions of hundreds of statutes were for the first time made generally accessible. The value of this procedure was initially demonstrated to a Select Committee of the Commons in 1824, taking forgery as the example: see the Reports of the Select Committee on the Criminal Law of England, 1824 (205, 444), IV; IUP Criminal Law 2.

45 For the passage of the Forgery Bill see N. Gash, *Mr. Secretary Peel* (1961) pp. 478-85.

46 Though not yet burglary (i.e. housebreaking at night) or housebreaking where someone was put in fear. See generally Radzinowicz *History* I, pp. 600-07. The courts in 1834 still passed 494 death sentences, of which only 17 were carried out: *ib*, IV, p. 309.

sioners.[47] The progress that had been made already demanded a penetrating investigation of the arguments, and the Commissioners' Report provides an altogether more sophisticated analysis than the 1819 Committee.[48] It develops an attack on the three tenets of Paleian faith: that capital punishment carried out occasionally for aggravated instances of a substantial range of offences formed an economical deterrent; that the cases to be selected for this exemplary treatment could not be defined in advance; and that if any attempt were made to delimit the circumstances that bore the death penalty many offenders would escape merited punishment. The Commissioners disliked the arbitrary fashion in which the selection was actually made by the judiciary and the executive, particularly the manner in which collateral circumstances, such as the defendant's conduct and character, might be taken into account without any proper attempt to find out the truth.[49] There was further and deeper injustice to offenders in failing to specify in advance the circumstances in which they would, as opposed to those in which they might, actually be executed. The Commissioners considered that the time was not yet ripe for total abolition of capital punishment; it should be retained for high treason, murder and certain other crimes aggravated by violence or the direct endangering of life.[50] This programme of reform Russell was ready to carry out and by 1841 he had largely achieved it. Only the outraged sentiment of the House of Lords forced him to abandon his attempt to make the 'infamous crime' of buggery non-capital.[51]

The long dispute over the death penalty lay near the very eye of political life. The eighteenth-century ruling class — small in number, hungry for property and its attendant power — had to maintain stability and order without the civil police of modern times. Capital punishment formed an ugly apex to a system of social control through legal processes which functioned to a significant degree at the pleasure of the governors. Paley's argument that capital statutes should only occasionally be carried out to the letter as an ultimate deterrent suited many of his readers. As Douglas Hay has shown, a reprieve often depended upon the good offices of a person of standing.[52] At earlier stages also — when magistrates and victims decided whether to prosecute, when the grand jury pronounced upon the indictment, when the trial jury returned its verdict — there was room for expression of upper-class

47   For the establishment of this Commission, whose major task became to codify the substantive and procedural criminal law, see below, p. 52.

48   Second Report 1836 (343), XXXVI; IUP Criminal Law 3, and the evidence there referred to.

49   Report, pp. 26-27.

50   pp. 32-33.

51   Radzinowicz *History* IV, pp. 316-26.

52   'Property Authority and the Criminal Law', in D. Hay and others, *Albion's Fatal Tree* (1975).

views of what was right and what was expedient.

These were the barbed legal fibres in a social fabric of variegated texture, patterned with a motif of vertical loyalties. A clear appreciation of the strands of criminal law is a necessary corrective to 'an historiography that is increasingly about the social harmonies of that society'.[53] But it may be doubted whether this justifies an account of the manner in which criminal processes were put to work in denunciatory terms that imply an implacable conspiracy to suppress dissidence. The landed aristocracy chose to increase the gamut of capital offences, with a particular eye on the protection of their own kinds of property. But they did not move so extravagantly in the direction of other forms of repression. True they did something to by-pass the trial jury, that 'bulwark of liberty', by increasing summary trial before justices. True also that some new policing arrangements were beginning to develop where robbery and theft were most prevalent. But in these matters, as in the actual execution of capital felons, they stopped at a certain point. The motivation for going no further was probably mixed. One man might fear that greater severity would only spark an uncontrollable reaction, another that the threats to the established order were not grave enough to warrant further repression. One might fear that new measures might be used to curb his own liberty, another might take an idealistic pride in the liberal and moderate criminal system in which the rule of law and fair process could be said to prevail to an extent unknown in Europe.

What is apparent is that under the disturbed conditions of the French wars a marked feeling of retrenchment developed among the governing class. One of its manifestations was their outraged reaction to Romilly's campaign. But the case against capital property offences was quickly supported by middle-class interests, anxious to protect their own typical forms of wealth—merchandise and money, rather than land and game. The particular issue was only part of a wider demand for reorganisation of the whole structure of criminal justice—detection, prosecution and punishment. And this in turn is but one manifestation of the claims of the newly rich to a stouter share of political power. Concessions on the death penalty and police flank the events of 1832. They form part of the same watershed.

The history of capital punishment reform after 1840 is in the nature of a postscript. Executions were in practice only performed upon convicted murderers[54] and the focus of arguments about the death penalty changed. In 1830, when Bentham demanded its total repeal his arguments reflected the continu-

53   D. Hay, *ibid* at p. 253.

54   In 1861, a hanging took place in the case of a vicious attempted murder. But the feeling that only the actual loss of one human life justified the taking of another was reflected by the abolition later the same year of the death penalty for attempted murder: 24 and 25 Vict. c. 100, s. 11.

ing existence of capital crimes against property.[55] While he objected to the 'irremissibility' of execution and to the undesirable effects of investing the government with a wide discretion to pardon, his fire was primarily directed at the 'inefficiency' of the punishment as a deterrent; those who had to put the law in motion were unwilling to act, with the consequence that men were left free to commit other crimes with equal impunity. But once the argument, in practical terms, had become one about murder, it was necessary to recognise the deep-rooted desire to avenge a life taken by the taking of another, an emotion that sometimes had an ugly showing at executions, which were still held in public. Certainly it was hard to carry the argument that the law of murder was not enforced because of public antipathy to its punishment, and neither the protagonists of capital punishment nor its opponents had convincing statistics about its deterrent effect in relation to that crime.[56]

It was Russell, rather than radicals like William Ewart, who recognised how far capital punishment could be repealed without provoking a serious reaction on the part of the upper classes. Ewart's attempts, through the 1840s and 1850s, to win total abolition, though they gained a temporary following in literary and other liberal circles, gradually lost support. Even when in 1861 a new consolidation of offences against the person was finally enacted, the Lords required some persuasion that lesser crimes than murder should not, formally at least, be kept capital. The campaign for total abolition became one of the lost causes of mid-century radicalism and was finally interred by a Royal Commission on Capital Punishment.[57] The report of this body only recommended two rather minor reforms. Both matters had in their time provided useful ballast in the abolitionist fire-ship: one was the extreme reluctance to see a mother convicted of murdering her recently-born child; the other, an increasing disapproval of the huge crowds that would gather to watch a public hanging. The Commission favoured the introduction of a lesser crime of infanticide,[58] and wanted executions removed within the privacy of the prison walls.[59]

---

55   On Death Punishment, Works (Bowring ed.) I, p. 251; cf. his earlier view that capital punishment should be retained for murder: ib. 441.

56   Radzinowicz, History IV, pp. 327-28, 337 reviews the evidence that was used in this part of the debate.

57   1866 [3590], XXI.

58   In the event, nothing was done until the Infanticide Act 1922. The doctors who gave evidence to the Commission of 1866 said that they would testify at such a trial that the child might not have been born alive. Doubtless they continued the practice, but a sufficient number of women were convicted of murdering their children for the judges in the end to lead the protest against having to pronounce a death sentence that they knew would not be carried out: see D. Seaborne Davies, 'Child-Killing in English Law' in Turner and Radzinowicz (eds.) The Modern Approach to Criminal Law (1945).

59   Public executions were abandoned in 1868: 31 Vict. c. 24; Radzinowicz, History IV, pp. 343-53.

Secondary Punishments

For treason and felony, the law's allotted punishment was death. By 1800, capital punishment was in practice largely being replaced by lesser substitutes, in particular the secondary punishments, transportation and imprisonment. The fact that in law they were substitutes continued to exert its influence long after death ceased even theoretically to be the sentence for most felonies. A chart of the punishments for different crimes during the nineteenth century shows two distinct streams whose channels draw into close parallel as time passes. In the one, the central authorities of the state at all stages bore the responsibility for carrying out secondary punishment. Down this channel passed those convicted of crimes, originally capital, where the death penalty was, for one reason or another, not carried out: because the offence had always remained clergyable,[60] because the sentence was commuted by royal pardon on the recommendation of the trial judge or the 'hanging cabinet',[61] or because parliament had substituted a secondary sentence in place of capital punishment. The usual form of commutation or substitution in the first half of the nineteenth century was transportation (for life or a long term of years), though only a minor proportion of those sentenced to transportation were actually sent. With the collapse of the transportation system there was substituted a period of penal servitude in one of the national penitentiaries whose original purpose was to house those awaiting transportation.

The other stream was made up of the convicts incarcerated in the local gaols of county and borough.[62] The obligation to maintain these gaols in the name of the king was of long standing. The duty had early fallen on the sheriff of the county, and it had been extended by charter or custom to boroughs and other franchise-holders.[63] By 1800, the local gaols were receiving, as well as those awaiting trial, convicts awaiting transportation, civil debtors (alleged and adjudged), and those who had been sentenced by the higher courts and petty sessions to terms of imprisonment. The sentencing of convicts to imprisonment had happened by accretion rather than by planned development and it formed one contributory factor in the deterioration of the gaols.

60   One technical reform carried out by Peel was the replacement of benefit of clergy with a sentence of transportation for seven years or imprisonment for not more than two: 7 & 8 Geo. IV, c. 28, ss. 6, 7.

61   See F. Bresler, *Reprieve* (1965); D. Hay, *op. cit.*, n. 52.

62   The local gaols included the houses of correction originally established to set vagrants to work. By the nineteenth century, many had become allied with local gaols and the distinction was formally abolished in 1865.

63   See generally R. B. Pugh, *Imprisonment in Medieval England* (1968).

As John Howard demonstrated to those willing to listen, cells that might have served for short-term lock-ups had become filthy, overcrowded death-traps, once prisoners were left in them for months or years. In *The State of the Prisons* (1777) Howard first catalogued the results of years of apathy and neglect. Though the justices had the authority, if they wanted it, to rebuild and repair their common gaols, and to use rates to maintain poor prisoners, they were content to leave everything to contractor-gaolers, whose reward comprised what they could extract from their prisoners.[64]

Between 1774 and 1791, a small band of reformers secured new legislation and used it in some places to build new, healthier prisons, which were run by salaried gaolers on quite novel lines of order and discipline. In 1823, Peel secured a Gaols Act which, at least in theory, placed justices under a duty to run their prisons in accordance with statutory rules reflecting these new ideas.[65] By the 1830s gaol reform had advanced far enough for the merits of different prison regimes to be passionately debated, and in 1835 the Home Office acquired four inspectors to supervise the administration of the local gaols. The inspectors had few legal powers until 1865, when they acquired the crucial authority to compel the local authorities to provide separate cells for prisoners in their gaols. In 1877 the central Prison Commissioners were appointed to take over the administration of the local prisons. Since the Commissioners were also the Directors of the Convict Prisons the prisons were effectively brought under a single administration, though the legal basis of the two systems remained distinct.[66]

The progression from death to imprisonment as the standard penalty for serious crime is a tortuous one, the details of which must be sought elsewhere. Fortunately there exist scholarly accounts of transportation to Australia and imprisonment in the British Isles. Here no more is attempted than to draw attention to certain relationships between the major integers in the whole machine, and to point briefly to lesser parts that warrant closer examination by historians than they have yet received.

Transportation

Capital punishment had definite and simple aims: upon persons other than the offender it was intended to work as a deterrent; as far as the offender himself was concerned it could achieve nothing other than an end to his career as a criminal. Transportation was an acceptable substitute for death because it

64 S. and B. Webb, *English Prisons under Local Government* (1922) Ch. 2.
65 See below, p. 29.
66 For the continuing gal differences see H. B. Simpson, 'Penal Servitude: its Past and Future' (1899) 17 L.Q.R. 33.
67 The leading history of transportation to Australia is A. G. L. Shaw, *Convicts and the Colonies* (1966) (cited as 'Shaw').

fulfilled similar functions: it removed the criminal from the society that he knew.[68] Yet the very fact that the transported convict remained alive created complications.

The first growth of transportation of vagrants and then criminals had been to the American colonies. Its attraction in the seventeenth century was that it helped supply labour in the new plantations. Later, however, the negro slave formed a cheap and more manipulable substitute; transportation was already unpopular in the colonies when the Declaration of Independence put a stop to it. At first, the government met the crisis by cramming those awaiting transportation into old warships. These were the notorious Hulks,[69] a temporary expedient whose cheapness kept them operative for eighty years. The first generation of prison reformers secured an act in 1779 that provided for the construction of two national penitentiaries.[70] These reception prisons for those awaiting transportation were to be run on reformed principles. The government, however, had no enthusiasm for the proposal which was shelved. Instead it eventually entered the abortive arrangement with Bentham for the construction of his Panopticon as a national prison.[71] This in turn was succeeded by the actual building of the Millbank Penitentiary between 1812 and 1816. Only the most advanced thinkers were beginning to regard imprisonment at home as the proper method for punishing serious criminals. A ruling class that was still adding capital penalties to the statute-book regarded imprisonment on a reformed plan as insufficiently frightening and unduly expensive.

In the 1780s the expedient that Pitt finally decided upon was to create a penal settlement in New South Wales — six months' journey away in a terrain known only from Cook's exploration. The choice was the more remarkable in that it seems to have been a response only to the problem of how to banish the country's least desirable elements; the government apparently did not entertain hopes, at any rate consciously, of a new colony across the globe. Audacious as the plan was, the early arrivals managed somehow to survive the rigours of journey and settlement. Not only did the number of transportees grow,[72] but so did the influx of free immigrants. Soon enough the

---

68   Though it was not illegal for those transported to return home after the expiry of their sentences, not many did. Between 1810 and 1820, for instance, only 389 left New South Wales: Shaw, pp. 65-66, 103-04.

69   See below, p.32.

70   19 Geo. III, c. 74.

71   On the Panopticon plan, see Bentham *Works* (1843) iv; Margery Fry, in Keeton and Schwarzenberger (eds.) *Jeremy Bentham and the Law* (1948) pp. 47-55.

72   According to Shaw (Appendix), between 1788 and 1853 152,170 were enshipped from Great Britain and Ireland, and 149,507 arrived. The records are not complete: for some variations see C. Bateson, *The Convict Ships* (1959). Some of the relevant returns are included in the IUP Transportation 6, 7, 11 and 15.

capacity of Australian settlements to outgrow their purely penal role produced the central tension of the transportation system. The more prosperous they became the less horrifying to be sent there as a convict, or so it was felt among the propertied classes of England. From the very beginning, the maintenance of discipline proved a major problem for the administrators of the settlements, and they sought to keep order not only by threats — lashings, chain gangs and (later) incarceration in special settlements for the refractory — but also by inducements to good behaviour. These included grants of lands to those whose sentences had expired, remission of sentences by the grant of tickets-of-leave and, during sentence, assignment of work under private masters which might put the convict in the position of an ordinary domestic servant or agricultural labourer. Under the governorship of Macquarie (1809-1821) the colony of New South Wales began to grow and the use of assignments and tickets-of-leave was expanded. This provided the route by which the emancipist was eventually absorbed into the free community.

Increasingly on bad terms with leading colonists, Macquarie also provoked the first upsurge of feeling at home that the lot of the transportee was becoming too easy.[73] A Commissioner, Bigge, was despatched to the colony in 1819 to investigate with a view to tightening the administration.[74] Bigge's first report[75] settled the main lines of development in the Australian penal colonies over the next twenty years. Though unduly hostile towards Macquarie, the report favoured the continuance of much that he had done. Bigge commended the system of assigning convicts to work for free settlers or emancipists. This Macquarie had already expanded by securing the relaxation of restrictions on free emigration, especially of persons with capital enough to take a number of convicts 'off the store'. Inevitably, in times of scarcity, transportation became a source of cheap labour to the colonists. Those prisoners who were not kept for government works were assigned on arrival and remained in that condition until given a ticket-of-leave. The general practice, settled by 1830, was to give the well-behaved convict his ticket after four years if transported for seven years, after six years if transported for fourteen, and after eight if transported for life.[76]

73   See the evidence to the Select Committee on State and Description of Gaols 1819 (579), VII; IUP Prisons 1; Shaw, p. 101 ff.

74   The furious dispute which led to Bigge's appointment — over the admission of ex-convicts into legal practice in the colony — was aired before the Select Committee on the State of Gaols (see n. 73). See generally J. M. Bennett, 'The Day of Retribution – Governor Bigge's Inquiries in Colonial New South Wales' (1971) 10 American Journal of Legal History 85.

75   Report on the State of the Colony of New South Wales 1822 (448), XX; IUP Australia 1.

76   Seven years became the minimum sentence of transportation, particularly when secondary sentences were prescribed by statute in place of death. An Act of 1832 (2 & 3 W.IV. c.62) forbade early grants of tickets of leave, among other privations.

The treatment afforded to an assigned convict differed markedly from master to master. It was the unequal effects of transportation which made it so objectionable to Bentham and his followers.[77] Their arguments mingled with the doubts of those who continued fearful that transportation was positively desired by the poverty-stricken masses. Inevitably, too, there was a growing dislike of the convict establishment amongst the colonists themselves.

As Shaw has shown, the gap widened between what was being done in the colony and the understanding of the situation in Britain.[78] The pressures, on the one hand to abandon transportation and on the other to increase its severity while it lasted, had various manifestations in the 1830s,[79] and reached its height with the Molesworth Select Committee.[80] Both Russell and Howick (the future Earl Grey) were members and the Report reflected the government's position concerning the future of the system. Assignment stood condemned in the Committee's eyes because, quite apart from a host of incidental abuses, the masters were too lenient or too tyrannical. If they treated their convicts with consideration they might hope for reformed conduct in return; if they did not, they became embroiled in a running battle to subdue insubordination, drunkenness and crime. In future the governors were to ensure that the convicts laboured in gangs on public works such as road-building. The Molesworth Committee took little account of evidence concerning the likely consequences to the settlers of this change.[81] It was in any case persuaded of the superior advantages of imprisonment and proposed the abandonment of transportation to settled colonies.[82] This began when in 1840, the last load of convicts for New South Wales departed.[83] Thenceforth most of the burden had to be borne by the settlement in Van Diemen's Land, a decision which within six years had so overwhelmed the resources of the island that transportation there had to be suspended.[84]

77 Bentham found transportation to lack, among his catalogue of desirable qualities for punishment, exemplarity, possibility of reformation, incapacitation, compensation and economy: *Works*, i, pp. 490-97.

78 Shaw, Ch. 11.

79 Notably Stanley's instruction in 1833 to subject the worst offenders to road-work in chains, an instruction which produced protests from the colonial governors and was found to have been made without legal authority: Shaw, pp. 250-52.

80 1837-38 (669), XXII; IUP Transportation 3, and see the evidence collected in the previous session 1837 (518), XIX; IUP Transportation 2.

81 The views of colonial settlers and officials are abundantly illustrated in the voluminous evidence to the Committee, in correspondence published as parliamentary papers (see the papers of 1834-41 included in the final part of IUP Transportation 6), and in other official and private correspondence reviewed by Shaw, p. 268 ff.

82 *Cf.* the use of hulks and shore prisons at Gibraltar and Bermuda, mentioned below, p. 33.

83 See the Order-in-Council 1840 (352), XXXVIII; IUP Transportation 6.

84 During this period, the Colonial Secretary, Stanley, instituted his 'probation' system, which was in essence an economical variant of assignment: Shaw, p. 295 ff.

Nonetheless there were many in Britain and Ireland who, far from accepting the Molesworth Committee's philosophy, wanted transportation to continue because of the dread that it was believed to excite and because it rid the country of its least desirable elements. A last attempt was therefore made by Russell and Earl Grey to use 'exile' to a colony as a final stage, following some years of separate confinement and gang labour in convict prisons at home, in a process of rehabilitation. By 1853, however, that system had been replaced by penal servitude, under which the convict, instead of a ticket-of-leave abroad, was released on licence from his prison in the United Kingdom. This change will, however, be better appreciated when more has been said of the development of British gaols.

Imprisonment in Britain[85]

In nineteenth-century terms the reform of British prisons meant the substitution of order and discipline for neglectful squalor. Since change tends to dominate the historian's stage, it is as well to emphasize how slow was the spread of new ideas, how long some of the smaller gaols survived in their eighteenth-century condition,[86] how parsimonious were the benches of justices in the face of requests for prison expenditure on a novel scale. Despite this there were many plans for new prison regimes, which ranged between two poles. At one extreme lay proposals which expressed the hope that prisoners might be led, by useful work, trade training and moral instruction, back to a respectable life in the world outside. At the other, were schemes to impose an arduous and lonely regimen that would deter the prisoners themselves and all other potential criminals. Humanitarians such as Howard, Mrs Fry and Maconochie are the best-remembered exemplars of the first, optimistic tradition. Even Jeremy Bentham, for all the quirkiness of his Panopticon plan, shared their essentially sympathetic approach. But there can be little doubt that the bulk of reformers were drawn towards the second pole. A strongly puritanical streak marked the enthusiasm with which the cause of prison reform was so often taken up.

Among the practical proposals two ranges of improvements may be distinguished — those relating to the basic physical requisites of prisoners, and those concerned with the discipline to which they were subjected. In the early

85   The leading history of nineteenth century developments remains that of Sidney and Beatrice Webb, *English Prisons under Local Government* (1922) (cited as 'Webb *Prisons*').

86   Even in 1865, the year when central powers of inspection were much increased, the two inspectors were drawing attention to such survivals as the Berkshire gaol at Abingdon, 'which is so universally admitted to be unnecessary and unfit for carrying out any system deserving of the name of discipline', and expressing the hope that it 'will ere long be abandoned': 1865 [3474], XXIII at p. 21.

nineteenth century it was coming to be accepted that the gaol authorities would provide such staples as food, clothing and bedding. This meant replacing the contractors with salaried gaolers, making the visiting committees work as supervisory bodies, particularly over the administration of punishments for breaches of the rules, forbidding the sale of liquor and requiring periodic cleansing of the premises. These were among the basic standards prescribed in the Gaols Act 1823, incomplete and ineffective though that statute was.

A reformed discipline came more slowly. The alternative plans that were considered practicable fell within a constricted compass and ideas recurred · from generation to generation. They revolved around three central preoccupations — work, association and diet — each of which deserves some separate consideration. But it should be remembered that until the late 1830's the main problem was to turn imprisonment into an effective short-term punishment. The transportation system removed the convicts thought to be most dangerous. It is only when the prospect of abandoning transportation looms that ideas are generated for a prison regime lasting for four years or more instead of at most two.

Work

The lack of discipline in the old gaols arose from the fact that prisoners were left in a state of complete idleness, and so all reformers agreed. Idleness bred 'contamination', for unrestricted opportunities were afforded to hardened old-timers to impress upon young newcomers the advantages of the criminal life. Work was therefore essential to a reformed discipline. The notion that useful work should be extracted from persons in institutions had been familiar for centuries, and it was supposed, in particular, to be imposed on the idle and disorderly, the rogues and vagabonds who were subjected to the quasi-criminal discipline of the Houses of Correction. The kind and amount of work to be done proved one of the key issues dividing the improving reformers and the stern dissuaders. Howard's preference seems to have been for useful labour.[87] His energetic disciple, Sir George Onesiphorus Paul, who reformed the Gloucestershire prisons, introduced labour that would teach a trade and relieve the mind of the burden of solitude.[88] The Revd J. T. Becher, who saw to the rebuilding of the Southwell House of Correction, went even further. He introduced outwork for local manufacturers of cotton goods, mats, shoes and stockings. From their earnings, the prisoners paid for some of their keep and

87 'The Keeper should be the master of some manufacture . . .' *The State of the Prisons* (Everyman ed.) p. 185.

88 Select Committee on the Laws relating to Penitentiary Houses 1810-11 (199), III, p. 25; IUP Transportation 1.

were able to earn a sum to be paid to them on release.[89] Becher's hope that worthwhile work would inculcate industrious habits and a sober life likewise informed the better-known activities of the Quaker, Elizabeth Fry. Her remarkable influence upon the wild inmates of the women's wards at Newgate was partly effected by providing regular laundering and other work — a task which was to become common for women prisoners in many parts of the country.

The remunerative aspect of productive work had its special appeal for justices whose concern was less for the souls of the prisoners than for the state of rateable pockets. As the Webbs point out, a productive system was open to grave objections: it inevitably favoured the strong and alert, it led to indiscriminate association, and it became increasingly the subject of criticism from rival employers and their labour forces who objected to the competition from incarcerated employees. Yet until the prisons were put under central administration, many justices continued to organise paid employment as a substantial part of their prison regimen.

Work could, however, be turned to purely disciplinary ends. The Penitentiary Act of 1779 required the work given to be 'of a base nature, such as treading the wheel, sawing stones and beating hemp'.[90] The tread-wheel could be used to give a short period of vigorous exercise and at the same time furnish power — for instance to raise water. This was one part of the system in Paul's Gloucestershire gaol. But other justices enthusiastically adopted tread-wheels (particularly once Cubitt had invented a simple version suitable for long hours of intentionally pointless labour). Already by 1823 considerable controversy had been aroused over the physical and mental dangers of requiring such exhausting and degrading work.[91] The advocates of stern discipline found their champions in Baron Western and Sydney Smith. 'There should be no tea and sugar', wrote the latter, with a baleful glare in the direction of Mrs. Fry, 'no assemblage of female felons round the washing-tub — nothing but beating hemp and pulling oakum and pounding bricks — no work but what was tedious, unusual and unfeminine'.[92] It was a perennial attitude in the administration of the prisons as in that of the poor law.

Association

Keeping prisoners from the evils of idleness did not necessarily eliminate

89   *Ibid.*, pp. 35-43.

90   *Ibid.*, at p. 25.

91   The generally complacent attitude of the justices who adopted the tread-wheel is reflected in the opinions that they expressed in published correspondence with Peel: 1823 (113), XV; 1824 (45,247), XIX; IUP Prisons 11.

92   See Webb *Prisons*, pp. 87-89.

'contamination'. Closely entwined with the question of labour was that of association: for if prisoners worked together they would talk, if not openly then surreptitiously. There were three possibilities: prisoners could work in association without restraint, they could work together but under threat of punishment if they communicated with one another (the Silent system, as it came to be called), or they could be kept at work in their individual cells (the so-called Separate system).[93] In each case, they might be provided with useful or useless work. It was never easy to find interesting tasks that could be performed in separate confinement. Frequently, however, those most impressed by the need for separation were advocates of unproductive labour. Those who saw work as a reformative influence, tended also to accept that prisoners might associate together during the day without the oppressive effects of enforced silence.

Among the early reformers this optimistic spirit was well-represented. Howard's proposal was that separate sleeping cells should be built, but that work should be carried on in communal day-rooms. This was the plan followed, for instance, by Becher at Southwell, and (of necessity) by Mrs Fry at Newgate. Bentham's Panopticon plan, in its completed version, inveighed against the idea of leaving prisoners in solitude and proposed cells for two, three or even four prisoners. Through all the early vicissitudes in the management of Millbank, the visiting committee attempted to maintain a series of useful trades which were carried on without any strict day-time separation.[94]

From these experiments was distilled the concept of classification: the dangers of contamination were to be met by grouping prisoners together according to their status, but keeping the groups apart. This principle was given an important place in Peel's Gaol Act of 1823. The justices in charge of the prisons and bridewells covered by the Act were obliged to separate male and female prisoners, those awaiting trial for misdemeanours and those for

---

93 In the writings of its British adherents, the separate system was carefully distinguished from solitary confinement, which was kept as a punishment for prison offences. Under the Separate system the prisoner was to be afforded wholesome contacts, with governor, chaplain, warders and so forth. 'The extent to which his solitude was, in practice, mitigated by "social intercourse" . . . was, we fear, to say the least, uncertain'. (Webb *Prisons*, p. 118).

94 E.g. Arthur Griffiths, *Memorials of Millbank* (1875) I, pp. 56-58; Report from Select Committee on the General Penitentiary at Millbank 1823 (533), V; IUP Prisons 10. One prominent member of the Millbank Visiting Committee was G. P. Holford, M.P., the chairman of the Select Committee that had recommended that the Penitentiary be built, but not according to Bentham's plan: see the Committee's First and Second Reports 1810-11 (199,217), III; and Third Report 1812 (306), II; IUP Transportation I. He was a diligent worker for prison reform throughout this period: see Webb *Prisons*, pp. 47-49.

felony, those convicted of misdemeanours and those of felony, debtors and vagrants.[95] But while the institution of these divisions marked an improvement on the old lack of discrimination, it was a very crude device and only survived formally for fourteen years.[96]

From Howard's time onwards, there were always those who maintained the virtues of separate confinement. In perhaps the most complete statement of the case for separation, the Third Report of the Inspectors for the Home District, its ancestry is traced back to ecclesiastical sources, such as the writings of Bishop Butler and the Revd Samuel Denne.[97] Overtones of monastic contemplation were always prominent in such arguments; indeed they resound in the very word 'penitentiary'. The case was not so much that this cruelly lonely fate would arouse loathing and fear both in those subjected to it and in all potential criminals, but rather that the opportunity for reflection away from all save the wholesome influence of governor, warders, chaplain and medical officer would have a positively reformative effect.

Nor was strict separation merely a plan in contemplation. Howard's first visit to Sussex inspired the Lord Lieutenant, the Duke of Richmond, to rebuild the county gaol at Horsham and then the House of Correction at Petworth. The regime of isolation instituted at Horsham was so severe that it was said to have halved the number of inmates. The same attitude was manifest in the statute for the national penitentiaries of 1779, which was the response of Blackstone and Eden to the teachings of Howard. The motivation of the enactment was made clear in a preamble: 'whereas if many Offenders, convicted of Crimes for which Transportation hath been usually inflicted, were ordered to solitary Imprisonment, accompanied by well-regulated Labour, and religious Instruction, it might be the Means, under Providence, not only of deterring others from the Commisssion of the like Crimes, but also of reforming the Individuals, and inuring them to Habits of Industry'. The drudge-like forms of labour required by the Act have already been mentioned.[98] It was also provided that where possible the work should be done separately. If the nature of the work brought prisoners together, then they should be kept under constant supervision.[99] This same plan of solitude was

---

95   4 Geo. IV, c. 64, s. 10. The degree to which this injunction was carried out was substantial: see Webb *Prisons*, pp. 92-94.

96   The classification provisions of the 1823 Act were repealed by 2 & 3 Vict. c. 56.

97   1837-38 [141], XXX at pp. 71-72.

98   Above, p. 28.

99   19 Geo. III, c. 74, s. 33.

written into the local act which gave Sir Onesiphorus Paul power to reform the Gloucestershire prisons,[100] and as the case for the separate system lost ground in the first decades of the new century,[101] his prison remained the one well-known example of its application.

Between the poles of solitary drudgery and productive association there were many possible courses, and in the period up to 1865 the regimes of prisons differed considerably. The treatment that a prisoner received varied with the degree to which the justices or franchise holders had been shaken out of their eighteenth-century lethargy by the ardour of the prison reformers, the extent to which they had been prepared to rebuild or modify their gaols, their attitude to work, the kind of work that could be found and possibility of performing it in the isolation of a cell. Moreover, it was soon enough appreciated that, at least for long-term prisoners, the system could be organised in stages, progressing from the severe to the more lenient. The Millbank Act of 1812, for instance, had two such stages. While any stage system involved some degree of association towards the end, the idea was so obviously useful as a means of enforcing discipline that in time it became as normal to the management of prisoners at home as of those who had been transported abroad.

Diet

In 1865, one of the Prison Inspectors mentioned an increase in rick-burning in Breconshire and explained it as the work of tramps who wanted to be sentenced to penal servitude.[102] Given the prevalence of destitution, prison reformers had always to face the prospect of their gaols, for all their discipline, becoming havens from the rigours of ordinary existence. Plans to make conditions 'less eligible' inside than out were given a sympathetic hearing, but particularly so if they concerned the most basic of all staples — food. Diet, therefore, is the third crucial element in the debates about reform. It had important relationships with the other essentials, especially with work, since the amount and quality of the food had to some extent to depend on the severity of the labour demanded. Moreover there was an inevitable temptation to force prisoners to work by threatening to withhold food, and this was one root of the scandals exposed at Birmingham and Leicester in 1854.[103]

The discussions about diet have been extensively treated by the Webbs[104] and need not be elaborated here. We may, however, note the practical

100   25 Geo. III, c. 10.
101   Separate confinement, for instance, was given up at Petworth in 1816.
102   Thirtieth Report 1865 [3474], XXIII, p. 24.
103   See below, p.36.
104   Webb *Prisons*, pp. 133-44, 225-26.

exercise in making a prison less eligible that was started at Millbank in 1822, both for its date and for the amount of public attention that it attracted. The pared rations that were then introduced caused an outbreak of scurvy which could not be eradicated by specially supplemented diet and the whole prison had to be evacuated for some months. The lesson was one that could not easily be forgotten, and perhaps was a reason why the dietaries later recommended by the Home Office, while scarcely abundant, were not as meagre as some advocated.

The central bureaucracy of the prisons

The dual system of national and local prisons meant that the Home Office in the mid-nineteenth century bore direct responsibility for some prisoners and supervised the manner in which local authorities treated others. For its period in Britain, the arrangement was unique. Those who directed the convict prisons remained distinct from the prison inspectors, but there were close links between them in the early years. The crucial importance to the subsequent history of the subject of the ideas then worked out suggests that the relationship of the two branches deserves more attention than it has yet received.

The old tradition of parsimonious neglect was the spirit in which the national system of imprisonment was first developed, just as it continued to dominate the gaols of the common law courts — the King's Bench, Marshalsea, and Fleet. The old warship hulks in which those awaiting transportation were held after 1776 proved to be, 'of all the places of confinement that British history records, . . . apparently the most brutalizing, the most demoralizing and the most horrible'.[105] An expedient seized upon to cope with a temporary hiatus, as was initially supposed, was found to have the fatal attraction of cheapness.

At first, the hulks were run by contractor-overseers. Conditions were over-crowded and disease-ridden; the convicts were given only intermittent labour on shore and spent a large part of their time unsupervised under battened hatches.[106] The contractor system, for all its dreadful evils, was allowed to survive for a quarter-century. Not till 1802 was a Government Inspector appointed. But he soon became the chief administrator of the hulk establishment and the contractors disappeared. The shift of opinion against prison contractors can be seen in the decision to abandon Bentham's contract with the Treasury for the erection and management of the national Panopti-

---

105   *Ibid.*, pp. 45-46.

106   Howard was an early visitor and gave a highly critical account of the conditions to a Select Committee which reported in 1778; 36 H.C. Journals 926.

con penitentiary.[107] The Committee which made this recommendation was responsible for the start on Millbank, but it was too appreciative of the savings effected by using the hulks to recommend their abandonment.[108] Some modifications followed, such as the building of cells to make separate confinement possible at night, and gradually there were improvements in the organisation of shore labour. But overall the hulks remained vicious, demoralising and physically disgusting places, alike for those who were subsequently transported and those who spent their whole period of confinement there.

Between 1814 and 1847, they were left to the charge of the same supervisor, J. H. Capper. During the first half of his long period in office, the numbers of convicts on the hulks grew from 2,000 to 4,000 and they were kept, by his estimate in 1832, at an annual cost (after deducting the value of labour performed) of only £6 11s. 6d. Yet the laxity of the regime — with its opportunities for 'contamination', for robbery of one prisoner by another and so forth — brought outspoken condemnation from a Select Committee on Secondary Punishments,[109] and the same view was echoed three years later by the Duke of Richmond's Committee.[110] As a result the regimen was made somewhat more severe. In addition, under a plan begun in 1824, the hardier men not sent to Australia were shipped off to hulks in Bermuda and Gibraltar, leaving the British hulks to cope with the old and sickly who were incapable of hard work in a hot climate.

The years of continuing neglect eventually produced a scandal. As a result of charges levied in 1847 by Thomas Duncombe, M.P., the Prison Inspector, Captain W. J. Williams, conducted an investigation in which evidence was actually taken from convicts still on the hulks.[111] The whole administration was roundly condemned, the ageing Capper resigned and the medical officer, Bossy, whose neglect of duty had been peculiarly serious, was summarily replaced.

Scandal played a prominent, if varied, rôle throughout nineteenth-century prison reform, but this exposure of conditions on the hulks was particularly effective. In the course of a decade they were phased out of operation.[112] This was not a necessary corollary of the abandonment of transportation, since the

107   First Report of the Committee on Laws relating to Penitentiary Houses 1810-11 (199), III, p. 11-16; IUP Transportation 1.

108   Third Report 1812 (306), II; IUP Transportation 1.

109   1831-32 (547), VII, pp. 12-16, Qs. 1130-1586; IUP Transportation 1.

110   Select Committee (H.L.) on Gaols and Houses of Correction, Third Report 1835 (440), XII, pp. iv-v; IUP Prisons 4; Second Report 1835 (439), XI, App. No. 21; IUP Prisons 3.

111   Report upon an Inquiry into . . . the Hulks at Woolwich 1847 [831], XVIII; IUP Prisons 12.

112   The hulks in Bermuda continued in use until 1862 and one in Gibraltar until 1875.

hulks had long been not only collection points for those being transported but also convict prisons in their own right. They were given up because, for all their cheapness, they could not be made to conform to the standards of sanitation and discipline that had become articles of faith in the other sections of the Home Office administration. By 1847 these standards, with cellular isolation as their keystone, had acquired an irresistible momentum.

The way in which this force had built up deserves consideration. Part of the pressure — represented in the handling of the exposure by Captain Williams' sharply uncompromising report — came from the Inspectors of Prisons. They had been given few powers of compulsion in the execution of their main task of inspecting the local gaols.[113] But some at least of their number showed that selfless determination to combat abuse and neglect that was so characteristic of the new inspectors in the years after 1832. The most forceful were William Crawford, who in 1815 had become Secretary to the London Prison Discipline Society, and Whitworth Russell, previously the Chaplain of Millbank. Crawford had been a member of an imposing European delegation which in 1832 went to inspect prisons in the United States.[114] The report that he made to the government on his return[115] focussed attention in political circles on the merits of the Separate system of cellular confinement, as exemplified by the new Eastern Penitentiary in Philadelphia, as opposed to the Silent system, imposed under threat of the whip, at Auburn Gaol, New York and elsewhere. Coming at a time when the classification plan of the Gaols Act 1823 was admittedly failing, it attracted great attention. Crawford was appointed with Russell to the Home District inspectorate under the Act of 1835,[116] and their Third Report, which restates with great eloquence the case for separate confinement, is a good example of the manner in which the early inspectors made public their personal views on questions of policy.[117]

Appended to that report, is an elaborate plan for a 'separate system' prison, which was the technical brain-child of Captain Jebb, R.E. The link that is there so close can be seen again in the fact that Jebb was the man brought in to implement Williams' Report on the Hulks, and the man who resolutely strove for their replacement by specially-designed prisons which allowed for cellular

113   For comparisons with other inspectorates see D. Roberts, *Victorian Origins of the Welfare State* (1962) Ch. 4, esp. pp. 116-17. The one significant power they did have was to license cells as fitted for separate occupation by prisoners: see 2 & 3 Vict. c. 56. If justices chose to ignore advice as to the virtues of cellular isolation, the inspectors could do nothing.

114   Webb *Prisons*, p. 115 discusses the other participants, who included de Tocqueville.

115   Penitentiaries of the United States 1834 (593), XLVI; IUP Prisons 2.

116   He was not made Inspector-General (no such office being created) because of Melbourne's antipathy: Roberts, *op. cit.*, n. 113, p. 123.

117   1837-38 [141], XXX.

isolation and effective discipline. That the man who was to exert so powerful an influence on the central prison system was a military engineer suggests a characteristic attitude of the day. Indeed, since the time of Howard and Bentham, building plans had played a uniquely important role in this field of social policy, a development which reached its climax with the execution of Jebb's design for the model prison, Pentonville. During the 1840's Jebb was immersed there in an experiment in the confinement of prisoners to single cells for long periods. This was tried first on men specially selected for their hardiness and then on male convicts indiscriminately. While the former was pronounced a success, the latter produced a disturbingly high incidence of insanity and suicide. This forced a cut in the period of isolation from eighteen to twelve and then to nine months.

Jebb, increasingly involved in the central prisons, saw beyond the unitary systems which so concerned the inspectors, with their oversight of mainly short-term prisoners. Upon the initial base of separate confinement Jebb began to build a second stage, intended to be more constructive, in which the convicts were put to hard productive labour in association on public works.[118] In this the influence of the labour gangs that had been developed in the colonial penal settlements is obvious, and when penal servitude was formally instituted in 1853, the model of transportation was again followed in the addition of a third stage — release on licence under police supervision. In the middle years of the century, the prison system occupied public attention more continuously than at any other period and through it all Jebb stood as a powerful defender of his own procedures. Their merits he asserted dogmatically with little apparent concern that the benefits of initial separation might be dissipated by the contamination spread during the subsequent period of associated labour. But then he was working against considerable public suspicion of a kind epitomised in the Report of Brougham's Select Committee in 1847:

'That imprisonment as usually practised is not an efficacious Punishment, though accompanied with hard Labour, and with Separation or with Silence, as it is in some Prisons, is likewise the result of the Evidence. Only those who undergo it for the first Time appear to feel it much; this Suffering soon wears off. A second Commitment finds the Criminal by no means unprepared to undergo it, and it ever after ceases to exercise a deterring Effect. The Number of Times that young Offenders have been committed, some of them Twelve or Fifteen Times within a few Years, seems strongly illustrative of this position; whereas Convicts returned from Transportation either by Escape or by Expiration of their Sentences, regard with the utmost Terror Repetition of that Punishment.

118   For this special prisons were built at Portland and Chatham and the Napoleonic war-prison on Dartmoor was refurbished.

How far imprisonment can be so far altered as to be efficacious, either as preparatory to Transportation or as a Punishment by itself is a Question of Difficulty, upon which little Evidence could be given, inasmuch as no sufficient Experience has yet been had of the improved Systems, which are now in partial Operation.'[119]

The idea of stages as an aid to discipline and reformation had long appealed to prison reformers, and was capable of many variations. In the writings of Jebb's contemporary, Alexander Maconochie, it was given an emphasis that carried forward the slender tradition of humane optimism in prison administration. Maconochie believed that prisoners could be induced to form responsible, industrious habits by earning marks for work and good conduct, the marks counting towards improved conditions of imprisonment and eventual freedom. Sentences would comprise so many marks, rather than so much time, and would be worked out in conditions which emphasised productive labour rather than solitary penance.[120] A marks system was introduced in Western Australia, Bermuda and Gibraltar and, after some modification, in Ireland. In each case it achieved some success.[121] Eventually, it was partly adopted into the regime of penal servitude in Britain.[122]

But in his own time Maconochie's ideas mostly aroused antagonism. His one opportunity to put them into practice — at the barbaric penal settlement on Norfolk Island — was soon brought to an end and that experience alone was enough for Jebb and Earl Grey to condemn the system as too extreme.[123] After returning to England, Maconochie was for a short time governor of Birmingham Prison before his sympathetic and clement attitude to the prisoners brought dismissal by the justices.[124] This episode indeed was followed by a disgraceful backlash. William Austin, who replaced Maconochie, instituted a reign of terror with long hours on the tread-wheel as the principal instrument. Similar harshness at Leicester Gaol meant that the two prisons

119 Second Report of the Select Committee on Juvenile Offenders and Transportation 1847 (534), VII, p. 4; IUP Juvenile Offenders 1.

120 Maconochie set forth his ideas in a series of pamphlets (for which see Sir J. V. Barry, *Alexander Maconochie of Norfolk Island* (1958) Ch. 4, 263-65). See also his Report on Prison Discipline in Van Diemen's Land 1837-38 [121], XL; IUP Transportation 6.

121 Information about progress of the marks system recurs in the voluminous published despatches concerning transportees in IUP Transportation 7, 14-16.

122 Both the Carnarvon and the Gladstone Committees approved of it: 1863 (499) IX, para. 3; 1895 [C. 7702], LVI; para. 43; IUP Prisons 6 and 19.

123 See their evidence to the Commons Select Committee on Transportation 1856 (244), XVII, Qs. 1415, 1416, 1688; IUP Transportation 4.

124 Maconochie was, however, warmly supported by the Recorder of Birmingham, Matthew Davenport Hill (see e.g. his evidence to the 1856 Select Committee, above n. 123, Second Report, App. 190). Hill's role as an advocate of liberal penal reform deserves reassessment.

were subjected to condemnatory investigations in the same year.[125] Yet the full horror of a regime of separation and long hours of useless labour for weeks or months — the rebelliousness, depression, insanity and suicide that it generated — seems to have evoked little enough response. Some of the prison inspectors became opponents of useless hard labour. But Jebb undoubtedly represented a common feeling in influential circles when he stated that, while long sentences gave time to exercise a reformatory influence, imprisonment for a matter of weeks could only hope to deter, and the local gaols should therefore provide treatment for such offenders that was as repellent as practicable.

When Jebb died in 1863 he had just given evidence to two official inquiries: to a Royal Commission which still hoped that the final stage in penal servitude could remain transportation to Western Australia or some other colony;[126] and to Lord Carnarvon's notorious Select Committee, which adopted Jebb's conception of the proper regimen for local prisons and recommended that all sentenced imprisonment with hard labour should be subject to work that was 'penal, irksome and fatiguing'.[127]

The Carnarvon report was decisive for penal administration over the ensuing thirty years. Its proposals were largely implemented by the Prisons Act 1865, which also *required* local authorities to build separate cells in their gaols. So substantial a measure of central compulsion, coming only in the 1860's, produced little local reaction, though justices closed some gaols rather than remodel them. The change paved the way for the unique step of 'nationalisation' twelve years later, which likewise caused only a passing ripple of antagonism on constitutional grounds.[128] During this transitional period not only the legal basis and administrative responsibility for penal servitude and imprisonment remained distinct, so did the aims. After 1877, only the legal authority is separate. The placing of the former local prisons under central commissioners led to the domination of their administration by the Chairman, Sir Edmund du Cane, who was already the Director-General of Convict Prisons.

It has become traditional to regard the Du Cane regime as the final achievement of 'reformers who have . . . made the neglect, oppression, corruption, and physical torture of the old common gaol the pretext for

125   Royal Commission on Birmingham Borough Prison 1854 [1809], XXXI; IUP Prisons 15; Royal Commission on Leicester County Jail 1854 [1808], XXXIV; IUP Prisons 13.

126   Royal Commission on Transportation and Penal Servitude 1863 [3190], XXI, IUP Transportation 5.

127   Lords Select Committee on Gaols and Houses of Correction 1863 (499), IX; IUP Prisons 6; Jebb's evidence: pp. 107-30.

128   Webb *Prisons*, pp. 199-200; Gordon Rose, *The Struggle for Penal Reform* (1961) pp. 36-42.

transforming it into that diabolical den of torment, mischief, and damnation, the modern model prison';[129] just as the reaction against it in the Gladstone Report of 1895 is treated as 'courageous and radical',[130] 'a milestone in English penal history'.[131] But Du Cane's system only put into practice the attitude to the imprisonment of offenders that had predominated in the middle of the century, when transportation had been given up. There had been two main views of transportation, both of which had as their corollary that imprisonment at home by way of substitute should be made as severe a deterrent as possible. One was that criminals really dreaded the long separation from their families and homes; the other that, in practice if not in intention, transportation held out too rosy a prospect of a new life upon release. However much the latter was a reality in the growing Australian colonies, no one supposed it to be a likely consequence of imprisonment at home. Accordingly, as the rehabilitation of prisoners began to occupy public attention, it became clear that only during the term of the sentence could such a possibility be realised. The Gladstone Committee was set up in response to a growing dissatisfaction with the regime administered by Du Cane, his most influential critic being the Chaplain of Wandsworth Prison, the Revd W. D. Morrison. The Committee accepted much of Morrison's case and took an optimistic view of what might be achieved:

'[T]hat some of (the community's) worst and most dangerous products, and that many of those who would lead honest lives under different surroundings, can be reclaimed by special and skilful prison treatment is emphatically maintained by many of the most capable and experienced witnesses.'[132]

The Committee was not seriously concerned about the conditions to which prisoners would return upon release, though the Report made a few suggestions for developing the existing arrangements for after-care;[133] apart from this, 'the improvement of general social conditions is the work of the com-

129   G. B. Shaw in his Introduction to Webb *Prisons*, p. vii.

130   L. W. Fox, *The English Prison and Borstal Systems* (1952) p. 53.

131   Rose, *op. cit.*, n. 128, p. 58.

132   Report of the Departmental Committee on Prisons 1895 [C. 7702], LVI, para. 29; IUP Prisons 19.

133   Ideas concerning the help that should be offered to discharged prisoners remained very limited throughout the Victorian era. The moment of discharge was thought to be an appropriate moment for payment of a small sum and there were early examples of dole charities for this purpose. Peel's Gaol Act (4 G. IV, c. 64, s. 16) had allowed justices to pay up to 20s. to prisoners released upon remission for 'extraordinary diligence and merit', and after 1862 this sum (increased to 40s.) could be administered through voluntary prisoners' aid societies. The central prison administration subsequently used the same system. But at a time when, in other fields of philanthropy, the idea of sustained support was beginning to replace the occasional dole, it took a long time to gain much of a footing in relation to discharged prisoners. The Gladstone Committee was not complimentary about the work of the societies as a

munity'. The recommendations focussed instead upon what might be achieved during the term of imprisonment by way of mollifying the existing harshness: separate confinement was to be reduced and unproductive hard labour eliminated, the diet was to be reconsidered and the educational and trade-training services developed.[134]

The Gladstone Report was the first official document to derive its general tone from the humane tradition of Howard, Fry and Maconochie, and therein has lain its attraction for later generations. It has become the classic text of those who treat rehabilitation as the governing consideration in the treatment of offenders, both within and without the walls of prisons. But it is important to remember that the Committee itself was primarily concerned with imprisonment and that it did not suggest that deterrence should be abandoned as the principal aim of punishment for crime. The first question that it asked was, 'Is the present Prison System sufficiently deterrent?'. What the Report does is to express the cautious hope that deterrence and reform could be pursued at one and the same time within the existing prison structure. In this it appears a document of its time; greater sympathy, in the same careful measure, was also beginning to affect the treatment of the poor. The limited changes that the Committee suggested were accepted by the government, and the Prison Commissioners, under a new chairman, Ruggles Brise, set about implementing them.[135] Yet a quarter-century later, when his administration came under criticism quite as heavy as that which had provoked the appointment of the Gladstone Committee, it emerged that little had really changed.[136] There were many who accepted that the indictment of the 'modern model prison' still stood.

It had been put to the Gladstone Committee by Sir Godfrey Lushington, Permanent Under-Secretary at the Home Department, that 'the true mode of

whole (paras. 34-36), and their view is supported by a subsequent investigation made on behalf of the Prison Commissioners: (The Operation of Discharged Prisoners' Aid Societies 1897 [C. 8299], XL; IUP Prisons 20). But subsequent reorganisation by no means brought about an adequate system of after-care, as the Salmon Committee on Employment in Prisons was to report in 1935 (Cmd. 4897, Part II). The whole history is treated in more depth by L. W. Fox, *op. cit.*, n. 130, ch. 15.

134 The Gladstone Report was followed by special investigations into the questions of education and diet: see the Report on Education and Moral Instruction of Prisoners 1896 [C. 8154], XLIV; Reports on Prison Dietaries and Prison Dietaries (Scotland) 1899 [C. 9166 and 9514] XLII; IUP Prisons 20, all of which share the cautiously reformative spirit of the main report.

135 Special records of their progress were published: see 1896 [C. 7995, 7996] XLIV; 1898 [C. 8790] XLVII; IUP Prisons 19.

136 The nationalisation of prisons placed an effective cordon around them, and it was rare for ex-prisoners to complain about how they had been treated. Ruggles Brise's regime came under intelligent scrutiny once conscription brought conscientious objectors into the prisons. Hobhouse and Brockway's *English Prisons Today* (to which the Webbs' *Prisons* forms a companion volume) raised their criticisms to the level of a highly-developed and well-informed impeachment.

reforming a man or restoring him to society is exactly in the opposite direction' from life in a prison, where inevitably 'the status of a prisoner throughout his whole career was unfavourable to reformation'.[137] The history of the attempts to implement the Gladstone Report suggests that Lushington's despondency was realistic, and that the Committee sought to reconcile two unalterably opposing forces. Certainly the real achievements of the period after Gladstone lie where Lushington suggested — outside prison. Ruggles Brise was himself responsible for the development of the Borstal system for adolescent delinquents[138] and he was a strong supporter of the Criminal Justice Act 1914, which did much to keep fine defaulters out of prison.[139] It was also during his period in office that the initial experiments in the probation of offenders were transformed into a regular system.[140]

Among adults who were confined for their offence, there were two major changes of principle. It was at last recognised that the mentally sick required treatment in separate institutions.[141] And persistent offenders, who caused the Gladstone Committee much anxiety, were made the subject of preventive detention orders.[142] Otherwise, the continuing feature of prison administration was its dreary uniformity, summed up for Hobhouse and Brockway by Ruggles Brise's boast that 'It is now 4.30 in the afternoon, and I know that just now, at every Local and Convict prison in England, the same things in general are being done, and that in general they are being done in the same way'.[143]

There are many aspects of punishment and the administration of penal institutions which at best have received only passing reference in this brief account. The case of young offenders, however, is of such importance that it must be separately mentioned, and some further comment is also offered upon the task of sentencing and the imprisonment of debtors in the hope of pointing up the special problems raised.

137   Op. cit., n. 132, para. 25.

138   See further below, p. 44.

139   S.1 allowed courts to order those who could not pay fines immediately to do so over time. Between 1910 and 1921 the numbers imprisoned annually for non-payment of fines dropped from 85,000 to 15,000.

140   Probation of Offenders Act 1907.

141   Mental Deficiency Act 1913; Webb Prisons p. 229.

142   By the Prevention of Crime Act 1908, Part II, a defendant sentenced to penal servitude for the crime for which he had been prosecuted, might in addition be charged and sentenced in respect of his habitual criminality to a further period of 'preventi e detention' (up to 10 years). This was intended to rid society of the competent, unscrupulous professional criminal, but in the event it was little used.

143   English Prisons Today (1922) p. 97.

Juvenile offenders

The extreme measure of how crude, indeed how desperate, was the eighteenth century policy of general deterrence lies in the fact that some children of nine and ten were actually executed,[144] and a great many more were imprisoned and transported in the same way as adults. The idea that punishment should be adjusted to the particular criminal, which Bentham supported on utilitarian grounds and which could also be justified in retributive terms, was denied by such actions. The principle of individualisation continued to be regarded with suspicion by those reformers of transportation and imprisonment who sought to make the lot of all convicts harshly punitive. However, there were always classes of prisoner who marked themselves out for special treatment, and of these juvenile offenders were the most obvious. It was natural to hope that those whose minds and characters were still being shaped might be specially receptive to reformatory influences. From the late eighteenth century onwards much charitable endeavour began to be devoted to the provision of institutions where convicted children, and those deprived of their parents, might be brought up and taught a trade or some other means of livelihood. As early as 1756 the Marine Society had started a school for the children of convicts, and in 1788, the Philanthropic Society set up cottage homes for delinquent and destitute boys, first in Hackney, then in Bermondsey. At Stretton in Warwickshire, farm-colonies for similar purposes were started in 1818. Gradually a link was forged with the administration of criminal justice, as the Crown was persuaded to pardon convicted juveniles on condition that they went into one of these homes.

What is now so striking is the time that it took for these special concessions to blossom into general practice. The amount of juvenile crime was very considerable. For much of the nineteenth century the large cities harboured gangs of young thieves, often put to work by Faginesque employers. It was common enough to find a lad of thirteen or fourteen being transported after a string of convictions stretching back to the age of seven or eight. The transport ships, the hulks and government penitentiaries, and the local prisons all bore a burden of young prisoners. In the inquiries into prisons that coincided with Romilly's campaign to reduce the number of capital offences various witnesses showed great concern over these young delinquents. The treatment they received was accounted a disgrace,[145] yet little happened. Capper,

144 Radzinowicz, *History* I, pp. 11-14 describes the law on the criminal capacity of infants and cites a number of examples of actual executions. It is doubtful, despite some unauthenticated stories, that executions of children for crimes short of murder were carried out in the nineteenth century: B. E. F. Knell, 'Capital Punishment: Its Administration in Relation to Juvenile Offenders' (1965) 5 B. J. Criminology 198.

145 See esp. Second and Third Reports of the Select Committee on the Police of the Metropolis 1817 (484), VII; IUP Police 2; 1818 (423), VIII; IUP Police 3; Select Committee on the State of Gaols 181 **(579), VII; IUP Prisons 1. See also the Select Committee on Criminal Commitments and Convictions 1828 (419), VII, Report pp. 9-13.**

the Superintendent of the Hulks, did succeed in setting apart one vessel for the reception of boys,[146] but it was not until 1837 that the government began to build Parkhurst prison on the Isle of Wight for the same purpose. In its first eight years Parkhurst received 1,200 boys, mostly keeping them for two or three years before sending them to Australia to work for private masters.[147]

In this period, there was also a movement to provide summary trial for juveniles accused of most offences, so that they did not have to be held in contaminating custody during the weeks before assizes or sessions took place.[148] Despite the inevitable doubts among lawyers,[149] this procedure began to be introduced in 1847.[150] The provision was extended to cover all offences short of homicide in 1879.[151] At the same time, the magistrates acquired certain special discretions in the sentencing of juveniles. It was not until the 'Children's Charter' of 1908, that this magistrates' work was removed into juvenile courts, distinct in time or place from the general 'police courts'.[152]

As long as transportation lasted, there were few who disapproved of a system which treated youngsters accused of crime by the methods that applied to adults — imprisoning them to begin with, then if they persisted in iniquity, sending them off to a new life abroad. But the ending of the system coincided with the first period of experimentation in the special imprisonment and reformatory treatment of juvenile offenders. Their treatment suddenly became a matter of hot controversy.[153] Colonel Jebb had been the continuing mentor of Parkhurst and became its stout defender. On the other side a number of high-minded figures claimed the superiority of special institutions in which juveniles could be moulded into upright, employable citizens. Some, like the Reverend Sydney Turner,[154] seem to have approached the task with

146   See the Select Committee on Gaols and Houses of Correction, Third Report 1835 (440), XII; IUP Prisons 4; also the last two Reports mentioned in the previous note.

147   Select Committee (H.L.) on the Execution of Criminal Law 1847 (447), VII; IUP Juvenile Offenders 1; Qs. 2182 ff.

148   This proposal had been advocated for at least twenty years, attracting, for instance, the Criminal Law Commissioners, Third Report 1837 [79], XXXI; IUP Criminal Law 3.

149   See, e,g., the Second Report of the Select Committee (op. cit., n. 147) at p. 5.

150   10 & 11 Vict. c. 82: charges of simple larceny against children under 14 (from 1850, under 16) could be tried summarily with parental consent. See R. M. Jackson 'The Incidence of Jury Trial during the Past Century', 1 Mod. Law Rev. 132, where the extension of summary trial to cover adult offenders in more limited circumstances is also discussed.

151   Summary Jurisdiction Act, 42 & 43 Vict. c. 49, s. 10.

152   Children Act 1908, s. 111.

153   For details of the controversy see J. Carlebach, Caring for Children in Trouble (1970) pp. 39 ff. Between 1847 and 1853 there were extensive investigations of the problem by Select Committees: Execution of the Criminal Law 1847 (447, 534), VII; IUP Juvenile Offenders 1; Criminal and Destitute Juveniles 1852 (515), VII; IUP Juvenile Offenders 2; 1852-3 (674), XXIII; IUP Juvenile Offenders 3.

kindness and imagination, striving to secure some substitute for proper family life. Others were of sterner cast. Barwick Lloyd Baker brought to his Gloucestershire reformatory a determination to impose a deterrent regime of hard work. Mary Carpenter, who became the best-known publicist of reformatories and industrial schools, believed in a stern and rigid discipline that made her own establishment at Kingswood an unhappy place. She it was who chose to launch an emotional, rather ignorant attack against Parkhurst, in the belief that prison could never be an appropriate method of dealing with juveniles.[155]

The influence of the campaign for separate institutions was considerable. Their use soon ceased to be experimental and became standard.[156] The courts were given power to sentence offenders under sixteen, first to fourteen days or more in prison, then to a period of 2-5 years in a reformatory school.[157] The schools were to be privately run but would receive a *per capita* grant in return for Home Office inspection — the first instance in which central grants were used as a means of controlling penal institutions in Britain. In the same year industrial schools for children found by the courts to be vagrants were assisted by grants in Scotland, a system which was extended to England in 1857.[158]

Both kinds of school grew in number,[159] and with growth came the parsimony and indifferent leadership that infected other experiments in institutional care. The personal inspiration of the pioneers was not readily transmissible. Complaints against the institutions were put to a Royal Commission in 1884, which returned a complacent verdict, considering that: 'Over and above their effect in reducing the amount of both juvenile and adult crime, these schools are successfully training a vast number of children for honest and useful lives.'[160] A decade later the Gladstone Committee took the schools

154 Chaplain to the Philanthropic Society from 1841 and organiser of the Redhill farm colony that it set up under the inspiration of De Metz's *colonie agricole* at Mettray, he was later appointed Inspector of Reformatory and Industrial Schools.

155 *Reformatory Schools for the Children of the Perishing and Dangerous Classes and for Juvenile Offenders* (1851).

156 Parkhurst as a boys' prison survived only until Jebb's death in 1863.

157 17 & 18 Vict. c. 86.

158 17 & 18 Vict. c. 74; 20 & 21 Vict. c. 48. Subsequent legislation on reformatories and industrial schools is discussed by R. E. S. Hinde, *The British Penal System* (1951), pp. 103-06; Carlebach, *op. cit.*, n. 153.

159 The number of English reformatories rose to over fifty in 1858 but thereafter during the century the number remained roughly constant. The number of industrial schools, however, grew steadily, until in 1894 there were 141.

160 1844 [C. 3876], XLV, IUP Juvenile Offenders 4, p. xii. One of the issues on which it called for change, however, was the requirement that juveniles sentenced to a reformatory should first undergo the 'short, sharp shock' of 10 or more days imprisonment (reduced from 14 in 1866). This was stoutly opposed by the English managers of the schools and so came about only in two stages: courts ceased to be obliged to impose it in 1893 and it was abolished entirely in 1899.

as models for institutions that would cater for the next age group. They believed, on slender evidence, that 'it is certain that the ages when the majority of habitual criminals are made lies between 16 and 21' and that this propensity could best be combatted in a 'penal reformatory'.[161] The idea was fashionable in America and from it the Borstal system was soon to blossom.[162]

But against this prevalent optimism a less sanguine current of opinion had for some time been flowing. A Departmental Committee, under the chairmanship of Sir Godfrey Lushington, reported on the schools in the very year after Gladstone. A long and careful analysis of their philosophy and work led to a host of criticisms that virtually all the Committee were prepared to accept. Among them was disapproval of the 'Asylum theory' adopted by some magistrates and school authorities, which held that children should be placed in them whenever they would be 'better off', not just when such a step was *necessary* for the child's protection or the public's.[163] Nearly half the Committee were prepared to speak out very firmly indeed against policies that had swollen the numbers detained in the schools from about 6,000 in 1864 to some 24,600 in 1894, and to plead the case for leaving the child at home, for his own sake and his parents', instead of incarcerating him with a miscellany of those also plucked from the 'tens of thousands of children indistinguishable in character and circumstances'.[164] This statement, albeit a minority view, put in uncompromising form Lushington's pessimistic assessment of the reformatory prospects of institutional incarceration, which the Gladstone Committee had noted but had been too cautious to accept.[165]

The managers of the schools fought the criticisms, just as they had the milder recommendations of the 1884 Commission.[166] But it became clear that, as the new century dawned, opinion was moving in favour of much more discriminate use of their services. The experiments in probation, which started with the cooperation of police court missionaries, blossomed into a state-run probation service with legislation in 1907.[167] The courts — especially the new juvenile courts — were able (in time) to use probation officers to investigate an offender's background. At the same time non-institutional supervision by means of probation orders added an important new dimension to sentencing

161   C. 7702, para. 29.

162   For the development of the Borstal System see L. W. Fox, *The English Prison and Borstal Systems* (1952) Ch. 21; R. Hood, *Borstal Re-assessed* (1965).

163   1896 [C. 8204], XLV, with minutes of evidence 1897 [C. 8290], XLII, IUP Juvenile Offenders 5, 6.

164   *Op cit.*, n. 163, p. 158.

165   See above, p. 40.

166   For a detailed account, see G. Carlebach, *op. cit.*, n. 153 above, Ch. 2.

167   Probation of Offenders Act 1907.

practice, just as it did for adults. Institutional treatment as a specific against social ills no longer commanded such ready faith; the new century was to find new forms for its aspirations.

Sentencing

The history of punishment in the nineteenth century is dominated by the administrative problems of the different forms of sentence. Until 'nationalisation' of the local prisons, the nature of punishment to which a prisoner was subjected might vary greatly, depending where he was sent in Britain or the overseas penal settlements. Indeed his prospects were constantly changing. After 1877 the institution of a uniform, rigidly authoritarian system of imprisonment led to a single form of custodial sentence for adult offenders, varying only with its duration. Throughout the period little is heard of the initiatory step in the process: the passing of sentence by the court.

Yet as the reforms in penal administration took place the court's sentence gained in significance. In the days before the reduction of capital punishment, the court had the formal power to pass only one sentence — death — in respect of the bulk of serious crimes, though it was the trial judge in many cases who determined whether that sentence would be carried out.[168] The substitution of transportation (in the less serious cases, with the alternative of a sentence of imprisonment) provided the courts with a greater range of choice. But during the period of transportation, whether the sentence was actually carried out became a decision for those in charge of the hulks, the convict penitentiaries and the local gaols,[169] and often depended as much on such factors as the prisoner's conduct during the first portion of his sentence as on its prescribed length.[170] In the middle of the century, when penal servitude was conceived, at least by some, as different in kind from imprisonment, the choice made by the court began to be more decisive.

The sentencing process deserves more attention from historians than it has yet received. It had been part of Beccaria's plea for moderation that uncertainty and discretion in the administration of the criminal law should be eliminated. The Criminal Law Commissioners, who laboured to produce an

168   See above, p. 16.

169   For instance, it was the Visiting Justices at Gloucester gaol who decided which 'transport convicts exhibit a disposition favourable to penitence' and are therefore kept: First Report on the Laws Relating to Penitentiary Houses 1810-11 (199), III; IUP Transportation 1, p. 30. J. H. Capper, rather than the Secretary of State, decided which transports in the hulks should be sent abroad: Shaw, pp. 137-38.

170   But length did have its effect. The sentence of seven years transportation, much the most common since it was prescribed for simple larceny, had in the 1840s almost invariably been transmuted into some four years imprisonment. Hence the scale by which, in 1853, penal servitude replaced transportation.

acceptable criminal code,[171] sought to refine the varieties of sentence to forty-five classes, one of which was attached to each crime. The classes ranged from death to a fine of £40, some prescribing a fixed penalty, some a maximum and some both a maximum and a minimum.[172] This would have introduced a modicum of sense into a matter that had become increasingly illogical with the progressive repeal of the capital penalty. As it was, the consolidating statutes that were eventually passed in 1861 did little to mend matters and the problem remained long without remedy.[173]

In sentencing for many crimes the courts retained wide discretionary powers which they used with little concern for consistency. Earl Cathcart put it to Jebb that 'You are probably aware, from your knowledge of the sentences of criminals, that there is, throughout the country, an extraordinary diversity of sentences for the same offence.' And received the reply: 'Yes, that is the most marked failure of law.'[174] Differences in sentencing between courts could not begin to be eliminated until detailed comparative information was made available and there was some body able to lay down policies to be pursued. The former has only now been started, the latter had to await the founding of the Court of Criminal Appeal in 1907.[175] That grave disproportions were so long tolerated at least emphasises how small has been the role of retributive ideas in the development of Britain's penal system.

If sentences were to be other than arbitrary, it would seem necessary that those imposing them should understand what they entailed. Where the justices who sat at quarter and petty sessions were at all active in supervising their local gaols they had some appreciation of the nature of imprisonment there. After 1877, they lost this contact, for the Visiting Committees of justices, having no serious duties, were a failure. The professional judges concerned in criminal justice — the judges, recorders, chairmen of sessions and stipendiary magistrates — with only occasional exceptions, showed scant interest in penological matters. In the many official inquiries recorded in the parliamentary papers under review, their appearances are only occasional. The three judges who gave evidence to the Commons Select Committee in 1856 were probably typical: they thoroughly disapproved of the replacement of transportation by penal servitude and disliked the legislative scheme by which a reduced period of penal servitude was substituted for

---

171   See below, p. 58.

172   Criminal Law Commissioners, Seventh Report: Act of Crimes and Punishments 1843 [448], XIX; IUP Criminal Law 4, pp. 281-83; cf. Fourth Report 1839 [168], XIX; IUP Criminal Law 3, pp. xvi-xviii.

173   See 'Justice', Legal Penalties: the Need for Revaluation (1960).

174   Report of the Lords Select Committee on Gaols and Houses of Correction 1863 (499), IX; IUP Prisons 6, C. 1198.

175   See below, p. 60.

transportation.[176] Their views of appropriate punishment appear dominated by the deterrent effect produced at the one point — the passing of sentence — over which they exercised control, and they all agreed that in court a sentence of transportation produced a greater sensation of horror.[177] 'All I can do' said Mr Justice Cresswell, 'is to pass such sentence as, having had the case and tried it, I think my duty calls upon me to pass. I must leave others to exercise their discretion afterwards in consequence of what is to happen elsewhere.'[178]

Debtors in prison

The social and legal aspects of credit in nineteenth-century Britain have not received the attention from historians that their importance demands. Here we can touch only upon the role played by imprisonment as a means of forcing debtors to meet their obligations. The practice did diminish in importance, but nonetheless it long remained 'one of the chronic factors in prison disorder'.[179] At the beginning of the nineteenth century, there were three factors which made imprisonment of debtors popular. The creditor could not enforce judgment against both the body and the property of the debtor — he had to choose. Debtors who were not traders [180] could not seek the protection of bankruptcy proceedings against liability to meet their debts in full. And where the debt was over £10[181] the debtor could be imprisoned by the exceedingly summary step of arrest upon mesne process: a writ claiming the amount was all that was necessary; there was no need to proceed as far as judgment. The result was the Dickensian horror of the debtor who found himself unable ever to escape from gaol, since his means of earning were cut off and his gaol fees continued to mount.

176   Commons Select Committee on transportation 1856 (296,355), XVII; IUP Transportation 4. Qs. 2963 ff. (Cresswell J.); 3306 ff. (Erle J.); 3962 ff. (Lord Campbell C. J.). Similar views concerning transportation were expressed in returns made by virtually all the judges to the Lord's Committee on the subject in 1847: Second Report 1847 (534), VII; IUP Juvenile Offenders 1. pp. 3-4 and Appendix.

177   Henry Mayhew, on the other hand, expressed the view that the habitual criminal, with his feckless lack of concentration, was attracted by the vagabond life of the Australian outback, rather than the prospects of imprisonment at home. He claimed, to the evident surprise of the Committee, to have spoken to many such convicts: 1856 Select Committee, cited n. 176, Qs. 3546-50.

178   *Ibid*. Q. 2977.

179   Webb *Prisons*, p. 192.

180   The distinction of traders and non-traders was a matter of legal nicety: see generally E. Welbourne, 'Bankruptcy before the Era of Victorian Reform' (1932) 4 Camb. Hist. J. 51.

181   From 1827, over £20.

The barbarity of these rules had many repercussions upon the state of the law. For instance, the rules were one factor which restricted the development of the criminal law in its application to confidence tricksters. There is little moral distinction between obtaining goods, money or services by telling lies and removing goods or money by force or stealth; yet the judges persisted in requiring some further element than mere dishonesty if the trick was to be accounted a crime.[182] The person duped, after all, had civil remedies to pursue which in reality might inflict punishment enough.

Technically, however, because failure to pay a debt was not itself a crime, the purpose of imprisoning a debtor was merely custodial and not punitive. There was therefore a special reason for making prison conditions as little eligible as possible. If a man unable to make ends meet in ordinary life could have himself and his family fed and housed in gaol, the pressure upon him to pay up would be diminished. Yet it was scarcely appropriate to submit him to the new notions of discipline — separation, hard labour, compulsory exercise. The debtors' prisons and the debtors' wings in the general gaols continued in the eighteenth century mould.[183] Their inmates were mostly left to provide for themselves[184] and were required to do no work. The canny might live in comfort for considerable periods, an idea which greatly upset prison reformers. How the luckless, truly penurious debtor fared is still a shadowy story. But with 12,000-15,000 debtors going into prison annually between 1830 and 1834, there must have been many pitiful cases.[185]

The problems of imprisoned debtors were met only by the gradual elimination of the procedure for imprisonment. In 1813, the eighteenth-century practice of passing occasional acts of indemnity releasing honest debtors from prison developed into a regular system with the setting up of insolvent debtors' courts.[186] This extended to non-traders some of the advantages of

---

182   The common law offence of cheating, for instance, was committed only where there was some element of danger to the public at large (as where a trader used false weights and measures), not where there was merely a private fraud which the victim might have escaped by common prudence. The common law crime of larceny by a trick and the statutory crime of obtaining by false pretences were also made the subject of careful limitations apparently in response to the same feeling: the fear was strong that 'mere' breaches of contract might be treated as criminal.

183   The shocking conditions to which the less fortunate debtors were subjected are detailed in the Reports of the Committees to investigate the London gaols: 1813-14 (157), IV; 1814-15 (152), IV; IUP Prisons 7; 1818 (275, 392), VIII; 1819 (109) IX; IUP Prisons 8.

184   Those who could not receive some form of county food allowance, which might be eked out by charitable donations.

185   Return of the Number of Persons Confined for Debt 1830-34, 1835 (199) XLIV. The Duke of Richmond's Committee heard some interesting evidence concerning debtors. The Governor of Horsemonger Lane Gaol, for instance, stated that of 118 debtors received in 1834, many of whom owed less than £5, two-thirds maintained themselves: 1835 (438), XI, IUP Prisons 3, pp. 227-8.

186   53 Geo. III, c. 28.

bankruptcy.[187] While the creditor could never be forced to accept a composition that would leave him with part-payment, the debtor would be freed from the threat of imprisonment upon surrendering his assets.

In 1838, the scandal of arrest on mesne process was ended,[188] though not without widespread fears for the trading stability of the nation.[189] Imprisonment for non-payment of a judgment was somewhat restricted,[190] but still the numbers remained considerable.[191] It was not until 1869 that it was provided that debtors should be imprisoned only where they had the means to pay but were wilfully refusing to do so.[192] In the 1870s nearly 6,000 debtors were being imprisoned each year.[193] In the county courts, the judges were prepared to assume on slender evidence that the debtor was wilfully refusing to pay. A Select Committee in 1873[194] found that, while the system did induce the plausible and tricksy to pay (they rarely went into prison), it incarcerated, at public expense, the feckless muddlers incapable of ordering their own affairs. Yet the same system was to survive for another century. Only when the expansion of credit facilities in the late 1950's had the effect of raising the number of debtors imprisoned for wilful refusal to pay once more to some 7,000 per annum was the public conscience disturbed. The Payne Committee on the Enforcement of Judgment Debts found little change in the character of those actually going to prison for debt.[195] The Committee's recommendation that imprisonment be replaced by other sanctions, including the attachment of earnings, has been partly implemented in the Administration of Justice Act 1970

The Substantive Law

In the early nineteenth century the movement to express law in the form of codes spread through much of Europe. It had important political objectives. As Radzinowicz remarks, 'codification was adopted, not so much for its

187   And brought with it many of the opportunities for abuse that were so rife in bankruptcy proceedings: see generally, Welbourne, *op. cit.*, n. 180.

188   1 & 2 Vict. c. 110, ss. 1-3. This was the result of a recommendation of the Common Law Commissioners: Fourth Report 1831-32 (239), XXV, p. 44; IUP Legal Administration: General 3.

189   See the Report of the Royal Commission on Insolvency 1840 [274], XVI.

190   8 & 9 Vict. c. 127, repealing a provision of the Bankruptcy Act 1844 (7 & 8 Vict. c. 96) which, in showing greater favour to debtors, had aroused loud commercial protests.

191   For an attempt to prevent judges from too readily finding against debtors and imprisoning them, see 22 & 23 Vict. c. 57.

192   See the Returns of Numbers confined for Debt 1844 (292), XXXVIII.

193   The figures are conveniently summarised in the Report of the Committee on the Enforcement of Judgment Debts (Cmnd. 3909, 1969), Table 14.

194   1873 (348), XV.

195   Cmnd. 3909, 1969 paras. 982, 1005 (referring to the Report of 1873, *supra*. n. 194).

intrinsic advantages, but largely because it was regarded as an effective means for preserving a strong central government and gaining a coherent legal system, both of which in their turn would ensure the rule of a purer and more equitable justice'.[196] Because of the significance of the criminal law in attaining these objectives, it was generally among the first parts of a legal system to be reduced to a code. Where, as in India, the British, with only slender resources, faced a situation of intractable legal and political complexity, they too turned to codification, and codes of criminal law and criminal procedure were among the earliest achievements. At home, where this branch of the law was also treated as the paradigm for codification,[197] the efforts of the reformers failed. In this failure we may sense the general satisfaction that the system of criminal justice commanded among the governing and middle classes. It gave them the opportunity to participate as justices and jurors in controlling their local community, and it allowed them considerable flexibility in applying the law to individuals — liberal mercy could be bestowed in the one case, exemplary severity in the next. Part of this discretionary power flowed from the vague and sometimes ridiculous terms in which the law was couched. Exhortations to change the form of the law — to introduce clearer, more rational principles — were coldly received, particularly among those best able to understand the technicalities — the judges and members of the legal profession.

Yet there was no denying the crudity of the criminal law at the beginning of the nineteenth century. Indeed it was often difficult even to discover what the law was. Many offences were laid down in obscure statutes of varying antiquity. Forgery, for instance, was dealt with in over eighty Acts.[198] But more law — including fundamental matters such as the definition of murder, manslaughter, rape and larceny, and of defences such as insanity and self-defence — was to be found only in common law principles, to be extracted from the decisions of the judges. In civil actions, general issues of law were regularly reserved to be considered by a bench of judges at Westminster, and their decisions were reported widely enough to be known to the legal profession. Reports were also beginning to be published of the rulings of individual judges as they tried cases with juries at assizes. But on the criminal side, the opportunity to take questions of law on appeal to Westminster Hall was very limited.[199] The records of decisions in criminal cases were imperfect and

196 *Sir James FitzJames Stephen* (1957), p. 21.

197 Until three aspects of commercial law — bills of exchange, partnership and sale of goods — were codified between 1882 and 1893, the criminal law was the only field of substantive law in which a code was seriously discussed.

198 Nor were the texts of statutes easily accessible. It was only in 1797 that justices began regularly to receive copies of new legislation: Esther Moir, *The Justice of the Peace* (1969) p. 121.

199 Rights of appeal are further discussed, below

generally to be found only in private collections.[200] At assizes the presiding judge, who was one of the twelve judges of the common law courts, gave the jurors their directions on the law;[201] at county quarter sessions this function fell upon the chairman of the justices, who might well have no legal training.[202] When legal difficulties arose, there was only variable help to be had from the literature of the criminal law. Blackstone's great influence stemmed from the orderly exposition of his material but he did not profess completeness.[203] The older classics — Coke's *Institutes*, Hale's *History of the Pleas of the Crown*, Foster's *Crown Cases* — were likewise incomplete and often contradictory. Otherwise, there were ill-assorted compendia of miscellaneous information — intended either for justices[204] or for legal practitioners.[205]

The state of the criminal law made it an obvious target for Bentham, since as a standard by which the individual could calculate the amount of pain or pleasure to be produced by a particular course of action it was so evidently a failure. Legislative codification lay at the heart of all Bentham's writings on legal reform, and in his projects for a *Pannomion* he did, indeed, treat the Penal Code as the sanctionary mechanism of the entire legal system.[206] This proved too radical a reformulation of existing notions to afford much inspiration to his followers. But Bentham also discussed the need to bestow upon the criminal law as it was more generally understood a logical framework developed from new concepts,[207] and here he was more clearly influential.

The events which happened provide an interesting illustration of the play of his ideas upon those concerned to achieve actual reforms of the law. In 1834 Macaulay arrived in India as the Law Member of the newly-formed Legislative Council. Already seized with the belief that a uniform code of laws in place of the disparate and chaotic admixture of local custom and administrative regulation, he spent two years completing a draft penal code that in

200   See Sir E. H. East, *Pleas of the Crown* (1803), pp. v-xv.

201   In the main, capital offences were reserved for the assize courts.

202   His clerk of the peace, an attorney, could advise him if he desired. Most borough quarter sessions were presided over by a Recorder or his Deputy, who was generally a barrister.

203   See his *Commentaries* IV (1769): *Of Public Wrongs*.

204   The Revd. Richard Burn's *The Justice of the Peace and Parish Officer* was long a favourite. Thirty editions appeared between 1755 and 1869.

205   East's work (*cit*. n. 200) was soon followed by others, among which the works by Russell and Archbold have, in successive editions, continued to this day as the encyclopaedias of practitioners in the criminal courts.

206   'A civil law is that which establishes a right: a penal law is that which, in consequence of the establishment of a right by the civil law, directs the punishment in a certain manner of him who violates it': *Works* (Bowring ed.) III, p. 160.

207   See, e.g., *Introduction to the Principles of Morals and Legislation*, Works I, 96 ff; *View of a Complete Code of Laws ib*. III, 163 ff; *Theory of Legislation* (Ogden ed. 1931) pp. 239 ff.

considerable measure achieved the Benthamic virtues of clarity, conciseness and completeness.[208] Considered as a technical achievement in draftsmanship, it is useful to remember Fitzjames Stephen's comment on contemporary practice: 'from about 1820 to 1830 was, I think the period in which statutes were lengthier, more drawling and tedious, more crammed with surplusage and tautology than they ever were either before or since'.[209] Considered as a contribution to the development of law, it is interesting to determine how far the code is indebted to Bentham. Macaulay did not work from Bentham's own sketches for a penal code and in particular he abandoned the unduly schematic plan into which Bentham's love of classification had led him. 'The debt', as Professor Stokes remarks 'is rather to be sought in the design and informing spirit of the Code'.[210] Most characteristic of all was Macaulay's refusal to work from the model of any one existing system. Modern scholars reject the view of Stephen and Pollock that the code was merely a demystified and systematic version of the criminal law of England.[211] It was essentially a fresh start, freed from the bonds of inherited doctrine and acknowledging only an eclectic debt to the 'most celebrated systems of Western jurisprudence'.

This forms the point of contrast with contemporaneous developments in England that is most striking. In 1833, Brougham secured the appointment of a Royal Commission on Criminal Law. Its five members — Starkie, Amos, Wightman, Bellenden Ker and Austin (replaced in 1836 by Jardine) — had as radical and intellectual a bias as could reasonably be expected. But they brought to their task a lawyer-like determination to work upon the existing materials which would only have excited Bentham's scorn. Their first brief was to explore the possibility of codifying not only statutory but common-law principles of criminal law. They used the arcane and casuistic law of larceny (and related offences) to demonstrate the virtues of reducing both sets of rules to a single statutory code.[212] In consequence they were given authority to produce a complete criminal code, and this, after several distractions,[213] they

---

208   The work was to have been done by the Indian Law Commission, but illness seems to have left Macaulay as the only functioning member for much of the time: see Eric Stokes, *The English Utilitarians and India* (1959) pp. 223-24.

209   *History of the Criminal Law*, III, p. 302.

210   Eric Stokes, *op. cit.*, n. 208, 225.

211   S. G. Vesey-Fitzgerald, in Keeton and Schwarzenberger (eds.), *Jeremy Bentham and the Law* (1948), p. 229, points out that the four other members of the Indian Law Commission with Macaulay were Scots and that accordingly the Code at some points displays a greater affinity to Scots law than to English law.

212   Criminal Law Commission: First Report 1834 (537), XXVI; IUP Criminal Law 3.

213   Not only did Russell divert them to the question of the felon's right to counsel (below, n. 231), the trial of juveniles (above n. 148) and the reduction of capital punishment (above n. 48), but they also reported (under a separate commission) on the vital general question of the promulgation of statutes: 1835 (406), XXXV.

proceeded to draw up in the course of four reports.[214] If the substance of their draft Act of Crimes and Punishments differed in character from the Indian draft, in legislative method it showed the same advance towards logic and clarity of expression that Bentham had so insistently demanded. It defined particular offences so as to eliminate many obscurities and contradictions in the existing law; it also set forth general principles applicable to the law as a whole, governing, for instance, the effects of insanity, intoxication, age, duress and marital coercion on criminal liability, prescribing who were parties to offences and what constituted inchoate offences such as attempt and conspiracy to commit crimes; and with truly Benthamic rigour it classified penalties under forty-five heads, as already mentioned.[215]

Once this long task had been completed, the scruples of the legal profession began to appear. Brougham introduced a Bill consisting of the draft code, but it was opposed not only by the Tory Lord Chancellor, Lyndhurst, but also by the Whig Chief Justice of the Queen's Bench, Denman. Lyndhurst referred the draft back for revision to a reconstituted Commission, with instructions also to draw up a code of criminal procedure.[216]

The revisions were substantial and the final product was undoubtedly the clearest exposition of English criminal law that had to that date been made. But it was not completed until 1849. The general enthusiasm for reforming institutions, from which the project had originally sprung, had evaporated. The ultimate fate of the Code is in its way a reflection of the general waywardness of British government in mid-century.[217] Brougham tried again, but was unable to secure any immediate following for it. Later, when portions were taken up by the Conservative Lord Chancellors, St Leonards and Cranworth, the judges took an openly hostile attitude. They would accept consolidation

---

214   Criminal Law Commission: Fourth Report 1839 [168], XIX; Fifth Report 1840 [242], XX; Sixth Report 1841 [316], X; IUP Criminal Law 3; Seventh Report 1843 [448], XIX; IUP Criminal Law 4.

215   Above, n. 172.

216   A first draft of the procedure code was drawn by Ker and Starkie: *Criminal Law Commission:* Eight Report 1845 [656], XIV; IUP Criminal Law 4. They were joined on the reconstituted commission by Amos, who during the earlier Commission had also succeeded Macaulay for five years as Law Member of the Governor-General's Council and so had not participated directly in drafting the first code; and by Sir Edward Ryan, who as Chief Justice of Bengal had been concerned with the Indian Draft during Macaulay's and Amos's terms and was later to be a member of the London-based Indian Law Commissions of the 1850's.

217   The independence of members of parliament was strongly felt by those who sought to promote law reforms at this period. '[W]hen we had a House of Commons', wrote Brougham in 1859, 'which consisted of a great number of lawyers, magistrates and country gentlemen, and persons who were neither lawyers nor magistrates, any Bill for the consolidation of the criminal or civil law was sure to give rise to so much discussion that it became impossible to pass any Bill on the subject', 3 Sol. Jo. 684. See A. H. Manchester, 'Simplifying the Sources of the Law' (1973) 2 Anglo-Am. L. R. 395.

of statutes, but not the codification of common law rules. Their main objection was the criticism that has most generally been made in common law countries against codification: that enactment casts the law into an inflexible mould, a form that cannot thereafter be altered to meet changed conditions in the way that is possible when law is built upon judicial precedent. In the particular case of the criminal law there was, of course, the counter-argument that the public has a special right to know the law since ignorance of it is no excuse. But to this Mr Justice Coleridge returned the answer that the public already knew enough of the criminal law and had no need of a code for guidance.[218] Thus the only course left was to undertake a revision, in the light of the Commissioners' Reports, of the consolidations of statutes on various branches of the criminal law made by Peel in the 'twenties. Even so, there were numerous false starts before 1861 when Lord Westbury shepherded through a new set of consolidating statutes.[219]

By contrast, the changed atmosphere in India following the Mutiny at last allowed the draft criminal code— still Macaulay's, though the subject of later revisions— to become law in 1860, and it was followed a year later by a Code of Criminal Procedure. When, in 1869, FitzJames Stephen succeeded Maine as Law Member of the Governor-General's Council he was involved in a much-needed revision of the Criminal Procedure Code. The idea of codification appealed to his forthright, dogmatic personality.[220] On his return to England he drafted a Homicide Law Amendment Bill. The initial purpose of the endeavour had been to alter certain aspects of the law of murder,[221] rather than to restate it as a whole. And there was the added difficulty of codifying general principles in relation to one branch of the criminal law alone. The judges were mostly critical of the result and it made no progress.

As professor of Common Law at the Inns of Court, Stephen next produced a Digest of the Criminal Law which was cast in the form of a draft code. It

---

218   1854 (303), III, p. 401. 'The truth is you might as well make every man his own doctor as every man his own lawyer, to any useful purpose, by such means as these; nor do I believe that they would be happier or better if you did'.

219   24 & 25 Vict. cs. 94-100. At occasional non-controversial points, common law principles were given statutory force in these acts. Thus they were not purely consolidating measures, though they were far from the complete restatement of the law contained in the drafts of the Commissioners.

220   Professor Stokes demonstrates FitzJames Stephen's debt to the authoritarian strain in utilitarian thought. In Stephen's case this led not only to his well-known rejection of Millian liberty (*Liberty, Equality, Fraternity*), but also to his justification of imperial rule as a means of imposing government through law: *The English Utilitarians and India* (1959), p. 280 et seq.

221   The Royal Commission on Capital Punishment of 1866 (*op. cit,* n. 57) had been dissatisfied with the definition of murder, particularly the notion of 'constructive murder'. Bright, a member, solicited the aid of Russell Gurney, Recorder of London, in amending the law and he in turn brought in Stephen.

attracted considerable interest and Stephen was asked to revise it as a draft bill covering indictable offences, punishment and criminal procedure. When with prodigious application he had done so, a Royal Commission, of which he was a member, undertook a further revision. This was completed by 1879,[222] and early enactment seemed to be in the wind.

Then once more came a judicial intervention. Cockburn, Chief Justice of the Queen's Bench, in a letter to the Attorney-General, opposed any code which did not encompass the complete criminal law.[223] As the Stephen draft did not entirely repeal all pre-existing statutes, let alone start on the codification of summary offences, it fell far short of so exacting a criterion. Moreover, the letter made a plethora of detailed objections to the introductory and general sections of the draft, and ominously promised similar criticisms of the rest. Stephen made a spirited riposte[224] but it attracted little professional sympathy or public interest. He had to rest content with the Queen's Bench judgeship which was already the reward of his labours. However, his work was not in vain, for it became the basis of criminal codes in Canada, New Zealand, Queensland, Western Australia and Tasmania.

Stephen had no successors. Codification became a moribund cause which has begun to revive only very recently. But for all its lack of success in England, the nineteenth-century movement remains significant for those concerned with the impact of utilitarian thought on practical affairs. Codification of the criminal law was one of Bentham's central concerns and the campaign for a code remained to a unique degree a Benthamite cause. To trace in detail the influence that each generation of codifiers had on its successors is difficult and requires more work than has yet been attempted. Historians have in particular tended to neglect the part played by the English Commissioners of 1833-49. Perhaps this is because Stephen and his fellow Commissioners make virtually no reference to the proposals of their predecessors; the occasional comparisons in their Report are with novelties of the Indian Codes, which were undoubtedly a direct influence on Stephen. Yet the Criminal Code Bill of 1879 adopts the method not of Macaulay but of the first English Commissioners. Stokes sees in Stephen's approach a change in intellectual attitude, a contrast between the eighteenth century preference for logical coherence, so strong in the early utilitarians, and the nineteenth-century recognition of the strength of historical tradition.[225] But this ignores the

---

222 Royal Commission on the Law relating to Indictable Offences 1878-79 [C. 2345], XX; IUP Criminal Law 6.

223 Letter from the Lord Chief Justice of England containing Comments and Suggestions in relation to the Criminal Code (Indictable Offences) Bill 1878-79 (232), LIX.

224 'The Criminal Code (1879)' (1880) 7 *The Nineteenth Century* 136.

225 *Op. cit.* n. 220, p. 277.

fact that the Commissioners of 1878-79 learned their criminal law when the work of the 1840's was fresh; the failure of the earlier efforts in the face of professional opposition must have been a known object lesson, just as the difficulty of persuading lawyers to accept any code seems to have been acknowledged by the form of the very first Report of Brougham's Commissioners. Radzinowicz, in describing Stephen as 'the greatest draftsman and codifier of criminal law that this country has ever produced', selects as his most important contribution the fact that 'by extracting principles out of the endless myriad of precedents' and 'wilderness of single instances', he raised the status of the criminal law as a legal discipline in a most remarkable way.[226] But it should not be forgotten that, thirty years before, some of the most progressive lawyers of the day worked for years to achieve similar results. They were the first to bring order out of chaos and, once done, how could their work be forgotten in its entirety?

The Process of Prosecution

By the nineteenth century, England already had a procedure for trying serious criminal charges that was much more liberal than its European counterparts. The maxim that it is better that ten guilty men go free than that one innocent be convicted, though it did not go uncontested,[227] had been acknowledged by a variety of improvements in the position of the accused. Torture had been abandoned as a means of extracting confessions. Most cases were submitted to a grand jury before the accused was made to stand trial. The trial itself had a relatively mild and dispassionate tone — the accused was not, on the whole, subjected to merciless bullying by the court, after the French fashion. Issues of guilt or innocence were decided by a further jury equipped with an unimpeachable power to acquit. Contemporary foreign visitors wrote of the system with 'genuine admiration, not unmingled with wonder at how such a system could be reconciled with the exigencies of an effective defence against crime'.[228] Even with charges of treason, sedition and other political offences, common enough until the end of the Chartist period, prisoners had a right to defend themselves against the charges to a degree that two centuries earlier would have been inconceivable.

---

226 *Op. cit.* n. 196, p. 22.

227 See for example Paley's view that 'he who falls' by mistaken sentence may be considered as falling for his country; he suffers 'under the operation of those rules, by the general effect and tendency of which the welfare of the community is maintained and upheld': *Moral and Political Philosophy* (ed. of 1818) 428; Radzinowicz *History* I, p. 368.

228 Radzinowicz *History* I, pp. 25-27, App. 3.

These developments were, of course, intimately connected with the prodigal spread of capital offences, for they were part of the apparatus by which the severity of the law could be mitigated in practice. The desire to convict only those unquestionably shown to be guilty was much less marked when it came to non-capital offences. This tendency is most noticeable in the manner in which the justices of the peace exercised their growing jurisdiction to try minor crimes in petty sessions, sitting alone or in couples without the assistance of any jury. Summary justice, it came to be called, with unintended irony. Objective accounts of how justices went about this business are not easy to come by, but it is clear that the game laws, the Combination Acts, the master and servant laws were often administered partially, without a trace of sympathy or understanding for the accused, and it is not difficult to suppose that similar attitudes were common on a wider front.[229]

The pride which the established classes of England took in their manner of trying criminal cases is reflected in the absence of extensive debate on the subject in official sources such as the parliamentary papers. Such issues as arose were mostly discussed in legal circles, where prevailing attitudes were decidedly conservative.[230] Few deliberate reforms were undertaken. The first Criminal Law Commissioners played an important part in one. Persons accused of treason or misdemeanour already had the right to full representation by counsel at the trial, but those accused of felony — the category which included all the capital offences against the person and property — could have counsel only to examine witnesses and argue points of law, not to make a final speech to the jury. But upon the recommendation of the Commissioners this fetter was lifted,[231] despite the views of several judges who considered that they could sufficiently befriend a prisoner at his trial.[232] This change needs to be viewed with another that did not come about until 1898. Before then, with insignificant exceptions, the accused was kept from giving evidence on oath. He was, however, entitled to address the court in his own defence (though not

229 Important evidence of such attitudes can be found, e.g. in E. P. Thompson, *The Making of the English Working Class* (1968 ed.) pp. 221, 306, 551, 804.

230 Both the Criminal Law Commissioners of 1833-49 and Stephen and his colleagues produced draft Codes of Criminal Procedure (see 1845 [656], XIV; IUP Criminal Law 4; 1849 [1100], XXI, IUP Criminal Law 5; 1878-79 [C. 2345], XX, IUP Criminal Law 6). Their work digests existing practice and comments on some of the issues here discussed. Perhaps the most interesting aspect of all this work is the set of returns from judges, officials and practitioners on the working of the system, which is appended to the first of these Reports.

231 Second Report 1836 (343), XXXVI; IUP Criminal Law 3, pp. 2-18; 6 & 7 W.IV. c.114. As to its effects, see Tobias, *Crime and Industrial Society in the 19th Century,* p. 230.

232 Twelve of the fifteen judges opposed the reform, Mr. Justice Park even threatening his resignation: H. B. Poland, *A Century of Law Reform* (ed. Odgers, 1901) p. 50; G. Gardiner and N. Curtis Raleigh, 'The Judicial Attitude to Penal Reform' (1949) 65 L.Q.R. 196, 212-14.

as a sworn witness subject to cross-examination). Indeed, one motive for so long denying a person accused of felony the right to counsel had been to oblige him to speak personally as his own advocate.[233] Once allowed counsel, the guilty defendant might choose to shelter unheard in the dock.[234] It was with a view rather to breaking down this shield than to providing the innocent defendant with better weapons that the right to give evidence was finally conceded.[235]

Thus a long period elapsed between giving the accused the right to counsel and obliging him to choose whether or not to enter the witness-box. Perhaps it was so long simply because of the great difference between the right to be represented and the reality of procuring a lawyer. How far defendants were represented, and how adequate that representation was, are questions that have yet to be accurately investigated. The dock brief system allowed a defendant to procure counsel at the actual trial for the price of £1.3s.6d., or the judge might ask counsel to defend a poor prisoner as an act of charity. Otherwise he went unassisted. 'It is a melancholy sight to see a party trying for his life without any legal assistance, and, peradventure, with great legal talent arrayed against him', as one barrister remarked to the Criminal Law Commissioners.[236] Few attempts were made to improve this situation until the passing of the Poor Persons Defence Act 1903,[237] and a legal aid system for criminal defendants that is in any degree adequate has had to wait until the 1960's.

The lack of serious attention to matters of criminal procedure is well illustrated by the absence of any right to appeal against a conviction on indictment. In the case of summary offences disposed of before magistrates, it was possible to seek a review by quarter sessions, and the record of judgment, which had to comply with increasingly technical rules, was open to

---

233   Hawkins, *Pleas of the Crown* (7th ed. 1795), II, c. 39, s. 2: 'the very speech, gesture, countenance and manners of defence of those who are guilty, when they speak for themselves, may often help to disclose the truth, which probably would not be so well discovered from the artificial defence of others speaking for them'.

234   After some division of opinion the judges held that the accused could still make an unsworn statement from the dock, even when he had counsel to defend him: see Z. Cowen and P. B. Carter, *Essays on the Law of Evidence* (1956), p. 207.

235   By the Criminal Evidence Act 1898, s. 1. The measure was introduced by the Lord Chancellor, Halsbury, formerly a leading prosecuting counsel. In an earlier attempt at the same end, Lord Bramwell had argued that his Bill was not 'for the benefit of prisoners. He believed that more convictions would take place under it than before. He thought that it was a bad Bill for the guilty and a beneficial Bill only for the innocent': (1886) P.D. CCCIII, 1471.

236   1845 [656], XIV; IUP Criminal Law 4, p. 250.

237   On the development of legal aid in criminal cases, see R. Egerton *Legal Aid* (1946), pp. 20-22; R. M. Jackson *Machinery of Justice in England* (6th ed., 1972), pp. 174-90.

review in the King's Bench under the prerogative writ of *certiorari*.[238] Rights of appeal in England had tended to grow upon errors in formal documents, and at trial on indictment there was no equivalent 'speaking order'. Usually there was only the jury's verdict of guilty or not guilty and that was impenetrable.[239] Where a criminal case tried by one of the judges on assize raised a question of legal importance, he might reserve it for the opinion of his fellows, and this procedure was made rather more formal in 1848 with the establishment of the Court of Crown Cases Reserved.[240] But the luxury of such treatment was given only to a handful of cases each year. In the 1840's a substantial number of lawyers believed that a right of appeal on questions of law, similar to that in civil cases, should be introduced.[241] But the prevalent view was plainly put by Baron Parke:

> . . . in Questions of Criminal Law, the Decision upon Matters of Fact and upon Matters of Law is vastly more easy than it is in Civil Cases. The Facts in the Discussion of Civil Rights are very often extremely complicated, and the Law difficult to ascertain and apply; but in Criminal Cases the Law is, generally speaking, abundantly clear, and the Facts are always either so unambiguous as to lead to a Conviction, or if they leave any reasonable Doubt as to the Guilt of the Accused, the Duty of the Jury is plain. . . . Generally speaking, Questions of Civil Rights occur in Superior Courts only, between Persons of Property, who are capable of paying the expense.[242]

A regular Court of Criminal Appeal became a standing lost cause.[243] Even the exposure of the remarkable injustice done to Adolf Beck, twice convicted of another man's frauds on mistaken identifications, did not convince a Committee of Inquiry that more was needed than somewhat easier access to the Court of Crown Cases Reserved when a question of law was at issue.[244]

238   If the justices at sessions wished it, they might state a case to the judges in order to have a question of law settled. In 1857, this simpler procedure became the regular method of appealing from sessions in a summary case: 20 & 21 Vict. c. 43.

239   Accordingly, the lawyers fell to criticising the indictment, which had to accord strictly with the evidence proved. It was not good enough to lay a charge of stealing a sheep if the evidence showed that a ewe had been stolen. The desire to side-step the death penalty accounts for much of this pedantry. All those who replied to the Criminal Law Commissioners in 1845 were highly critical and the first general attempt at simplification was made in 1851: 14 & 15 Vict. c. 100; Stephen thought the Act left the law in a 'blurred, half-defaced condition': *History of the Criminal Law* I, pp. 285-92.

240   11 & 12 Vict. c. 78. It became possible for questions of law to be reserved at Quarter Sessions for the opinion of the judges.

241   See 1845 [631], XIV, IUP Criminal Law 5.

242   Lords S.C. on the Criminal Law Administration Amendment Bill 1847-48 (523), XVI, IUP Criminal Law 6, p. 6.

243   Some twenty-eight Bills for a Court of Criminal Appeal failed in the course of seventy years; B. Abel Smith and R. B. Stevens, *Lawyers and the Courts* (1967), p. 100.

244   1905 [Cd. 2315], LXII, pp. xviii-xix.

But the scandal caused too much misgiving and the Court of Criminal Appeal was finally set up in 1907.[245]

As important as the trial itself was the procedure that led up to it. Here there were important changes that are closely linked with the creation of the professional police forces. Traditionally the justice of the peace had played the role of consolidator, and sometimes of investigator, of the prosecution case, where an offence was to be tried on indictment by a jury.[246] In particular, the justice made a record, in the form of sworn depositions, of the evidence that witnesses were prepared to give for the Crown. These depositions were placed before the grand jury at the beginning of assizes and quarter sessions, and that body (sitting in secret and hearing such of the witnesses as it chose) decided whether the prosecution case was sufficient to support a 'true bill' of indictment. The accused was not entitled to be present when witnesses appeared before the justice to make depositions against him;[247] he would also appear before them and would be questioned, though he could not be compelled to answer.[248]

As the new police forces developed, in the day-to-day charge of a chief constable rather than a magistrate, the active investigation of crime passed to them. This included the interrogation of suspects and other witnesses. Yet if the police decided to prosecute, depositions had first to be taken before the magistrates and then the case had to be put to the grand jury; one step too many was developing. Even in the 1830's some shift can be seen in the conception of the procedure before magistrates. The judges gave it a judicial appearance by holding that the accused had the right to be present as each witness was heard, in order that he might know the case to be made against him at the trial.[249] So emerged the form of preliminary hearing that was to survive unchanged until 1967.[250] Its purpose was to determine whether a

245   Criminal Appeal Act 1907.

246   If a case was tried summarily two justices would be the judges. And if an indictable offence went to County Quarter Sessions, a bench of justices would sit with a jury.

247   Stephen (op. cit., n. 239, pp. 227-28), quotes Mr. Justice Park's direction to the Grand Jury in the trial of Thurtell and Hunt for murder in 1824, which stresses that the depositions were kept from the accused precisely so that he should not know the case against him.

248   One direction in which the judges, doubtless under the influence of the death penalty, strove to extend protection to accused persons was in developing the rule that confessions made before the trial were admissible only if made voluntarily, without the inducement of fear or favour. Many of the cases were concerned with confessions made to magistrates and their clerks. Coleridge and Maule were two judges who pressed the protection of this rule to extremes: even if the accused was led to believe no more than that his statement would necessarily be put in at the trial, this rendered it inadmissible. Later, this view was declared heterodox: R. v. Baldry (1852), 2 Den. 430.

249   R. v. Arnold (1838) 8 C. & P. 62; and see 6 & 7 Wm. IV, c. 114, s. 4 allowing the accused to inspect the depositions at his trial.

250   It was given statutory authority by 11 & 12 Vict. c. 42.

sufficient case existed against the accused to justify making him stand trial. This was also the function of the grand jury, which some accordingly argued should be abolished. But the grand jury had too settled a place in the government of the shires for such logic to prevail.[251] At the assizes, when it was composed of the leading magistrates of the county, it was the formal assembly in which the local ministers of justice and communal affairs met the assize judges to discuss matters of law and its administration. The grand jury maintained the legitimacy of the established order. It was to survive many changes in local government and the powers of the magistracy. It succumbed only to the financial stringencies of the 1930's,[252] even then amid sad regrets.

The preliminary hearing before justices imposed some control upon the institution of criminal proceedings by the police, just as much as by private prosecutors.[253] Perhaps the fact that the procedure was so simply adapted to the new circumstances prevented any close examination of its adequacy. But in the light of the extreme suspicion with which the new police were greeted it seems surprising that no attempt was made to give the magistrates immediate supervision over the questioning of suspects. As it happened, the police were left without the kind of check by an independent official that is to be found in many modern criminal systems.[254] The most that occurred was the establishment in 1879 of the office of Director of Public Prosecutions.[255] He was given charge over the decision to prosecute and the actual trial of certain very serious and legally difficult offences. It has never been part of his function to ensure that police investigations of crime are fair.

Herbert Packer has usefully posited the opposing models of a 'crime control' and a 'due process' penal system.[256] The development of the English system during the nineteenth century shows considerable activity, some of it the result of reasoned argument, more the product of political necessity, towards the more efficient control of crime. By the last years of the century the country was coming to be adequately policed. It had established a prison system of so uniform a dreariness that it was soon to be used only with greater circumspection. Moreover, crime appeared to be in substantial decline. In

---

251 'I can see no benefit produced by Grand Juries but the cooperation of the higher and middle classes in the administration of justice. But this I estimate very highly, and hope it may be preserved through all changes by some means or other.' (Lord Denman, Chief Justice of King's Bench) 1845 [631], XIV; IUP Criminal Law 6, p. 212.

252 Administration of Justice (Miscellaneous Provisions) Act 1933, s. 1.

253 Abuses of the system were mostly laid at the door of private prosecutors and their lawyers in the Answers of 1845; e.g., 'Hungry practitioners prefer bills for the sake of costs and in general it is not a bad speculation.' (Sir G. Lewin, Recorder of Doncaster) 1845 [656], XIV; IUP Criminal Law 4, p. 220.

254 Scotland is among the countries most deserving of comparison.

255 42 & 43 Vict. c. 22. Stephen, *op. cit*, n. 239, I, p. 501.

256 H. L. Packer, *The Limits of the Criminal Sanction*, (1969), Ch. 8.

reality much of this was probably attributable to the considerable changes in the conditions of the lowest social groups during Victoria's reign. But those in charge of the police and prisons naturally claimed success for their positive contributions to deterrence. It is only perhaps with the hindsight provided by the subsequent growth in crime rates amid increasing affluence that one sees myopia in their judgments.

Be that as it may, their activities at least produced considerable change. By comparison, little energy was devoted to making the process of accusation and trial fairer to the accused. He went without a voice in the political affairs of the nation, his fate entrusted to the propertied jurymen or the well-to-do magistrates who tried his case. It was to take the social crises and the political unrest of the inter-war years to make a significant cause of civil liberties in the criminal process.

Select Bibliography

(Volumes with particularly useful bibliographies are indicated by an asterisk)

1. *The Phenomenon of Crime*
Nineteenth-century studies of the social and personal causes of criminal behaviour are reviewed by Morris, T. P., *The Criminal Area* (1957) and Radzinowicz, L., *Ideology and Crime* (1966). The unique contribution of Henry Mayhew is best sought in his own three volumes, *London Labour and the London Poor* (1851-52) and, to a lesser extent, in the supplementary volume, Mayhew, H. and Binny, J., *The Criminal Prisons of London and Scenes from London Life* (1862).

A wider range of nineteenth-century opinion about crime is surveyed by Tobias, J. J., *Crime and Industrial Society in the 19th Century** (1967) (see also his collection of readings, *Nineteenth Century Crime: Prevention and Punishment* (1972)). The reliability of such opinion has, however, been doubted, and the relative value of statistical indicators suggested, by Gattrell, V. A. C. and Hadden, T. B., 'Criminal Statistics and their Interpretation', in Wrigley, E. A. (ed.), *Nineteenth Century Society* (1972).

The social characteristics of Australian transportees are analysed by Robson, L. L., *The Convict Settlers of Australia* (1965); see also Hobsbawm, E. and Rudé, G., *Captain Swing** (1969).

2. *The Criminal Law*
The role of criminal law as a method of social control in the nineteenth century should be viewed against the eighteenth-century inheritance revealed in Thompson, E. P., *Whigs and Hunters: the Origin of the Black Act* (1975); Hay, D., Linebaugh, P. and Thompson, E. P. (eds.) *Albion's Fatal Tree* (1975); and Radzinowicz, L., *History of English Criminal Law*, vols. 1-4, (1948-68).

On the movement for codification of substantive and procedural criminal law, see Manchester, A. H., 'Simplifying the Sources of Law' (1973) 2 Anglo-American Law Review 395, 527; Radzinowicz, L., *Sir James FitzJames Stephen* (1957); Stephen, L., *The Life of Sir James Stephen* (1895); Stokes, E., *The English Utilitarians and India* (1959); Stephen, J. F., *History of the Criminal Law in England* (1883).

Stephen's own *History* and Pike, L. O., *A History of Crime in England* (1873-6) provide an overview of their subject that remains of considerable interest to the historian of the nineteenth century. Only a brief introduction to the criminal law in this period is to be found in Holdsworth, W. E. S., *A History of English Law*, vol. 15 (1965), pp. 141-67.

A few aspects of the substantive law have received modern historical treatment: Hall, J., *Theft Law and Society* (2nd ed., 1952), Walker, N., *Crime and Insanity in England*, vol. 1 (1968). There is much of historical interest on general principles of substantive law in Williams, Glanville, *Criminal Law: The General Part* (1961); and see also Turner, J. W. C., *Russell on Crime*, 12th ed., 3 vols. (1964), Fifoot, C. H. S., *Judge and Jurist in the Reign of Queen Victoria* (1959) Ch. 5.

The law relating to political offences and public order is examined in its historical context by Williams, D., *Keeping the Peace* (1967). The history of its application at different times can be traced in a large number of sources, including in particular: Darvall, F. O., *Popular Disturbances and Public Order in Regency England* (1934)*; Hobsbawm, E. J. and Rudé, G., *Captain Swing* (1969)*; Hammond, J. L. and B., *The Village Labourer* (1911); *The Town Labourer 1760-1832* (1919); Mather, F. C., *Public Order in the Age of the Chartists* (1959); Thompson, E. P., *The Making of the English Working Class* (rev. ed. 1968); Wickwar, W. H., *The Struggle for the Freedom of the Press,* 1819-1832 (1928).

Nineteenth-century developments of the procedures leading up to and governing criminal trials and appeals have received no complete modern treatment. But important aspects are discussed by Jackson, R. M., 'The Incidence of Jury Trial during the Past Century' (1937) 1 *Modern Law Review* 132; Abel-Smith, B., and Stevens, R. B., *Lawyers and the Courts* (1967) Ch. 2.

The peculiar technicalities of the law of evidence were the subject of voluminous comment by Jeremy Bentham in his *Treatise on Judicial Evidence* (1st English ed. 1825) and the *Rationale of Evidence* (edited by J. S. Mill, 1827; *Works* (1843) vols. 6 and 7); see also Thayer, J. B., *A Preliminary Treatise on Evidence as the Common Law* (1898); Wigmore, J. H., *A Treatise on the Anglo-American System of Evidence,* vols. 1-10 (1940); Cowen, Z. and Carter, P. B., *Essays in the Law of Evidence;* Williams, G., *The Proof of Guilt* (3rd ed., 1964).

3 Disposal of Offenders

The philosophical roots of the movement to reduce capital punishment and replace it with a moderate penal system, together with its actual achievements, are traced in great depth up to the 1860s, by Radzinowicz, L., *History of English Criminal Law,** vols. 1 and 4 (1948, 1968). See also Phillipson, C., *Three Criminal Law Reformers* (1923); Hay, D., 'Property, Authority and the Criminal Law', *Albion's Fatal Tree* (supra) Ch. 1; Heath, J., *Eighteenth Century Penal Theory* (1963) (readings).

Of the secondary punishments which grew in place of the death penalty, the history of transportation in the period is reviewed in scrupulous detail by Shaw, A. G. L., *Convicts and the Colonies** (1966); and see his 'Reformatory Aspects of Transportation of Criminals to Australia' in Morris, N. and Perlman, M., *Law and Crime* (1972). See also Hasluck, A., *Unwilling Emigrants* (1959); Bateson, C., *The Convict Ships* (1959); Forsyth, W. D., *Governor-Arthur's Convict System* (1935).

For the development of prisons, the most detailed account remains Webb, S. and B., *English Prisons under Local Government* (1922). The title however indicates the local perspective of the work. Accounts of the aims of the dominant figures in the first two periods of the national prison system can be found in their own works: Du Cane, E. F., *The Punishment and Prevention of Crime* (London, 1885) and Ruggles Brise, E., *The English Prison System* (1921). A more modern account by an administrator is Fox, L., *The English Prison and Borstal System* (1952). See also Cross, R., *Punishment, Prison and the Public* (1971); Grunhut M., *Penal Reform* (1948); Henriques, U. R. Q., 'The Rise and Decline of the Separate System of Prison Discipline' (1972), 54 P. & P. 61; Hinde, R. S. E., *The British Penal System,* 1773-1950 (1951); Howard, D. L., *English Prisons, their Past and Future* (1960); Mannheim,

H., *The Dilemma of Penal Reform* (1939); McLachlan, N., 'Penal Reform and Penal History: Some Reflections' in Blom-Cooper, L. *Progress in Penal Reform* (1974); Rose, G., *The Struggle for Penal Reform* (1962); Thomas, J. E., *The English Prison Officer Since 1850* (1972).

Further information on the changes impending at the end of the Victorian period can be found in Hobhouse, S. and Brockway, F., *English Prisons Today* (1922); Hood, R., *Borstal Re-assessed* (1965); Morris, N., *The Habitual Criminal* (1951).

Two recent accounts of nineteenth-century policies towards juvenile offenders (both part of wider studies) are Carlebach, J., *Caring for Children in Trouble* (1970), Chs. 1 and 2; Pinchbeck, I. and Hewitt, M., *Children in English Society** (1969, 1973), Chs. 6 and 16.

Important figures in the history of nineteenth-century penal reform have been the subject of biographies: Howard, D. L., *John Howard: Prison Reformer* (1958); Kent, J., *Elizabeth Fry* (1962); Barry, J. V., *Alexander Maconochie of Norfolk Island* (Melbourne, 1958); Clay, W. L., *The Prison Chaplain*, (1861); Davenport-Hill, R. and F., *The Recorder of Birmingham* (1878); Mannheim, H., *Pioneers in Criminology* (2nd ed., 1973).

Addendum
The Criminal Law
  Kurland, P. B. and Waters, D. M. W., 'Public Prosecutions in England, 1854-1879' (1959) 9 Duke Law Journal, 493.

The Documents
Criminal Law

Criminal Law Volume 1
REPORT FROM THE SELECT COMMITTEE ON THE CRIMINAL LAW RELATING TO CAPITAL PUNISHMENT, WITH MINUTES OF EVIDENCE AND APPENDIX, 1819

In the early nineteenth century the persistent efforts of Samuel Romilly to mitigate the severity of the Criminal Law aroused widespread public sympathy. By 1819, the House of Commons had received over 12,000 petitions as a result of which a select committee was appointed 'to consider so much of the criminal laws as relate to capital punishment in felonies'.

The witnesses before the committee were chosen so as to get an assessment of popular rather than professional opinion. They included members of various social classes and professional groups but excluded the judiciary.

The report was concerned mainly with capital punishment imposed for the offences of larceny without violence and forgery, though certain other branches of the law were also examined. It seemed a grave injustice that a man could be sentenced to death for stealing 'more than five shillings' or forging a bank-note just as easily as for murder. Statutes allowing such indiscriminate use of the death penalty had been useful deterrents at the time of their enactment but had long outlived their utility. As a first step towards reform, diminution of punishments for unaggravated larceny and forgery by the abolition or amendment of obsolete statutes was recommended. The appendix contains detailed statistical returns of convictions, executions etc., for various offences and a valuable chronological review of Criminal Law statutes from the sixteenth century. The merit of this report is based less on its immediate outcome, for this was comparatively little, than on the pattern of reform it founded and established as a model for the rest of the nineteenth century.

Original reference
1819   (585) VIII   Criminal Law relating to capital punishments in felonies, Sel. Cttee. Rep., mins. of ev., etc.

Criminal Law Volume 2
REPORTS FROM THE SELECT COMMITTEE ON THE CRIMINAL LAW OF ENGLAND WITH APPENDIX, 1824

Following in the footsteps of Romilly and Mackintosh, Sir Robert

Peel adopted the cause of penal reform. As Home Secretary, he was largely responsible for the appointment of a select committee in 1824 to consolidate and amend the Criminal Law—a task which he himself took up in earnest in 1826.

The committee agreed that consolidation was possible and studied the law of forgery as a working example. Forgery was chosen not because reform in this area was less complicated but because public opinion demanded that the widespread imposition of capital punishment for forgery should be discontinued. The first report examined the existing law and a draft bill to consolidate and amend it. The second report tabulated under various headings the enactments relating to forgery. In both reports the principal issues were analysed and the reasoning behind suggested modifications was given.

The reports gave an excellent review of the law but made no effort to solve the capital punishment issue. In 1830, Peel introduced a Forgery Bill which adopted the consolidated provisions of this committee but he also chose to ignore the pleas for a diminution of the penalties.

Original references

1824	(205) IV	Criminal Law of England. Sel. Cttee. Rep., appendix.
	(444)	Criminal Law of England. Sel. Cttee. Rep., appendix.

Criminal Law Volume 3

REPORTS FROM THE ROYAL COMMISSION ON CRIMINAL LAW WITH APPENDICES AND INDICES, 1834–1841

After the earlier inquiries there was continued dissatisfaction at the injustices of the Criminal Law system, particularly that arising from the vagueness of the unwritten laws. Codification was considered to be the most logical solution and Thomas Starkie and other legal writers and reformers were appointed commissioners to consolidate all the statutory criminal law in one statute and all the provisions of the unwritten law in another. Furthermore, the commissioners were instructed to examine the possibility of combining both written and unwritten law in one statute—they eventually adopted this course.

Enormous difficulties were encountered when the commissioners attempted to draft a digest containing all the provisions of the Criminal Law. Information on the unwritten law was based on unreliable text-books, contradictory principles and unprecedented judgements, while the statute law contained numerous discrepancies.

Added to these problems were the diverse reforms which were considered necessary. These included insuring the right of exercising defence through counsel in felonious offences; revising the imposition of capital punishment; improving the procedure for the trial of juvenile offenders; and clarifying the niceties of the substantive law.

Despite these impediments, the commissioners drafted in the fourth, fifth and sixth reports a remarkable digest in clear and intelligible language with explanatory notes giving the reasons for the amendments proposed.

Even before its completion in 1841, the impact of the Royal Commission's work was considerable. The Trials for Felony Act (1836) extended the right of defence through counsel to all persons accused of felony; the Punishment of Offences Act (1837) reduced the number of offences for which capital punishment could be imposed and the Abolition of Pillory Act (1837) helped remove some of the barbarity of the Criminal Law.

Original references

1834	(537) XXVI	Criminal Law, R. Com. 1st Rep.
1836	(343) XXXVI	Criminal Law, R. Com. 2nd Rep.
1837	[79] XXXI	Criminal Law, R. Com. 3rd Rep.
1839	[168] XIX	Criminal Law, R. Com. 4th Rep.
1840	[242] XX	Criminal Law, R. Com. 5th Rep.
1841	[316] X	Criminal Law, R. Com. 6th Rep.

Criminal Law Volume 4

REPORTS FROM THE ROYAL COMMISSION ON THE CRIMINAL LAW WITH APPENDICES AND INDEX, 1843–1845

The two reports in this volume conclude the digest of the Criminal Law. In the seventh report, a complete digest of all indictable offences and the punishments relating to them was submitted. All petty offences and those triable by summary procedure were omitted but a reduced and organized text of praemunire offences was included. The eighth report contains a digest on the procedure for trying indictable offences.

In both reports the same tabulation as in the previous volume was followed—the digest enumerated all the provisions of the Criminal Law while explanatory memoranda explained the reasons for the amendments proposed.

The sweeping reforms recommended in the law relating to defences on the grounds of criminal incapacity showed a clear-sighted understanding of the problems involved. The effects on criminal capacity of insanity, intoxication, age, duress and marital coercion were thoroughly examined. Inchoate crimes too, came under close scrutinization, especially the crime of attempt. Despite the efficiency and originality of the commissioners' work the digests were never adopted in toto. Much legislation, however, was based on them, notably the statutes passed in 1848–49 and 1851–52 dealing with criminal procedure. The judgements of the courts were also affected by the rationalization and it is clearly reflected in the M'Naghten Rules on Insanity of 1843. The immediate outcome of the inquiry, however, was the appointment of another commission to revise and consolidate the Criminal Law with special reference to the present digests.

Original references

| 1843 | [448] XIX | Criminal Law, R. Com. 7th Rep. |
| 1845 | [656] XIV | Criminal Law, R. Com. 8th Rep. |

Criminal Law Volume 5

REPORTS FROM THE ROYAL COMMISSION ON REVISING AND CON-SOLIDATING THE CRIMINAL LAW WITH APPENDICES, 1845–1849

The achievement of the 1834–45 Royal Commission in compiling a highly efficient digest of the Criminal Law was diminished only by the unsatisfactory manner in which the recommendations were drafted in a bill for parliament. As a result, a new commission in 1845 was instructed not only to revise and consolidate the Criminal Law but also to draft a bill of their codification suitable for statutory enactment. Sir Edward Ryan was appointed chairman because of the knowledge and experience he had gained in drafting a penal code in India.

In the first report, the antiquated laws relating to praemunire offences were examined in detail and such provisions as transportation for recusancy were severely criticized. Although the Ecclesiastical Courts rarely enforced these laws their abolition was necessary in order to establish a non-denominational code.

The subsequent four reports contain the draft of a bill encompassing all indictable offences and the law of procedure. The commissioners agreed with the modifications proposed by the previous commission and suggested further amendments submitting explanatory notes for each. Dissenting opinions were expressed on several controversial issues such as the definition of capacity, the presumption of marital coercion, and homicide as a result of a duel. In procedural law the Coroner's inquisitions were reorganized and the abolition of such relics of the age of barbarism as 'hue and cry' was recommended.

In 1849 Lord Brougham introduced the draft bill to the House of Lords but the political furore caused by the Chartist Movement stayed its enactment. It never went any farther and like the previous attempts at codification the draft bill served as a basis on which subsequent criminal law acts were founded.

Original references

1845	[631] XIV	Revising and consolidating the Criminal law, R. Com. 1st Rep. (Disabilities in regard to religious opinions).
1846	[709] XXIV	Revising and consolidating the Criminal Law, R. Com. 2nd Rep.
1847	[830] XV	Revising and consolidating the Criminal Law, R. Com. 3rd Rep.
1847–48	[940] XXVII	Revising and consolidating the Criminal Law, R. Com. 4th Rep.
1849	[1100] XXI	Revising and consolidating the Criminal Law, R. Com. 5th Rep.

Criminal Law Volume 6

REPORTS FROM SELECT COMMITTEES AND A ROYAL COMMISSION AND OTHER REPORTS ON THE CRIMINAL LAW WITH MINUTES OF EVIDENCE, APPENDICES AND INDICES, 1847–1879

The practice of referring poorly drafted and controversial bills to select committees arose in the mid-nineteenth century. This volume contains the reports of select committees between 1847 and 1874 on the bills listed in the original references below, together with a Royal Commission Report on the law relating to indictable offences (1879) and reports on the state of the law relating to brutal assaults submitted to the Home Secretary in 1875.

The Amendment of the Administration of the Criminal Law Bill (1847–48) sought to establish a special court to decide questions of law in certain criminal cases. The committee which examined the bill heard evidence from a number of experts including several House of Lords judges and after considerable controversy approved it.

The 1874 committee on the Homicide Law Amendment Bill was chaired by Robert Lowe. The bill was an attempt to codify and clarify the law on homicide. This, however, was extremely difficult because much of the law was intangible and also because the definitions of malice aforethought, justifiable and excusable homicide, etc., were not sufficiently clear. The committee examined many of the difficult and obscure points and decided that the injustices of the existing law were preferable to the confusion which the proposed amendment would create.

The 1875 reports on the state of the law relating to brutal assaults were based on answers from the magistrates and police to circular questionnaires. The questionnaires sought to determine whether the law was sufficiently stringent. Statistics in the police replies showed that the numbers of brutal assaults had increased—this was attributed to the greater affluence of the working class. The majority of the replies considered that the law was too lax and more extensive use of flogging as a deterrent was widely recommended.

The last and longest paper in the volume, a Royal Commission report on the laws relating to indictable offences, was a further attempt to bring the criminal law into a uniform code. Valuable evidence was taken from members of the judiciary and the deliberations of previous inquiries on codification were widely consulted. Though admitting the impossibility of complete codification the commission approved the substance of a bill which had been referred to them and drafted it for enactment.

The commission was chaired by Colin Baron Blackburn and included Sir James Fitzjames Stephens, a tireless worker for legal reform.

Original references

1847–48	(523) XVI	Criminal Law Administration Amendment Bill, Sel. Cttee. Rep., mins of ev., etc.
1861	(240) XIV	Offences against the person etc., Bills, Sel. Cttee. Reps., etc.
1870	(183) VI	Felony Bill, Sel. Cttee. Rep., etc.
1874	(315) IX	Homicide Law Amendment Bill, Sel. Cttee. Special Rep., mins of ev., etc.
1875	[C.1138] LXI	Brutal assaults (state of the law), Reps.
1878–79	[C.2345] XX	Law relating to indictable offences, R. Com. Rep.

Prisons Volume 1

REPORT FROM THE SELECT COMMITTEE ON THE STATE AND DESCRIPTION OF GAOLS WITH MINUTES OF EVIDENCE, 1819

This Select Committee was appointed to inquire not only into the conditions in jails in the British Isles, but also into the state of the convict settlements in New South Wales. The material dealing with jails in Great Britain and Ireland covers almost all aspects of prison life and prison conditions and includes a special section on juvenile offenders. Despite a wealth of evidence pointing to the appalling

state of the jails, the committee's only recommendation was to
suggest possible ways to alleviate crowding in Newgate. William
Crawford, a leader in the prison reform movement (see IUP volume
Prisons 2), was one of the witnesses in this part of the inquiry.

The evidence dealing with Australia centres on the dispute between
Lachlan Macquarie, governor of New South Wales, and Geoffrey
Hart Bent, who had been first judge of the supreme court in the
colony. The argument was over the question of admitting convict
solicitors to practise in the court; the outcome was the commission-
ing of J. T. Bigge to inquire into the general conditions of the
convict population and the settlement as a whole (see IUP volume
Australia 1).

Original reference
1819   (579) VII   State of gaols, etc., Sel. Cttee. Rep., mins. of ev., etc.

Prisons Volume 2
REPORT OF WILLIAM CRAWFORD ON THE PENITENTIARIES OF THE
UNITED STATES, 1834

In 1833 William Crawford was sent as a commissioner to report on
the prison system in the United States; the result of his visit was the
suggestion, formulated in this report, that the system of penitentiaries with separate cells (as existing in the Walnut Street penitentiary
in Philadelphia and the Auburn and Sing-Sing penitentiaries in New
York state) should be applied generally to jails in England. Crawford
was also impressed by the profitable labour of prisoners which was a
marked feature of these American penitentiaries. The Gaol Act of
1822 had actually provided for the principles of separate cells and
employment of prisonsers but, because of disorganization and lack
of centralization, this provision was not put into practice. This
confused situation existed until 1835 when the system of prison
inspectors was introduced and Crawford's report began to achieve
results. Crawford was one of the first four inspectors and also one of
the framers of the laws which firmly established the separate cell
system in the jails of the three kingdoms.
This volume also includes descriptions of penitentiaries in twenty
American states, estimates of the expense involved in enlarging the
English county prisons and contains a statement on the several jails
in Ireland and Scotland.

Original reference
1834   (593) XLVI   Penitentiaries of the U.S., William Crawford, Rep.

Prisons Volume 3

FIRST AND SECOND REPORTS FROM THE SELECT COMMITTEE OF THE HOUSE OF LORDS ON GAOLS AND HOUSES OF CORRECTION IN ENGLAND AND WALES WITH MINUTES OF EVIDENCE, 1835

The first report in this volume deals with discipline as it already existed in prisons and seeks to find a uniform system of prison discipline. This gave rise to evidence on the efficacy of silence, separation, religious instruction, employment and transportation. Much of the testimony was supplied by William Crawford. Another important witness was Elizabeth Fry, whose chief concern was prisons for women. She told the committee that 'the begging, swearing, gaming, fighting, singing, dancing, dressing-up in men's clothes' that went on among women prisoners was 'too bad to be described'. Mr. J. Mance, keeper of the Petworth house of correction, submitted his designs for a tread-wheel and an ergometer for measuring prison labour.

The second report continued the inquiry but reserved for a later report the conclusions regarding prisons in Scotland (see IUP volume Prisons 4). The committee recommended a system of discipline centring on separation, religious instruction and employment. The expense which would be incurred would be great, but as a deterrent and reforming influence the new system would prove an economy.

Legislation to establish a uniform system of prison discipline was passed in 1835 and 1837. The system of prison inspectors, also advocated by this committee, was set up by an Act of 1835. Separate confinement was legalized in 1839.

Original references

1835	(438) XI	Gaols and houses of correction, England and Wales, Sel. Cttee. HL. 1st rep.
	(439)	Gaols and houses of correction, England and Wales, Sel. Cttee. HL. 2nd rep., mins. of ev.

Prisons Volume 4

THIRD, FOURTH AND FIFTH REPORTS FROM THE SELECT COMMITTEE OF THE HOUSE OF LORDS ON GAOLS AND HOUSES OF CORRECTION IN ENGLAND, WALES AND SCOTLAND, 1835

These reports deal with prison conditions generally, prison discipline and jail regulations. Shepton Mallet, Bridewell Hospital and Bethlehem Hospital, all in London, were three of the more important prisons given detailed attention. The committee assessed the suitability of jails for the efficient carrying out of the sentences under which prisoners were confined. As a corollary, the committee considered the necessity for changes in current laws governing administrative and disciplinary procedures in order to ensure uniformity from prison to prison. Various ways of improving prison construction were also explored.

In its third report the committee paid particular attention to conditions on the hulks—prison ships used for temporary confinement of convicts under sentence of transportation. The committee supported the recommendations of a House of Commons report of 1832 which emphasized that separation and silence could not be maintained on board ship and that the hulks should be considered solely as intermediate stations between the jails and the colonies (see IUP volume Transportation 1).

The fourth report deals exclusively with conditions in Scottish prisons, which were found to be in a deplorable state. Glasgow jail was given particular attention.

The fifth report related principally to the system of private reformatory schools for juvenile offenders and recommended their establishment as a public service.

Original references

| 1835 | (440) XII | Gaols and houses of correction, England and Wales, Sel. Cttee. HL. 3rd rep. |
| | (441) | Gaols and houses of correction, England and Wales, Sel. Cttee. HL. 4th and 5th reps. |

Prisons Volume 5

REPORT FROM THE SELECT COMMITTEE ON PRISON DISCIPLINE WITH MINUTES OF EVIDENCE, 1850

This committee investigated and considered possible improvements in the system of rules and discipline currently in force in England and Wales. Particular attention was paid to the extent to which uniformity both in prison discipline and construction had been promoted since the House of Lords' committee report of 1835 (see IUP volume Prisons 4).

The system of separate confinement both before and after trial was considered at length; the reformatory character of the system and the tendency of separated prisoners to develop symptoms of insanity were discussed within this sphere. The modified separate system, as practised at Pentonville, was also examined. In this system, the prisoners, were gradually brought from separation towards association at the last stages of their term. The committee concluded that, if properly regulated, the separate system was more efficient than any other as a deterrent and a reform measure. The question of prison labour was also examined, along with the problems of inequality of the methods used in carrying out sentences of hard labour. Foreshadowing a comparatively modern development in the British prison system, Mr. Pearson, a member of the committee, presented detailed proposals for the erection of prison farms. Other topics covered were the merits of transportation as opposed to imprisonment in Britain and the rehabilitation of prisoners.

Original reference
1850   (632) XVII   Prison discipline, Sel. Cttee. Rep., mins. of ev., etc.

Prisons Volume 6
REPORT FROM THE SELECT COMMITTEE OF THE HOUSE OF LORDS ON THE STATE OF DISCIPLINE IN GAOLS AND HOUSES OF CORRECTION WITH MINUTES OF EVIDENCE, 1863

Discrepancies in prison construction, diet, labour and general discipline which existed among the prisons of England and Wales formed the main topic of this committee's investigations. In the majority of prisons the diet was supposed to form part of the punishment; as Joshua Jebb, the surveyor-general of prisons, remarked in evidence, 'The deterring elements of the punishment are hard labour, hard fare and a hard bed.' The committee criticized the official Home Office scale of prison diet and stressed the need for uniformity of food from prison to prison. (In the following session, Commons' committees investigated this same subject. See IUP volume Prisons 17.) The committee also dealt with the problems of separation of prisoners. Despite laws passed many years before, there was still no uniformity of the system. The question of hard labour in prisons was analysed and a minimum scale of hard labour fixed. Among other topics covered were school instruction and the provision of books, the amalgamation of certain smaller jails with larger prisons, the need for yearly inspection of all prisons, the necessity for uniformity in prison dress and the use of photography as a means of identifying prisoners.

The outcome of this investigation was the Prison Act of 1865, which set up a uniform but excessively rigid, system of prisons and punishments.

Original reference
1863   (499) IX   State of discipline in gaols and houses of correction, Sel. Cttee. HL. Rep., mins. of ev., etc.

Prisons Volume 7

REPORTS ON VARIOUS PRISONS, 1808–1815

The five reports included in this volume cover investigations into
conditions at Coldbath Fields, Lancaster, Lincoln Castle, and
various London prisons. The three commissioners' reports deal
chiefly with the treatment of prisoners, while the Select Committees
concentrated on surveying the general state of the prisons in London.
The Lincoln Castle inquiry stemmed from a petition to parliament
from the journalist Peter Finnerty, who had been sentenced to
eighteen months' imprisonment for libelling Lord Castlereagh.
Finnerty, supported in his memorial by John Drakard and others
sentenced for political libel, accused the jailers of misconduct and
mismanagement. The three commissioners exonerated the prison
administrators, but Finnerty's petition gave rise to considerable
discussion in the Commons, where he was supported by several
prominent politicians. One of the recurring problems raised in all
these investigations was that of separation or classification of
prisoners. Felons, murderers, debtors and 'political' prisoners were
usually all mixed together in English jails at this time. By the time of
the London jails inquiries, it was apparent that architectural changes
were needed in most prisons in order to alleviate this problem.

Original references

1809	(216) IV	Coldbath Fields prison, Com. Rep.
1812–13	(3) V	Lancaster prison, Com. Rep., mins. of ev., etc.
	(4)	Lincoln Castle prison, Com. Rep., mins. of ev., etc.
1813–14	(157) IV	London gaols, Sel. Cttee. Rep., mins. of ev., etc.
1814–15	(152) IV	London gaols, Sel. Cttee. Rep., mins. of ev., etc.

Prisons Volume 8

REPORTS AND RETURNS RELATING TO PRISONS AND PRISON DISCIPLINE,
1818–1822

The bulk of the reports in volume eight relate to London jails—with
emphasis given to Newgate—and are chiefly descriptive, containing
information on classification, food, clothing, health, etc., of prisoners.
The report on Scottish jails is primarily on prison financing and
administration. Each royal burgh in Scotland was to provide a jail,
but many of the burghs were unable to make adequate provision for
the support of jails. The lengthy appendix to this paper contains
information from all the royal burghs respecting the problem of
prisons in each area. The short report from the 1822 committee on
laws relating to prisons contains the recommendation that constant

labour should be provided in every prison, although the kind of labour is not specified. Included also are four sets of jail returns which consist of county-by-county listings of prisons—their capacity, kinds of prisoners detained there, types of labour done and general observations on the state of the prison.

In addition, this volume contains five plans that were originally meant to accompany the 1819 report on the state and condition of jails (see IUP volume Prisons 1). These plans were not printed until 1821 and thus were not bound originally into the volume for which they were intended.

Original references

1818	(346) VI	Scottish gaols, Sel. Cttee. Rep., appendix.
1818	(275) VIII	London and Southwark prisons, Sel. Cttee. 1st rep., mins. of ev., etc.
	(392)	London and Southwark prisons, Sel. Cttee. 2nd rep.
1819	(109) XI	State of the prisons of the Fleet, Marshalsea, etc., R. Com. Rep., mins. of ev., etc.
1819	(135) XVII	Gaols, etc., England and Wales, returns.
	(136)	Gaols, etc., Scotland, returns.
	(137)	Gaols, etc., Ireland, returns.
1821	(400) XXI	Gaols, etc., England, Wales, Scotland, returns.
	in XXI	Plans to accompany 1819 (579) VII.
1822	(300) IV	Laws relating to prisons, Sel. Cttee. Rep., appendix.

Prisons Volume 9

REPORTS AND PAPERS RELATING TO ILCHESTER JAIL, 1822

Henry Hunt, the radical politician, was sentenced to two years' imprisonment in Ilchester for matters rising out of the Manchester riots (August 1819—the Peterloo Massacre). Hunt brought charges of misconduct against William Brindle, the keeper of the prison, and commissioners were appointed to investigate the situation. Their inquiry upheld Hunt's claims, as did the report of the sheriff and the magistrates. Apart from Hunt's immediate charges, the commissioners also devoted a part of their report to the problems of prisoners' health, the site of the jail and the structure of the prison, including plans of the buildings as a part of the material submitted.

Original references

1822	(7) XI	Ilchester gaol, R. Com. Rep.
	(54)	Ilchester gaol, R. Com. apps., mins. of ev.
	(30)	Ilchester gaol, High Sheriff and Magistrates, Rep.
	(70)	Ilchester gaol, Coroner's inquests.

Prisons Volume 10
REPORTS AND PAPERS RELATING TO MILLBANK PENITENTIARY, 1823–1824

The reports and papers included in this volume deal mainly with the health of the Millbank prisoners. In the winter of 1822–23 an epidemic broke out in the prison; two doctors, Peter M. Lathem and Peter M. Roget, were asked to investigate. They found that the disease, a form of scurvy accompanied by nervous disorders, was due chiefly to scanty diet. When their recommendations—that prisoners be given more solid food, better bread and one and a half pounds of meat per fortnight—were adopted, the epidemic ended. The seriousness of the situation led to the formation of two Select Committees to inquire into the state of the penitentiary, concentrating on the epidemic, prison diet and prison discipline in general. The reports also contain a history of Millbank and recommendations for improvement of the site. The entire volume provides an excellent overall picture of conditions in Millbank during the years covered and contains detailed information on dietary problems in relation to the problem of punishment.

Original references

1823	(256) V	Millbank penitentiary, physicians rep.
	(309)	Millbank penitentiary, further papers.
	(545)	Millbank penitentiary, further papers.
	(533)	Millbank penitentiary, Sel. Cttee. Rep., mins. of ev., etc.
1824	(408) IV	Millbank penitentiary, Sel. Cttee. Rep., mins. of ev., etc.

Prisons Volume 11
REPORTS AND PAPERS RELATING TO PRISONS AND PRISON DISCIPLINE, 1823–1845

The years covered by these reports and papers were a period of confusion and change in the British prison system. The Gaol Act of 1823 required better organization of prisons, closer inspection by the magistrates and a five-group classification system. However, there were other influences at work apart from the Act of 1823. The enthusiasm on the part of some for the silent system, of some for the separate system, of still others for the plan of hard labour led to great discrepancies between prisons. During this period the influential

Crawford Report (see IUP volume Prisons 2) was published and finally, in 1835, a centralized administration was established through the appointment of prison inspectors. The separate system advocated by Crawford came to be accepted, and new prisons—several of them designed by Joshua Jebb who became surveyor-general of prisons in 1837—were built to this plan.

These reports and papers reflect many of the changes of the time. The first group of short papers deals with hard labour, specifically, the much-favoured tread-wheel. There are papers relating to abuses and mismanagement in specific prisons—Bradford, Warwick, Carnarvon, Knutsford, etc.—and two long reports on the financing of Scottish prisons. Also included are recommendations for amending the Gaol Act, a report of the prison inspectors advocating the useful employment of prisoners and an extensive collection of plans for the new model prison at Pentonville with Jebb's explanations on the relation between prison construction and the separate system.

Original references

1823	(113) XV	Tread-wheels, communications from magistrates.
1824	(45) XIX	Tread-wheels, communications from magistrates.
	(247)	Tread-wheels, statement.
1825	(34) XXIII	Tread-wheels, papers.
1825	(330) XXI	Bradford gaol, correspondence.
1826	(381) V	Scottish prisons, Sel. Cttee. Rep., mins. of ev., etc.
1836	(454) XXI	Laws relating to prisons, Sel. Cttee. Rep., etc.
1836	(414) XLII	Newgate gaol, Rep. of the cttee. of the court of aldermen on the inspectors' rep., mins. of ev., etc.
	(486)	Newgate gaol, inspectors' reply.
1839	(462) XXXVIII	Warwick gaol, allegations in the petition of Messrs. Lovett and Collins, Rep. of visiting magistrates, mins. of ev., etc.
1843	[457] XXV, XXVI	System of prison discipline, inspectors of prisons, Rep., etc.
1843	(422) XLIII	Conduct of the governor of Carnarvon gaol, Rep.
	(126)	Treatment of prisoners in the house of correction at Knutsford, inspector of prisons for Northern District, Rep., mins. of ev., etc.
	(518)	Treatment of prisoners in the house of correction at Knutsford, visiting magistrates' reps.
1844	[594] XXVIII	Construction of Pentonville prison, Lt.-Col. Jebb, surveyor-general of prisons, Rep., etc.
1845	(460) XIII	Prisons, Scotland, Regulation of assessment, Sel. Cttee. Rep., mins of ev., etc.
1845	(366) XXV	Circumstances which occurred on the occasion of the condemned sermon in the chapel of Newgate gaol in the case of Hocker, and the circumstances which took place on the morning of his execution, W. Russell, Rep., etc.
1845	(380) XXXVII	Millbank prison (light, ventilation), Reps.

Prisons Volume 12

REPORTS ON THE TREATMENT AND CONDITION OF THE CONVICTS IN
THE HULKS AT WOOLWICH, 1847

In 1847 Thomas Slingsby Duncombe, the radical M.P. for Finsbury,
published a statement in *The Times* accusing the superintendent of
convicts, J. H. Capper, with gross neglect of duty and mismanagement of the hulks on which the convicts were confined. Capper
replied to Duncombe with a report to the Home Secretary exonerating himself. However, one of the prison inspectors, W. J. Williams,
was appointed to inquire into the situation on the hulks at Woolwich.
The report and evidence of Williams's investigation make some of
the grimmest reading of all the prison papers. Williams dismissed
several of Duncombe's specific charges but found that conditions on
the hulks could hardly have been worse. Cleanliness—even on the
hospital ship—was non-existent, the diet caused scurvy (the oatmeal
was so bad that the prisoners threw it overboard), regulations for
punishments were completely disregarded, the superintendent
mismanaged the earnings of the convicts, lunatics were permitted to
remain among the other prisoners and, finally, Superintendent
Capper had hardly visited the hulks at all, leaving his visitorial
duties to his secretary. For years Capper had been submitting
reports about things he had not personally inspected. The result of
Williams's inquiry was the easing of the elderly Capper out of his
office and the reform of the hulks (which were gradually phased out
of use).

Original references

1847	(149) XLVIII	Treatment of convicts in the hulks at Woolwich, superintendent of convicts, Rep.
1847	[831] XVIII	Treatment and condition of convicts in the hulks at Woolwich, Rep., mins. of ev., etc.
	[831–II]	Treatment and condition of convicts in the hulks at Woolwich, index.

Prisons Volume 13

REPORTS ON MILLBANK PENITENTIARY AND LEICESTER COUNTY JAIL,
1847–1854

The ubiquitous Thomas Slingsby Duncombe appears again in this
volume, once more as a champion of the oppressed. Edward Baker,
a warder at Millbank, petitioned against the conduct of the prison's
governor, Capt. J. R. Groves. Duncombe assisted Baker in bringing
the case to the attention of the House of Commons. The resulting
inquiry centred chiefly around the question of corporal punishment

in the prison. While the commissioners agreed that Millbank should be subjected to an independent system of inspection, they refused to uphold Baker's charges against Groves.

The Leicester inquiry came about through the discovery by one of the inspectors that prisoners were made to operate cranking machines as a form of punishment. The machines were weighted in order to make the prisoner's tasks more difficult. A set number of revolutions was assigned and the prisoner deprived of food until this goal was reached. The report is extremely critical of crank labour—apart from the fact that the weighting and possible lack of proper diet were definite health hazards, the concept of unproductive labour had become obsolete in the thinking of most of Britain's prison experts by this date.

Original references

1847	[760] XXX	Management of Millbank prison, R. Com. Rep.
	[768]	Management of Millbank prison, R. Com. mins. of ev.
1854	[1808] XXXIV	Leicester county gaol, R. Com. Rep., mins. of ev., etc.

Prisons Volume 14

REPORTS OF THE SURVEYOR-GENERAL OF PRISONS, 1847–1853

Joshua Jebb, surveyor-general of convict prisons, began submitting annual reports in the late 1840s. Most of his reports were accompanied by detailed plans and drawings, not only of the structure of prisons but also for such items as locks, sanitary facilities and even good conduct medals for well-behaved prisoners. As an advocate of the separate system, Jebb naturally emphasized its advantages whenever possible. Much space in the reports is also devoted to prison labour. However, one of the most interesting aspects of these reports is the way in which they reflect the changing attitude toward transportation as a solution to problems of crime and criminality. Jebb constantly stressed the need for reducing the number of transported convicts and removing prisoners from the hulks to regular prisons. All the reports contain statistics relating to the convict prisons. The 1847 report includes some case studies of prisoners in Pentonville. The final report in this volume contains plans for Dartmoor prison.

Original references

1847	[867] XXIX	Prisons. Lt.-Col. Jebb, 2nd rep., etc.
1850	[1176] XXIX	Portland prison and its connection with the system of convict discipline, Lt.-Col. Jebb, Rep.

1851   [1419] XXVIII   Discipline and management of the convict prisons,
                         1850, Lt.-Col. Jebb, Rep.
1852–53 [1572] LI   Discipline and management of the convict prisons,
                         Lt.-Col. Jebb, Rep.

Prisons Volume 15

REPORT ON THE CONDITION AND TREATMENT OF PRISONERS IN
BIRMINGHAM BOROUGH PRISON WITH MINUTES OF EVIDENCE, 1854

This investigation was brought about when charges of excessive
cruelty were levelled against Lieut. William Austin, the governor of
the Birmingham prison. The commissioners found that the prison
authorities, even before Austin took office, had constantly punished
prisoners beyond the limits of the Gaol Act. Among other punishments, the Birmingham prisoners were required to work weighted
cranking machines. Prisoners who proved 'difficult' were placed in
strait-jackets for long periods. The separate system was used in the
prison but was interpreted so strictly that the commissioners felt it
was more a system of solitary confinement. The report, which
contains summaries of specific cases, condemned Austin, certain of
the warders, the medical officer and some of the visiting magistrates—
these last for not reporting conditions they knew to be wrong.

Original reference
1854   [1809] XXXI   Treatment of the prisoners in Birmingham borough
                         prison, R. Com. Rep., mins. of ev.

Prisons Volume 16

REPORTS FROM THE SURVEYOR-GENERAL OF CONVICT PRISONS, 1853–
1855

During the period covered by these reports, penal servitude became
the legal substitute for transportation—a factor which added to
Jebb's tasks as surveyor-general. Like the earlier reports (see IUP
volume Prisons 14), these are divided into categories—discipline,
reports on various prisons, prison construction, etc.—and contain
many plans. In the first report Jebb puts great emphasis on the
causes of crime and on crime prevention, particularly among
juveniles. The second report, which includes plans of Brixton
prison, contains the observation that short-term prisoners should be
separated from association with long-term, hardened prisoners. The
final report stresses the need for a comprehensive system of prison
discipline because of the abolition of transportation. The plans

accompanying this report are of Chatham prison.

Original references

1852–53 [1659] LI	Discipline and management of convict prisons, Lt.-Col. Jebb, Rep.	
1854 [1846] XXXIII	Discipline and management of convict prisons, Lt.-Col. Jebb, Rep.	
1854–55 [2004] XXV	Discipline of convict prisons and on substitution of penal servitude for transportation, Lt.-Col. Jebb, Reps.	

Prisons Volume 17

REPORTS RELATING TO PRISONS, 1857–1870

The first two reports in this volume are those of Sir Joshua Jebb, who died in 1863. His last reports are of a more historical nature than his earlier ones—those included here contain summaries of the system of convict discipline from 1842, a general history of the British prison system, evolving ideas of prison construction, and so on. Jebb also emphasized the idea that reform is equally as important as punishment, especially in cases of long-term prisoners. The plans included with his reports are for the prisons at Fulham and Woking.

The short reports on prison diet present an attempt to equate the diets in various prisons and to adjust the content of diet to the classification of the prisoner. Jebb's successor, Lt.-Col. E. Y. W. Henderson, was among the signatories of the first of these reports. The Select Committee on the Prisons and Prison Ministers Acts turned their attention to the problem of the lack of Roman Catholic priests as prison chaplains. Appointment of non-Anglican chaplains was usually left to the local authorities, with the result that Catholic prisoners were frequently bereft of spiritual guidance. The committee recommended that Catholic priests should, by law, be assigned to prisons where Roman Catholics were confined. The evidence contains interesting accounts of the role of the church in the British prison system.

Original references

1857–58 [2414] XXIX	Discipline of convict prisons and on substitution of penal servitude for transportation, Lt.-Col. Jebb, Reps.	
1862 [3055] XXV	Convict prisons, Lt.-Col. Jebb, General Rep. for 1860–61.	
1864 (467) XLIX	Dietaries in convict prisons, Rep.	
(313)	Dietaries in the county and borough gaols, Cttee. Rep. and correspondence on prison discipline.	
1870 (259) VIII	Prisons and Prison Ministers Acts, Sel. Cttee. Rep., mins. of ev., etc.	

Prisons Volume 18

REPORTS RELATING TO PRISONS, 1878–1889

Of the reports contained in this volume, the majority deal with the problem of accommodation for prisoners awaiting trial—that is, the jail facilities available in such places as court-houses and police courts. All the investigations revealed that these accommodations were usually defective. In the Scottish report, for example, only 13 of the 190 courts investigated had suitable jail facilities. The most frequent complaint was overcrowding of prisoners and/or lack of separation of the sexes.

Prison diet papers are also included here. The report of the committee recommended that the programme of different diets for different types of prisoners be reduced if not abandoned. This report included a summary of earlier reports on diets (see IUP volume Prisons 17) but contains information on nutrition and cooking methods that the previous papers lack. The investigation into the death of John Nolan in Clerkenwell prison is related to the diet question—the coroner's jury decided that Nolan died because of the repeated bread-and-water diet ordered for him by the prison's governor. The commission disagreed, saying the death was due to lung trouble caused by a change in the weather.

The two other subjects covered in this group of papers are convict labour on public works, particularly harbours, and prison dress. In the latter case the recommendation was advanced that British prisons should follow the Irish system of issuing prisoners with uniforms and requiring haircuts.

Original references

1878	(95) XLII	Dietaries of the prisons in England and Wales subject to the Prison Acts, 1865 and 1877, Cttee. Rep., etc.
1878–79	(79) LIX	Death of John Nolan in Clerkenwell prison, Com. Rep., mins. of ev.
1882	[C.3427] XXXIV	Employment of convicts in the United Kingdom, Cttee. Rep.
1887	[C.4971] XLI	Accommodation for prisoners awaiting trial at assizes and sessions, Cttee. Rep.
1888	[C.5439] LVIII	Accommodation for prisoners in the police courts of the metropolis and all buildings in England and Wales, Cttee. Rep.
1889	[C.5683] XLI	Accommodation for prisoners awaiting trial at courts in Scotland, Cttee. Rep.
1889	[C.5759] LXI	Prison rules (wearing of prison dress, etc.), Cttee. Rep., mins. of ev., etc.

Prisons Volume 19

During the 1890s British prisons and prison administration were the
subjects of many articles in newspapers and magazines. Most of
these accounts were sweeping indictments of the system of administration as stringently enforced under the Acts of 1865 and 1877. The
committee of 1895, under the chairmanship of H. J. Gladstone, was
called upon to investigate the prisons in the light of the journalists'
charges. The committee's report and evidence form the basis of this
volume—the three remaining papers are illustrative of the outcome
of the inquiry. The report is one of the most important documents
in the prisons series, as it sets out the principles that in many ways
still govern the British penal system. According to the committee,
'Prison discipline and treatment should be designed to maintain,
stimulate, or awaken the higher susceptibilities of prisoners . . . and
whenever possible to turn them out of prison better men and women
than when they came in.' The report condemned separate confinement and useless or excessively hard labour and went on to say,
'Prison treatment should have as its primary and concurrent objects
deterrence and reformation'—an idea that had been virtually
ignored since Jebb first tentatively mentioned it almost fifty years
before.

The papers showing how the committee's recommendations were
carried out indicate the resentment the report must have caused
among those responsible for the administration of the system.

Original references

1895	[C.7702] LVI	Prisons, Dept. Cttee., Rep.
	[C.7702–I]	Prisons, Dept. Cttee., mins. of ev., etc.
1896	[C.7996] XLIV	Prisons, steps taken to carry out the recommenda-tion, prison commissioners, statement.
	[C.7995]	Prisons, observation on the recommendation by the prison commissioners.
1898	[C.8790] XLVII	Prisons, steps taken to carry out the recommenda-tion, statement.

Prisons Volume 20

The four reports included here can all be traced to the important
report of 1895 (see IUP volume Prisons 19), which urged better
educational facilities for prisoners, guidance for ex-prisoners and

an investigation of standard prison diets. The committee investigating the education of prisoners generally encouraged a certain amount of regular schooling given by qualified teachers. The appendix to this report contains papers showing the then current educational standards in prisons. The Merrick report on the Discharged Prisoners' Aid Societies is a summary of the work done— or not done—by the organization, which had recognized branches affiliated with every prison in England and Wales. Rev. Merrick concluded that the work of the society was extremely uneven, and he called for several reforms. The two remaining reports are on the subject of diet and are quite similar. The Scottish report, however, includes information and critical comment on prison diets in other countries, including England. Apart from general nutritional improvements and the reduction of the number of diets served in individual prisons, the reports emphasized the need for trained cooks, the use of enamel (rather than metal) dishes and the appointment of an inspector of food.

Original references

1896	[C.8154] XLIV	Education and moral instruction of prisoners, Dept. Cttee. Rep., etc.
	[C.8155]	Education and moral instruction of prisoners, Dept. Cttee. mins. of ev., etc.
1897	[C.8299] XL	Operations of Discharged Prisoners' Aid Societies, G. P. Merrick, Rep.
1899	[C.9166] XLIII	Prison dietaries, Dept. Cttee. Rep.
	[C.9514]	Prison dietaries in Scotland, J. C. Dunlop, Rep.

Prisons Volume 21

REPORTS AND PAPERS RELATING TO TREASON-FELONY PRISONERS, 1866–1890

By an Act of 1848 treason-felony was removed from the list of capital offences and those convicted of the crime were given prison sentences or transported. This volume deals with the prison treatment of some prominent Fenian leaders convicted for treason-felony—Jeremiah O'Donovan Rossa, James Stephens, Daniel O'Sullivan (Borano) and others. These men had sworn the Fenian oath of allegiance to 'the Irish Republic now virtually established'. A facsimile of this oath is included in this volume.

The escape of James Stephens from Richmond jail and the causes of his escape—a badly guarded and insecure prison and the aid of a prison guard who was a member of the Fenian brotherhood—is dealt with in the first of the reports. The treatment of Fenian prisoners in Pentonville and Woking prisons and an examination of their complaints (which were considered to be unfounded) appears in another report. However, the commissioners in 1871 found the excessive use of the dark cell and manacles on treason-felony prisoners was abusive. This report contains summaries of the character and behaviour of individual prisoners, including O'Donovan Rossa. The final report deals with the treatment of treason-felony prisoners at Chatham prison. The investigators claimed that the convicts were probably better treated than other prisoners and that their grievances had all been righted by the prison authorities. The charge against the prison warders of attempting to poison convict Michael Daly was refuted.

This series of reports which deals exclusively with one type of prisoner provides an important supplement to the prisons set. The papers are also illustrative of the methods used by the British government to handle the rebellious Fenians, most of whom became heroes in their own country.

Original references

1866	(147) LVIII	Treason-felony; arrest and escape of James Stephens, inspectors general of prisons in Ireland, Rep.
	(307)	Treason-felony; persons charged with Fenianism, Papers.
1867	[3880] XXXV	Treatment of treason-felony convicts in English convict prisons, Com. Rep.
1871	[C.319] XXXII	Treatment of treason-felony convicts in English prisons. Com. Vol. I, Rep., etc.
	[C.319–I]	Treatment of treason-felony convicts in English prisons. Com. Vol. II, Mins. of ev.
1890	[C.6016] XXXVII	Treatment of certain prisoners convicted for treason-felony, visitors of the convict prison at Chatham, Rep., mins. of ev., etc.

Transportation Volume 1

REPORTS FROM SELECT COMMITTEES ON FINANCING CONVICT ESTAB-LISHMENTS, ERECTING PENITENTIARY HOUSES AND OTHER MATTERS RELATING TO TRANSPORTATION AND SECONDARY PUNISHMENTS WITH MINUTES OF EVIDENCE, APPENDICES AND INDICES, 1810–1832

During the period covered by the reports, the penal system in Britain was undergoing revision and rationalisation. The investigating committees were concerned with the collection of facts regarding penal conditions and costs and examining the effectiveness of methods of imprisonment and punishment. Transportation in operation as a form of punishment for a wide range of crimes, was regarded with horror by sentenced prisoners (the evidence claims that three prisoners in Newgate Jail chose to be hanged rather than transported) and the conditions in the penal colonies were severe, consisting of arbitrary and often savage punishments, poor diet and hard labour. The reports contain valuable accounts of these conditions, on the state of prisons, houses of correction and hulks in Britain and the penal colonies, on the labour, diet, classification and treatment of prisoners and on the effectiveness of such punishments as solitary confinement and transportation. A special feature of the volume is Jeremy Bentham's prison reform plan and the extensive discussion of it. The recommendations of the committees were incorporated in the transportation laws of 1814, 1816, 1823 and 1824, and by 1840 many of the reforms proposed had been made. As a result transportation developed into an efficient, fairly rapid means of supplying labour markets in the colonies with large numbers of convicts.

Original references

1810	(348) IV	Convict establishments, Sel. Cttee. Rep. with Appendix.
1810–11	(199) III	Penitentiary houses, transportation, Sel. Cttee. 1st Rep. with Appendix.
	(217)	Penitentiary houses, transportation, Sel. Cttee. 2nd Rep.
1812	(306) II	Penitentiary houses, transportation, Sel. Cttee. 3rd Rep. with Appendix.
	(341)	Transportation sentences, Sel. Cttee. Rep. with Appendix.
1831	(276) VII	Secondary Punishments, Sel. Cttee. Rep., mins. of ev., etc.
1831–32	(547) VII	Secondary Punishments, Sel. Cttee. Rep., mins. of ev., etc.

Transportation Volume 2

REPORT FROM THE SELECT COMMITTEE ON TRANSPORTATION WITH MINUTES OF EVIDENCE, APPENDIX AND INDEX, 1837

By 1837 the notion of transportation to the colonies as a form of crime control was beginning to be questioned. Vast numbers of convicts, mainly criminal offenders but also political undesirables, were swelling the population of New South Wales and Van Diemen's Land and there were indications that serious conflicts between free settlers, convicts on tickets-of-leave and imprisoned convicts might arise. The Select Committee heard extensive evidence on the evil effects produced by transportation on the character of colonies, on the livelihood of the free settler and aboriginal populations and on the convicts themselves. A clear and often disturbing picture emerges from witnesses' descriptions of life in the colonies and convict settlements. Other topics covered by the inquiry include the employment of convicts, the increasing use of tickets-of-leave, crime, and in particular, prostitution among convicts, religious instruction and education, social habits in the colonies, methods of reforming the transportation system and the advisability of abolishing it entirely.

Original reference
1837   (518) XIX   Transportation, Sel. Cttee. Rep., mins. of ev., etc.

Transportation Volume 3

REPORTS FROM SELECT COMMITTEES ON TRANSPORTATION WITH PROCEEDINGS, MINUTES OF EVIDENCE, APPENDICES AND INDICES, 1837–1861

The first of the two reports in this volume was the result of an exhaustive inquiry into the whole system of transportation as a punishment for convicts. The Select Committee provides in this report a useful survey of the history of transportation from Elizabethan times, describes its nature and investigates its efficacy as a deterrent and method of reform and examines its social and economic effects. Among the subjects analysed in depth are the use of convict labour in public works, the system of assignment of convicts to settlers and the influence of emancipated convicts on the opening up of the colonies.

Although transportation to New South Wales and Van Diemen's Land had been discontinued, convicts were still sent to Western Australia, Bermuda and Gibraltar. The 1861 Select Committee examines the current situation on similar lines to those of the earlier committee and presents a valuable picture of Australian official attitudes to the system. This report also considers the overall crime situation in Britain since the abolition of transportation in 1853 and 1857 and notes a significant decrease in convictions, attributed to the effectiveness and the better use of penitentiaries.

Original references
1837–38 (669) XXII   Transportation, Sel. Cttee. Rep., mins. of ev., etc.
1861   (286) XIII   Present system of transportation, its utility, economy and effect upon colonisation, Sel. Cttee. Rep., mins. of ev., etc.

Transportation Volume 4

REPORTS FROM SELECT COMMITTEES ON THE PROVISIONS AND OPERATION
OF THE ACT TO SUBSTITUTE OTHER PUNISHMENT IN LIEU OF TRANS-
PORTATION WITH MINUTES OF EVIDENCE, APPENDICES AND INDEX, 1856·

The conclusions reached by both the House of Commons and House
of Lords Select Committees which inquired into the system of
transportation are basically the same: transportation should be
continued as the best system of secondary punishment; efforts should
be made to placate anti-transportation colonists; the Marks System
should be ended. These reports are valuable, coming at a time when
the system had reached its peak, and was the subject of prolonged and
vigorous argument. The witnesses included Colonel Jebb, chairman
of the Directors of convict prisons, who felt transportation had no
deterrent effect and spoke on the employment of convicts; Captain
Croften who gave details on the operation of the Irish prison system;
Earl Grey who gave his views on Maconochie's system; Governors
Fitzgerald, Ronnie and Caldwell who reported on Western Australia,
the Falkland Islands and the Red River Settlement of Canada.
Valuable evidence was given by Henry Mayhew on his study of
criminal classes, on the tickets-of-leave system and on the need for
rehabilitation. These reports and minutes of evidence are an important contribution to a study of the reform of the transportation
system and of the development of the British prison system.

Original references

1856	(244) XVII	Punishment in lieu of transportation, Sel. Cttee. 1st Rep., mins. of ev., etc.
	(296)	2nd Rep., mins. of ev., etc.
	(355)	3rd Rep., mins. of ev., etc.
	(355–I)	Index to Reps.
	(404)	Punishment in lieu of transportation. Sel. Cttee. HL. Rep., mins. of ev., etc.

Transportation Volume 5

REPORT OF THE COMMISSIONERS ON THE ACTS RELATING TO TRANS-
PORTATION AND PENAL SERVITUDE WITH MINUTES OF EVIDENCE,
APPENDIX AND INDEX, 1863

The Acts which form the subjects of investigation by the Royal
Commission are the 1853 and 1857 Acts by which penal servitude
replaced transportation as a secondary punishment. This lengthy
report provides a final official examination by Parliament on trans-

portation and is a major document on the reform of British criminal law, being a study of the transition from one form of punishment to another. The report describes in detail how the Acts operated, analyses defects and proposes improvements. Evidence is taken from governors and members of the staff of prisons, from representatives of the courts, from the police and from officials in Southern and Western Australia. The practice of penal servitude, the system of sentencing, prison conditions and labour and the use of the Marks System originated by Captain Alexander Maconochie of Norfolk Island penal colony in 1840 (see IUP volumes Transportation 6 and 7) are investigated. The value of penal servitude and the management of prisons are also discussed.

Original references

| 1863 | [3190] XXI | Transportation and the Penal Servitude Acts, R. Com. Rep., etc. |
| | [3190–I] | Mins. of ev., etc. |

Transportation Volume 6

CORRESPONDENCE AND PAPERS RELATING TO TRANSPORTATION, 1810–1841

This volume contains the large number of papers relating to transportation which were presented to the House of Commons in the course of the first forty years of the century. These include the statistical returns of convicts transported, particularly in the new colony of New South Wales. The figures provided indicate the great extent of transportation and its cost. During this period, transportation as a form of crime control was acceptable in Britain but there was a growing resentment to this constant influx of convicts by the colonial settlers and immigrants. This opposition is reflected in the correspondence from Australia. The despatches between the British Foreign Office and the Governors of the Australian colonies deal with the treatment of convicts, discipline and assignment of labour. The whole system of secondary punishments is examined in detail and the function of convict establishments analysed. The Order in Council of 1840, revoking regulations of 1824 and 1825 and declaring Van Diemen's Land and Norfolk Island the only penal colonies in Australia, is included.

The correspondence on secondary punishment and other papers on prison discipline in the penal colonies of New South Wales and Van Diemen's Land provides information on the development of the famous Marks System, which was later refined and adopted as the Irish System and used extensively at the end of the century in United States reformatories. The volume also includes a letter from Captain Maconochie opposing the system of transportation.

Original references

1810	(45) XIV	Convicts transported to New South Wales, returns.
	(52)	Persons under sentence of transportation, returns.
1812	(97) X	Convicts transported to New South Wales, returns.
1814–15	(354) XI	Persons transported to New South Wales, account.
	(255)	Discharge from convict ships, New South Wales, returns.
1816	(314) XVIII	Convict deaths on route, returns.
	(315)	Convicts landed in New South Wales, returns.
	(366)	Transportation costs, returns.
	(431)	Transportation costs, returns.
1817	(276) XVI	Convicts transported, returns.
1818	(334) XVI	Transportation costs, returns.
	(418)	Persons transported, returns.
1819	(191) XVII	Transportation, costs.
1821	(172) XX	Irish convicts, returns.
1821	(171) XXI	Convicts transported to New South Wales, returns.
	(439)	Convict ships, returns.
1822	(136) XXII	Convicts transported to New South Wales, returns.
	(281)	Convicts transported to New South Wales, returns.
1824	(144) XIX	Convicts transported, returns.
1829	(108) XVIII	Male convicts transported, returns.
1830	(600) XXIII	Convicts in England and Bermuda, returns.
	(585)	Employment of convicts, returns.
1831–32	(161) XXXII	Convicts in New South Wales, returns.
	(335)	Regulation of penal settlements, papers.
1834	(81) XLVII	Surgeons and masters of convict ships, instructions.
	(427)	Loss of Amphitrite convict ship, papers.
	(82)	Secondary punishments, correspondence.
	(614)	Secondary punishments, correspondence.
1837–38	[121] XL	Prison discipline in Van Diemen's Land, rep.
1837–38	(309) XLII*	Convict discipline, despatch.
1839	(76) XXXIV	Transportation and convict assignments, despatches.
	(524)	Transportation and convict assignments, despatches.
1839	(582) XXXVIII	Transportation and convict assignments, papers.
	(244)	Conveyance of convicts, returns.
1840	(352) XXXVIII	Transportation, Order in Council.
1841	(412) XVII	Secondary punishments, correspondence.

*The original Index reference XXII is incorrect and should read XLII as here.

Transportation Volume 7

CORRESPONDENCE AND OTHER PAPERS RELATING TO TRANSPORTATION AND CONVICT DISCIPLINE, 1843–1847

The correspondence between the colonial Governors (Wilmot, Gibb,

Grey and Fitzroy) and Lord Stanley and W E Gladstone, successive colonial secretaries, provides an interesting guide to shifts of policy on the treatment of transported convicts. The question of conditional and absolute pardons to convicts was a subject of growing importance. A major breakthrough on this matter was Gladstone's proposed colony of "emancipists" or pardoned convicts. The effects of this on all transported convicts, Gladstone felt, would be salutary, providing them with a reason for good behaviour and a hope for their future. The state of rebellion on Norfolk Island, the transfer of convicts to there from Van Diemen's Land, the regulation of female convict establishments and boys' prisons are also detailed. Of special interest is Lord Stanley's analysis of the uses of the Marks System in penal colonies and Maconochie's proposals (see IUP volume Transportation 6). Rejecting many of Maconochie's proposals, Stanley recognises the value in principle of a marks system based on good conduct but requests further study before it could be put into use in prisons. These papers provide data on Australian attitudes to transportation and statistics of convict ships and convicts transported between 1839 and 1846.

Original references

1843	(158) XLII	Convict discipline and transportation, correspondence.
	(171)	Transportation, letter.
	(159)	Convict discipline and transportation, correspondence.
1843	(166) LII	Convict ships and transports, returns.
	(84)	Ships "Abercrombie Robinson" and "Waterloo", papers.
	(222)	Merchant ships employed as transports, returns.
	(353)	Convict ships and transports, returns.
1845	(78) XXXVII	Prisoners unfit for transportation, returns.
	[659]	Convict discipline and transportation, correspondence.
1846	(692) XXIX	Convict pardons, returns.
	(36)	Convict discipline in Van Diemen's Land, rep. and correspondence.
	(402)	Convict discipline in Van Diemen's Land, rep. and correspondence.
	(401)	Convict pardons, returns.
	(169)	Transportation to Van Diemen's Land, letter.
1846	(573) XLV	Ships hired for conveyance of convicts, returns.
1847	(741) XXXVIII	Transportation, letter.
1847	[785] XLVIII	Convict discipline and transportation, correspondence.
	[800]	Convict discipline and transportation, correspondence.
	[811]	Convict discipline and transportation, correspondence.

Transportation Volume 8

CORRESPONDENCE AND PAPERS RELATING TO CONVICT DISCIPLINE
AND TRANSPORTATION, 1847–1850

The economic distress and administrative chaos in Van Diemen's
Land in the early 1840s opened the eyes of the settlers to the moral
evils of transportation. In 1846 Gladstone abolished transportation
to the island and New South Wales squatters took the opportunity
to demand a renewal of transportation to their colony to solve
their labour problems. The ensuing outcries from anti-transportation
groups of settlers are reported here by Governor Fitzroy and a
large number of petitions are included. Governor Denison's reports
from Van Diemen's Land provide detailed statistics for the island
for 1847. The arrival of convicts from the Cape of Good Hope
where settlers succeeded in preventing the establishment of a penal
settlement is recorded here with instructions to grant conditional
pardons to all except "prisoner Mitchell" (the Irish patriot). An
interesting feature of Governor Denison's account of Van Diemen's
Land is his criticism of Irish convicts who seem to him to be unduly
subservient to the Catholic chaplain. The different cultural and
religious backgrounds of British and Irish convicts provided an
interesting mixture in the penal colonies since their initiation.

Original references

1847–48	(941) LII	Convict discipline and transportation, correspondence.
1849	(393) VI	Transportation for treason (Ireland), Act.
1850	[1138] XXXVIII	Reception of convicts from the Cape of Good Hope, despatch.
1850	[1153] XLV	Convict discipline and transportation, correspondence.
	[1285]	Convict discipline and transportation, correspondence.
	(40)	Convict discipline and transportation, letter.

Transportation Volume 9

CORRESPONDENCE RELATING TO CONVICT DISCIPLINE AND TRANS-
PORTATION, 1849

The reluctance of the Australian colonies, except Western Australia,
to accept transported convicts, led the government to consider
establishing a penal settlement at the Cape of Good Hope. The

utter failure of this plan is evident in the Cape colonists' treatment
of the convict ship "Neptune". The famine years in Ireland led to
a marked increase in the number of Irish convicts. Governor
Elliot of Bermuda in correspondence with the Foreign Office
complains of the harsh treatment meted out to Irish prisoners. He
gives the example of a boy of thirteen sentenced to fifteen years
transportation for sheep-stealing. Elliot succeeded in obtaining
pardons for prisoners willing to emigrate to the Cape or Australia.
From Australia and Van Diemen's Land there is evidence of
continued strong opposition to transportation. The settlers plead
lack of discipline, insufficient protection and the dire poverty of
freed convicts as detrimental to the interests of the labouring
population and the economy of the colonies. Western Australia
alone, because inhospitable climate and physical conditions kept
immigration of labourers at a minimum, favoured the retention of
the system.

Original references

1849	(217) XLIII	Transportation, Cape of Good Hope and Bermuda, correspondence.
	[1022]	Convict discipline and transportation, correspondence.
	[1121]	Convict discipline and transportation, correspondence.

Transportation Volume 10

CORRESPONDENCE AND OTHER PAPERS RELATING TO CONVICT DISCI-
PLINE AND TRANSPORTATION, 1851

Vigorous opposition to any form of transportation to their colony
was the tone of huge public meetings held in Tasmania in 1850
objecting strongly to Governor Denison's suggestion that the free
settlers were not as opposed to transportation as formerly. Detailed
reports, fascinating and informative, of these meetings are included
in this volume. The arrival of the "Neptune" (see IUP volume
Transportation 9) is recorded and details on the disposal and
treatment of both male and female convicts are given. The use of
convicts under the Assignment system in the Moreton Bay district
and in the colony of Western Australia is proposed in a detailed
memorandum by A G Dumas, clerk in the convict department of
New South Wales. This paper provides a valuable guide to the
reasons for the continuance of transportation — economic and
expansionist. Details are given also in these papers of the public
works performed by convict labour; of the reaction of convicts on

their arrival at the colony, of the juvenile convicts from Parkhurst, and of the system of Conditional Pardons.

Original references

1851	[1361] XLV	Convict discipline and transportation, correspondence.
	[1418]	Convict discipline and transportation, correspondence.
	(130)	Convict discipline and transportation, petitions.
	(262)	Convict discipline and transportation, memorials.
	(280)	Convict discipline and transportation, petitions.

Transportation Volume 11

CORRESPONDENCE AND PAPERS RELATING TO CONVICT DISCIPLINE AND TRANSPORTATION, 1851–1854

Increasing dissatisfaction with convict labour and the existence of penal settlements for British and Irish transportees resulted in the formation of anti-transportation leagues. This volume includes details of the Australasian League which was strongly supported by the workers of New South Wales. Landed proprietors and employers in Van Diemen's Land tended to support transportation since it provided a constant and cheap supply of labour; but the workers and a large section of the population opposed it because it led to reduced wages and increased crime rates in the colonies. Reports from Western Australia provide details of convict welfare and employment and are favourable towards the continuance of transportation. The problem of Irish convicts is again raised and reasons are given for the difficulty of absorbing them into the community. The closure of Norfolk Island penal settlement, the need for increased immigration of free settlers, the request of Pitcairn Islanders to be settled on Norfolk Island, and the use of Australian aborigines as police are also discussed in the correspondence.

Original references

1851	(681) XLVI	Convicts, Van Diemen's Land, returns.
	(684)	Convicts and Emigration, returns.
	(572)	Transportation sentences, returns.
	(316)	Tickets-of-leave, Van Diemen's Land, despatch.
1852	[1517] XLI	Convict discipline and transportation, correspondence.
1854	[1795] LIV	Convict discipline and transportation, correspondence.

Transportation Volume 12

CORRESPONDENCE RELATING TO CONVICT DISCIPLINE AND TRANS-
PORTATION, 1852–1853

The material relating to the penal colony of Van Diemen's Land
reveals differences of opinion among the free settlers on the question
of the continuance of transportation to the island. A large body of
settlers express a strong repugnance to the presence of the convicts,
yet as each convict ship arrives the inmates are immediately employed. Supply of labour has become a major problem for the
colony because of the gold discoveries on the Australian continent.
The effects of the discovery of gold on the convicts in each of the
penal colonies, particularly in Norfolk Island, are examined. The
correspondence provides details and comment on the systems of
discipline now in operation and reveals a genuine and lively interest
by the British Government, in the person of Sir John S Pakington.
Reports on penal conditions are included and data on the working
of the probation and tickets-of-leave systems is extensive. The whole
approach of the British Government, under pressure from both
colonial legislatures and settler organisations, to the abolition of
transportation and the difficulties involved both in the penal
colonies themselves and in Britain are outlined. Among other
problems examined and discussed here are those of escaped convicts,
punishments, female convicts, expenses of convict establishments,
effects of convict labour on wages and employment, religious
instruction and education. The colonies involved are those of Van
Diemen's Land, Norfolk Island, New South Wales, Western
Australia, Victoria and South Australia and New Zealand. One of the
valuable features of this volume is the very detailed statistical
information provided on convict settlements and transportation.

Original references

1852–53 [1601] LXXXII	Convict discipline and transportation, correspondence.	
[1677]	Convict discipline and transportation, correspondence.	

Transportation Volume 13

CORRESPONDENCE RELATING TO CONVICT DISCIPLINE AND TRANS-
PORTATION, 1854–1856

The Penal Servitude Act of 1853 provided for the abolition of
transportation as a form of punishment. The papers in this volume
reflect the reaction of the penal colonies in Australia to this Act

which they had been urging for many years. The existing convict settlements, however, remained and the problems of administration, adjustment and gradual reduction of these now became more immediate and are considered in these series of despatches. Of special interest to a student of the penal colonies is the series of letters, memorials and reports on the settlements of Western Australia which provide, in addition to the general information, data on religious arrangements, health of convicts, administrative information on the arrival and disposal of convicts, tickets-of-leave, financial supervision, military protection for free settlers, etc. These papers provide a total view of the conditions within and surrounding a penal colony. Reports from the comptroller-general of the Tasmanian and Western Australian Convict Departments are included. Among the other topics documented here are the following: convict labour; invalid and lunatic convicts; the removal of the Pitcairn Islanders to Norfolk Island; the transfer of management of convict establishments to the colonial governments; convict labour and emigration. The volume contains copies of a number of colonial Acts relating to the substitution of penal servitude for transportation, to the establishment of Houses of Correction, to the control and disposal of offenders and to the prevention and punishment of certain offences.

Original references

1854–55	[1916] XXXIX	Convict discipline and transportation, correspondence.
	[1988]	Convict discipline and transportation, correspondence.
1856	[2101] XLII	Convict discipline and transportation, correspondence.

Transportation Volume 14

REPORTS, CORRESPONDENCE AND PAPERS RELATING TO CONVICT DISCIPLINE AND TRANSPORTATION, 1856–1859

The material contained in the papers relating to the Australian penal colonies provides further comment and information on the Marks System, the treatment of female convicts and the objections of the settler population to transportation of women. Superintendent Dixon of the Western Australian penal colony, with the approval of the comptroller-general, introduced the Marks System in his establishment for a trial period and there was still a demand for convict labour in the colony. However, the proposed introduction of Indian mutineers was rejected. The increasing cost of transportation was beginning to cause concern at this time. In Van Diemen's Land, after continual demands, some control of convict establishments was granted to the legislative government. The volume contains the 1859 annual report on the convict establishments in Bermuda and Gibraltar and the Select Committee report on the petition of W H Barber, a British attorney unjustly convicted of fraud and transported to Norfolk Island. This report provides a valuable account of the fearful conditions in that penal colony.

Original references

1856	(140) XLIV	Convict Department, Tasmania, correspondence.
1857 Sess 1	[2197] XIV	Convict discipline and transportation, correspondence.
1857–58	(397) XII	W H Barber, Sel. Cttee. Rep., mins. of ev.
1857–58	[2301] XLI	Convict discipline and transportation, correspondence.
1859	[2568] XXII	Convict discipline and transportation, correspondence.
1859 Sess 2	[2523] XXII	Convict establishments at Bermuda and Gibraltar, Annual Rep.
1859 Sess 2	(136) XXVI	W H Barber, memorial.

Transportation Volume 15

REPORTS AND CORRESPONDENCE RELATING TO CONVICT DISCIPLINE AND TRANSPORTATION, 1860–1864

The 1862 annual report on the convict establishments at Bermuda and Gibraltar indicates that no convicts were received at Bermuda in 1861 and that only 644 remain on the island. These annual reports (see IUP volumes Transportation 14 and 16) provide a breakdown of conditions on the Islands relating to the education, labour, religious instruction, diet and behaviour of the convicts and in general indicate an enlightened approach to these subjects. The cost of supporting convict establishments led to a conflict between the Tasmanian Government and the British Government but there was still a demand for transportation to Western Australia. Petitions from the other Australian colonies object to the promised continuation of transportation to Western Australia but Newcastle, the colonial secretary, rejects these stating that each colony should confine its demands to its own territory. There is further material on the Marks System in practice in Western Australia and the system is approved of by the Foreign Office.

Original references

1860	[2701] XLV	Convict discipline and transportation, correspondence.
	(454)	Convict establishments, Western Australia, returns.
	[2662]	Convict establishments at Bermuda and Gibraltar, Annual Rep.
	[2700]	Convict establishments at Bermuda, papers.
1861	[2796] XL	Convict discipline and transportation, correspondence.
	[2785]	Convict establishments at Bermuda and Gibraltar, Annual Rep.
1862	[2954] XXXVI	Convict establishments at Bermuda and Gibraltar, Annual Rep.
1862	[2981] XLV	Convict discipline and transportation, correspondence.
1863	(505) XXXVIII	Transportation, memorials.
1863	[3224] XXXIX	Convict discipline and transportation, correspondence.
	[3134]	Convict establishments at Bermuda and Gibraltar, Annual Rep.
1864	[3264] XL	Convict discipline and transportation, correspondence.

Transportation Volume 16

REPORTS AND CORRESPONDENCE RELATING TO CONVICT DISCIPLINE
AND TRANSPORTATION, 1864–1869

The Royal Commission of 1863 recommended the continuance of
transportation to Western Australia. The eastern colonies objected
and succeeded in having the system banned. Western Australia's
resentment is recorded here and demands are made for subsidies
to counteract the effects of the loss of convict labour. Western
Australia, Tasmania and Gibraltar were the only remaining penal
settlements and the annual reports on these to 1869 are included.
Transportation then came to an end as a penal system and the
remaining parts in this volume deal with complaints of the ill-
treatment of some convicts, the replacement of Tasmanian troops
by civilian police, the state of prison buildings and, in the report
from Gibraltar, the introduction and working of the Marks System
is recorded.

Original references

1864	[3305] XL	Convict establishment at Gibraltar, Annual Rep.
1864	[3357] XLI	Transportation, petitions.

1865	(247) XXXVII	Discontinuance of transportation, letters.
	[3524]	Convict establishment, Western Australia, paper.
	[3424]	Discontinuance of transportation, correspondence.
	[3454]	Convict establishment at Gibraltar, Annual Rep.
1866	[3735] XLIX	Convict establishments at Western Australia and Tasmania, Rep.
	[3642]	Convict establishment at Gibraltar, Annual Rep.
1867	[3804] XXXVI	Convict establishment at Gibraltar, Annual Rep.
1867	[3851] XLIX	Convict establishments at Tasmania and Western Australia, Annual Reps.
1867–68	[4074] XXXIV	Convict establishments, Western Australia and Tasmania, Annual Reps.
1867–68	(482) XLVIII	Punishment of convicts, letter.
1867–68	[4015] XXXIV	Convict establishment at Gibraltar, Annual Rep.
1868–69	[4189] XXX	Convict establishments, Western Australia and Tasmania, Annual Reps.
	[4129]	Convict establishment at Gibraltar, Annual Rep.

Penal Servitude Volume 1

REPORTS OF THE COMMISSIONERS APPOINTED TO INQUIRE INTO THE
WORKING OF THE PENAL SERVITUDE ACTS WITH MINUTES OF EVIDENCE,
1878–79

The commissioners introduce their report on the Penal Servitude
Acts with brief summaries of all the Acts relating to Penal Servitude
and to the circumstances which led to their enactment. The first of
those was the 1853 Act which imposed penal servitude in place of
transportation sentences of less than fourteen years duration. The
contents of this and succeeding Acts are reported on and the extent
of their implementation examined. The existing prison system in
Britain is reviewed in detail by the commission who make recommendations on discipline, prison sentences, hard labour, treason-
felony and the proper organisation of prisons. Among the important
suggestions are those relating to improvement of prison cells,
medical service, the appointment of probation officers to supervise
convicts on tickets-of-leave and the separation of first offenders
from habitual criminals. The report marks a major advance in
penal reform and the evidence received, the first part of which is
contained in this volume and the second part in IUP volume Penal

Servitude 2, indicates the increasing consciousness of the need for a more humanitarian approach to the treatment of criminals.

Original references
1878–79 [C.2368] XXXVII Penal Servitude Acts, Com. Rep.
     [C.2368–1]   Penal Servitude Acts, Com., mins. of ev.

Penal Servitude Volume 2
FURTHER MINUTES OF EVIDENCE TO THE REPORT OF THE COMMISSIONERS ON THE PENAL SERVITUDE ACTS WITH APPENDIX AND INDEX, 1878–79

The evidence received by the commission on the Penal Servitude Acts provides a valuable account of prison life in England and Ireland in the 1870s. The extent to which the penal servitude system was a means of reform is one of the principal themes throughout and there is a consistent regard for the rights of prisoners. On the need for further reform the main recommendations of various witnesses are the consolidation of the law and the stricter enforcement of the existing regulations. However, it is generally admitted that the classification of prisoners is very incomplete and inadequate. A balance of comment has been achieved by the commission through hearing evidence from both prison officials and prisoners as well as from magistrates, medical officers, chaplains, prison engineers and others. Two important witnesses were the chairmen of the directors of convict prisons in England and Ireland, Sir E F du Cane and Sir Walter F Crofton. Taken in conjunction with the evidence in volume 1 of this set, a complete picture of prison conditions and of the effects of the system on prisoners emerges side by side with a genuine desire for immediate practical reforms. The analytical index provides a quick guide to the complete evidence.

Original reference
1878–79 [C.2368–11]   Penal Servitude Acts, Com., mins. of ev.
     XXXVIII

Juvenile Offenders Volume 1
REPORTS FROM THE SELECT COMMITTEE OF THE HOUSE OF LORDS ON THE EXECUTION OF CRIMINAL LAW ESPECIALLY RESPECTING JUVENILE OFFENDERS AND TRANSPORTATION, WITH MINUTES OF EVIDENCE, APPENDICES AND INDEX, 1847

Retributive punishment, consisting of a sentence in jail or transportation, was the manner in which juvenile offenders were treated until the mid 1840s. One witness, giving evidence before the House of Lords' Committee (1847) told of children aged nine years being sentenced to transportation for house-breaking. The steady increase in juvenile crime—illustrated in this volume by a table showing the number of juvenile offenders convicted in 1843, 1844 and 1845—and the high proportion which they bore to the total amount of criminal offenders convinced the authorities that the system of retributive punishment was inadequate. The causes of the particularly high proportion of juvenile crime in Liverpool were discussed with particulars of the case of fourteen juvenile offenders selected in 1841 as examples of the frequency of recommitments in the city. Most of the witnesses acknowledged the extent of juvenile crime but condemned the British criminal code which did not discriminate between the ages of prisoners as the law of France did. The importance of reformatory and industrial schools where children might be trained in useful trades was realized and discussed. The Rev. William Russell, an ardent advocate of the reformatory system, suggested in this connection that juveniles who had behaved well in the reformatory should have their names placed upon a record of recommendation for employment. In Birmingham a system was in operation whereby children found guilty of an offence were returned to their masters who undertook responsibility for their conduct. The difficulties which juvenile prisoners experienced in obtaining work after their discharge from the House of Refuge in Glasgow was compared with the problems of discharges from Houses of Refuge in America. Another facet of juvenile crime was the attitude of parents. It was suggested that some responsibility be conferred on parents for their children's conduct by obliging them to pay fines or maintain their offspring while they were in jail or reformatory. The importance of conditions which affected the early development and character of the juveniles was realized and it was suggested that much good would come from the education and moral and religious training which the child might receive in an infant school. This education, it was envisaged, would lead eventually to industrial training.

Extracts from the reports of 1839 and 1844 on Parkhurst prison, show the circumstances under which juveniles were admitted and the state of their education. A return for the same prison tabulates the periods of school attendance prior to committal. Workhouse schools were severely criticized for failing to give adequate training. As an alternative, the committee recommended the establishment of district union schools. An Act following from this report provided for the

establishment of such schools. The replies of several High Court
Judges such as Lord Denham, the Lord Justice General for Scotland
and Lord Chief Baron Pollock to questions put by the committee on
the amendments to the law on juvenile offenders are included.

Original references

1847   (447) VII   Criminal law (juvenile offenders and transportation),
                          Sel. Cttee. HL. 1st Rep., mins. of ev., etc.
        (534)   Criminal law (juvenile offenders and transportation),
                          Sel. Cttee. HL. 2nd Rep., mins. of ev., etc.

Juvenile Offenders Volume 2

REPORT FROM THE SELECT COMMITTEE ON CRIMINAL AND DESTITUTE
JUVENILES, TOGETHER WITH PROCEEDINGS, MINUTES OF EVIDENCE,
APPENDIX AND INDEX, 1852

As the industrial age progressed, the expansion of towns and the
greater separation of classes, characterized by the overcrowded and
unhealthy sanitary conditions of the poor (see IUP Urban Areas:
Housing Set), resulted in widespread juvenile crime. The Select Committee appointed in 1852 to report on criminal and destitute juveniles
received evidence on the class of children particularly liable to crime
—children of criminals, illegitimate children and orphans; the
ineffectiveness of the law in dealing with such juveniles and the vital
necessity of reformatories and industrial schools. Four sets of
schools were suggested: reformatories for juveniles guilty of
serious offences, based on the principle of a 'painful' rooting out of
the pre-formed habits; industrial schools for minor offenders and for
destitute children whose circumstances were likely to induce them to
commit crimes; day schools for the poor; and the existing national
schools. The reformatory school at Mettray in France was discussed
and statistics on the ages of the boys remanded there and the results
obtained—85 per cent of those discharged were reformed—were
provided. The management of schools in America was examined
with details on the conditions of admission and periods of detention
in the New York House of Refuge.

Mary Carpenter, author of a book on reformatory schools and a
social worker with seventeen years experience of working among
juveniles, gave as her opinion that neglect not poverty was the cause
to be guarded against and that children should in all circumstances
be treated in accordance with the spirit of English law which defined
the child as being incapable of guiding himself. Related to this is a

draft bill, included here, for the commitment of boys to a reformatory should the parent be unable to provide sureties for good behaviour. Due to the prorogation of parliament, the committee under the chairmanship of M. T. Baines (appointed President of the Poor Law Board in 1849) recommended an early resumption of the inquiry. However, they submitted the evidence taken before them to parliament. Sir Joshua Jebb, Surveyor-General of Convict Prisons, was one of the more important witnesses.

Original reference

1852   (515) VII   Criminal and destitute juveniles, Sel. Cttee. Rep., mins. of ev., appendix and index.

Juvenile Offenders Volume 3

REPORT FROM THE SELECT COMMITTEE ON THE TREATMENT OF CRIMINAL AND DESTITUTE CHILDREN WITH THE PROCEEDINGS, MINUTES OF EVIDENCE, APPENDIX AND INDEX, 1852–53

This volume continues the inquiry terminated by the 1852 Select Committee because of the prorogation of parliament (see IUP volume Juvenile Offenders 2). The evidence and information brought to the notice of this Select Committee, pointed to the great amount of juvenile crime still existing in England and for which no final remedy had as yet been provided. The existence of similar evils in France, Germany, Switzerland, Belgium and the United States of America had been met by vigorous counter measures.

The aims of the inquiry were three-fold: to examine the treatment of criminal and destitute juveniles; to see what changes were desirable to provide industrial training and how to combine reformation with due correction of juvenile crime. One of the most important considerations for the prevention of juvenile crime was the rescue of the destitute child from the streets before the opportunity of committing an offence was put in his path. Various private reformatories were in existence to provide education and industrial occupation for these children—but were not sure of permanent support. The result of the establishment of District Union Schools in 1847 and the recommended extension of the principles of the Act which established these schools were discussed. The report also dealt with the ragged and industrial schools in Edinburgh, the Glasgow House of Refuge and the Philadelphia House of Refuge. The problem of parental neglect was discussed, one aspect of which was that parents would encourage their children to commit crimes in order to have them admitted to reformatory and industrial schools. To solve this problem, it was suggested that the detention of children should not relieve parents of the liability of maintaining them. The importance of training the child in a trade was realized and it was recommended that particular attention should be paid to the industrial aspect of the juvenile's education. The volume includes a map of Europe and America showing the percentage of the population which received primary education. There is an analysis of juvenile crime in Ireland for· 1851 and an interesting paper applying the continental farm-school system to England. As a result of this report, reformatory schools received legislative sanction in 1854.

Original references

1852–53 (674) XXIII	Criminal and destitute children, Sel. Cttee. Rep., mins. of ev., etc.
(674–I)	Criminal and destitute children, Sel. Cttee. index.

Juvenile Offenders Volume 4

REPORT FROM THE REFORMATORIES AND INDUSTRIAL SCHOOLS COM-MISSIONERS WITH MINUTES OF EVIDENCE, APPENDICES AND INDEX, 1884

Due to the establishment of the reformatory school system in 1854 and the industrial school system in 1857, there was a marked decline in juvenile crime in the fifties and sixties. This Royal Commission accepted that the gangs of young criminals had been broken up and that an end had been put to the training of young boys as professional thieves—in fact the reformatory school system marked the end of the 'artful dodger' era. The commission examined the operation, management, control, inspection, financial arrangements, conditions, of admission, limits of age and terms of detention in reformatories and industrial schools, and considered what amendments were necessary to make the institutions more efficient. The volume contains a summary of the legislation passed regarding the establishment of certified schools and the effects of these schools on crime in England and Scotland. There had been no increase in admissions to reformatory schools since 1864; however, the contrary was true of industrial schools. This latter was due principally to the Elementary Education Acts of 1870 and 1876 which permitted a child to be sent to an industrial school for a breach of a school attendance order and made the school authorities responsible for enforcing the industrial school acts. The abuse of the power of committal to industrial schools was also a factor in the increase in admissions to industrial schools; the law afforded facilities to parents to get rid of the burden of the support and education of their children by throwing it upon the industrial schools system. A table of admissions to industrial schools in England and Scotland, 1879–82, highlights this further. The management of industrial and reformatory schools was discussed and conflicting views on voluntary or state management and the respective functions of the Home Office and Department of Education appear in the evidence. Some witnesses were not satisfied with the manner in which educational efficiency in the industrial schools was being tested. The sytem of employment of boys after their detention in schools, apprenticeship, emigration and life on training ships were investigated. A separate report on industrial and reformatory schools in Ireland is included. Tables show the number of young offenders admitted into and discharged from reformatory schools in Britain, the manner of their discharge up to December 1881, statistics on the expenses of reformatories for the period 1859–82, and the number of children from reformatory and industrial schools in Ireland who were following the trades they had learned at school. Sir Michael Edward Hicks-Beach and Sir Ughtred James Kay Shuttleworth were two important members of the commission.

Original references

| 1884 | [C.3876] XLV | Reformatory and industrial schools. R. Com. Rep., Vol. I. |
| | [C.3876–I] | Reformatory and industrial schools, R. Com. mins. of ev., etc., Vol. II. |

Juvenile Offenders Volume 5

REPORTS FROM SELECT COMMITTEES OF THE HOUSE OF LORDS ON THE PROTECTION OF YOUNG GIRLS, THE TREATMENT AND PUNISHMENT OF JUVENILE OFFENDERS AND ON REFORMATORY AND INDUSTRIAL SCHOOLS WITH MINUTES OF EVIDENCE, APPENDICES AND INDICES, 1881–1896

Juvenile prostitution, an important facet of juvenile crime in nineteenth-century Britain, was investigated by House of Lords' Select Committees in 1881 and 1882. London had the highest rate of juvenile prostitution in Europe (statistics are included in this volume on the actual number of prostitutes in London). The causes of the high rate of prostitution were examined—endemic overcrowding and conditions in lodging houses, laxity in parental authority (in some cases juvenile prostitutes lived with their parents), lack of education

and according to one witness, the condition of the streets. Among
the various topics discussed were: juvenile prostitution in Liverpool,
the means employed by Liverpool town council to check street trading by children, the various classes of brothels and number of Irish
girls in the streets of Liverpool, the question of procuring girls in
Liverpool for brothels abroad and the white slave-traffic between
England and Belgium. Remedies suggested to arrest the high rate
of juvenile prostitution included: the proper enforcement of the
Industrial Schools Amendment Act, the prohibition of girls under
sixteen from entering brothels and the raising of the age under
which it would be an offence to have sexual intercourse with young
girls by three years from thirteen to sixteen. The general state of
reformatory and industrial schools, their control both by government and local authority, and the framing of model rules with
application to particular schools were the subjects of an inquiry
by a departmental committee in 1896. The report (with appendices)
of this committee is published in this volume; the minutes of
evidence and index form volume 6 of the set. The evidence of Dr.
Barnardo before the poor law school committee (1895) on his
interest in the education and rehabilitation of children, and the
number of children under his control is an interesting and important
feature of the volume.

Original references

1881	(448) IX	The law relating to the protection of young girls from artifices to induce them to lead a corrupt life, Sel. Cttee. HL. Rep., mins. of ev., etc. (Reprinted: 1883 (HL.109) IX)
1881	[C.2808] LIII	Juvenile offenders, Rep.
1882	(344) XIII	The law relating to the protection of young girls from artifices to induce them to lead a corrupt life. Sel. Cttee. Rep., mins. of ev., etc.
1896	[C.8204] XLV	Reformatory and industrial schools, Dept. Cttee. Vol. I Rep., appendices.

Juvenile Offenders Volume 6

MINUTES OF EVIDENCE TAKEN BEFORE THE DEPARTMENTAL COMMITTEE
ON REFORMATORY AND INDUSTRIAL SCHOOLS AND INDEX, 1897

The departmental committee, under the chairmanship of Godfrey
Lushington, visited over two-thirds of the reformatories, industrial
schools, truant schools, day industrial schools, working boys' homes
and all the ship schools in England. The evidence obtained by the

committee is, as a result, very comprehensive. Besides the evidence on the practical running and progress of the schools, an important memorandum on the government of the schools was discussed before the committee. This related to whether the Home Office or the Department of Education, should be the central authority for the schools. Conflicting views on voluntary management or management by local authorities were heard in evidence. Much attention was given to the question of technical education and the attitude of trade unions on the working at trades in the schools was discussed. It was observed that every school with fifty pupils had at least one certified teacher. Witnesses gave opinions on the amount of money per head which ought to be expended upon the inmates of the schools. It was decided that although a very large number of parents had the means to pay for their children's maintenance, the machinery for enforcing the collection of parental contributions was defective. Special attention was given to the particular position of feeble-minded children. The kindergarten system of education was discussed. Rev. Benjamin Waugh, Director of the National Society for the Prevention of Cruelty to Children gave evidence on the aims and objectives of the society; the immediate objects of the society were to require the parent to feed and clothe his children, and to prevent the necessity of sending children to industrial schools. Rev. Waugh would in the first instance make every offence on the part of the child a charge against the parent until the latter had proved that he had performed his duty adequately. In the seven years since the passing of the 1889 Act for the prevention of cruelty to, and protection of children, the society had sent 9,300 parents to jail for criminal neglect and cruelty. The home and institutions were compared in the evidence; some witnesses objected to the industrial school system because of the lack of home influence. In this context, the method of procedure to be adopted with destitutes, vagrants, refractory paupers and children of bad parents was discussed. Another important witness who appeared before the committee, was J. G. Legge, inspector of reformatory and industrial schools.

Original reference

1897   [C.8290] XLII   Reformatory and industrial schools, Dept. Cttee.
                           Vol. II, mins. of ev., etc.

Legal Administration

A. H. Manchester

Commentary

Introduction

Inevitably, the theme which runs throughout the whole of the nineteenth-century discussion of legal administration is that of the quest for a less expensive, more expeditious system. Justice 'is not only shamefully delayed', wrote a radical critic in 1820,[1] 'but from its dearness in many cases wholly unattainable.' It is some measure of the difficulty of remedying such a complaint that, despite the considerable efforts which were made over the years to reduce both delay and expense in the courts, similar allegations were made at the close of the century. Indeed, a distinguished judge stated that the result of the great reforming Judicature Acts, measures which had been introduced in the 1870s with a view to reducing both expense and delay, had been to increase by something like twenty percent the ordinary expenses of a common law action, whilst the Appeal Court had been 'staggering under a mass of arrears.'[2] And in 1897 a member of parliament alleged that with the possible exception of the French, English courts were 'the most extravagantly expensive in the world.'[3]

Accordingly, it is not surprising that these volumes (cited below, pp. 139-152) show a lively awareness of the allegations which were made regarding the delay and expense of the system, together with an appreciation of those qualities of convenience and economy for which we look in a modern court system.[4] They also display an instinctive understanding of the view that, if a court is to perform its social function effectively, it consists not only of a judge or judges but also, for example, of court officials and rules of procedure.[5] Indeed, the structure and role of the legal profession and, in our society, of the extent of legal aid are also germane to any study of legal administration.

Few changes in legal administration had been made during the latter half of the eighteenth century. In part such nonactivity may have reflected the contemporary view of government's limited role: there can be little doubt, however, that it reflected to a far greater extent a widely held complacency with our institutions. The 'forms of administring justice came to perfection under Edward the first', wrote Blackstone in his classic work, 'and have not been much varied, nor always for the better, since.' Blackstone's conclusion

---

1 (Wade) *The Black Book* (1820) p. 219.

2 Charles Bowen, The Law Courts under the Judicature Acts. *The Law Quarterly Review* Vol. 2 (1886), p. 1 at p. 8.

3 Cited in Brian Abel-Smith's and Robert B. Stevens's *Lawyers and the Courts*, (Heinemann, 1967), at p. 90.

4 See the *Royal Commission on Assizes and Quarter Sessions 1966-1969*. Cmnd. 4153 para. 112.

5 Geoffrey Sawer, *Law in Society* (Oxford, 1965) p. 72.

was that of 'a constitution so wisely contrived, so strongly raised, and so
highly finished, it is hard to speak with that praise, which is justly and
severely its due . . .' Blackstone did concede, however, that defects did exist
'chiefly arising from the decays of time, or the rage of unskilful improvements
in later ages.'[6] Equally, Paley's chapter on the administration of justice[7]
really amounts to no more than a justification of current practice. Such
attitudes were further hardened by that strong reaction against the French
Revolution which tended to condemn all change. The opening years of the
nineteenth century were not years which witnessed, therefore, any major
institutional reform: they were the years which Dicey has characterized as a
period of old Toryism or legislative quiescence.[8]

Yet even during this period law reformers were not inactive. In particular,
the efforts which had been made over the years by Sir Samuel Romilly, a
distinguished Chancery lawyer, to mitigate the number of offences for which
death was the punishment, came to fruition during the years following Romilly's death in 1818. And Peel's moves to simplify a number of the criminal
statutes was not only notable in itself but can be seen as part of a wider
movement for the overall simplification of the law.[9] Moves for reform within
the field of legal administration were less dramatic: with hindsight, however,
we can note the first stirrings of the changes which were to come. Inquiries
were held, for example, on saleable offices in courts of law in 1810, on delays
in Chancery in 1811, and on the nature of the offices held in the courts of
justice. The persistence of Taylor, a perennial critic of Chancery, was re-
warded by the appointment of a Vice Chancellor in 1813: and a Chancery
Commission was appointed in 1824.[10]

6   William Blackstone, *Commentaries on the Laws of England,* 5th ed. Vol. 4 (1773)
pp. 435-436. Blackstone commented on the 'solecism' of the distinction between Law
and Equity: see n. 16 *infra.* For an account of great, although ultimately unsuccessful,
efforts of Lord Mansfield, a distinguished judge, to mitigate the harmful effects of the
distinction between Law and Equity, see William Holdsworth, *History of English Law,*
Vol. 12 (Methuen, 1938) pp. 588-605.

7   William Paley, *The Principles of Moral and Political Philosophy* (1785) p. 497.

8   Albert Venn Dicey, *Law and Public Opinion in England during the Nineteenth
Century,* 2nd. ed. (1963) p. 62.

9   See generally William Holdsworth, 'The Movement for Reforms in the Law (1793-
1832)', *The Law Quarterly Review,* Vol. 56 (1940) pp. 33, 208, 340. Leon Radzinowicz,
A History of English Criminal Law, Vol. 1 (1948) p. 574 ff: Norman Gash *Mr. Secretary
Peel; the Life of Sir Robert Peel to 1830* (London, 1961); Courtenay Ilbert, *Legislative
Methods and Forms* (Oxford, 1901) p. 51.

10   *Report of Commissioners on Saleable Offices in Courts of Law* 1810 (358) LX, p.
125; *Report from the Committee Appointed to enquire into the Causes that retard the
Decision on Suits in the High Court of Chancery* 1811 (244), Ordered to be printed by
the House of Commons 18 June 1811; *Second Report from the Committee Appointed to
enquire into the Causes that retard the Decision of suits in the High Court of Chancery*
(273), Ordered by the House of Commons to be printed 13 June 1812; *Report by the
Commissioners appointed to inquire into the practice of the Court of Chancery* 1826
(56), Ordered to be printed 7th April, 1826.

Change did not come suddenly, then, and yet, aided perhaps by the advent of liberal Tories to the Ministry, reforms could be seen to be imminent several years before the Reform Act. Indeed Brougham's great six hour speech of 7 February 1828[11] on the common law system can be seen as the prelude to the period of legal reforms which followed — and in that speech Brougham acknowledged the work which others had already set in train in the areas of criminal law, real property, and Chancery reform. Following that speech two Commissions were issued, on Common Law practice and procedure and on Real Property respectively. Legal reform was in the air, therefore, for some years before the Reform Act and it may be that this 'ensured a continuity in legal development between the pre- and post-Reform Act eras.'[12] Naturally, there were sharp differences of view as to whether such continuity was desirable. Some argued that such a gradualist approach was the only possible way to secure reforms. On the other hand Benthamites believed that a more complete break with the past was necessary if worthwhile reforms were to be achieved.

Undoubtedly Jeremy Bentham exercised a great intellectual influence on many, including Brougham, during this period. Indeed Dicey has characterized the period 1825-1870 as the period of Benthamism or individualism. Bentham's influence, then, was a considerable factor in the advance of law reform. Yet too much should not be claimed for Bentham. Nor should the sheer momentum of reforms introduced in response to the very real pressure upon the courts be ignored.[13] Other factors are obvious. The rise in population, for example, together with the increase and change in commercial forms and practice were among the causes of strain upon a legal framework which was becoming irrelevant to the needs of the day. The period of the Reform Act was, too, a time when even wise conservatives appreciated full well the value of timely concession. In the field of legal administration, however, it may be that the period of real reform began not so much in 1828 or even in 1830, although useful reforms were introduced after 1830, as from the mid 1840s at a time when government inclined to a greater interest in law reform and the profession too was more receptive to ideas of reform.

---

11 18 Hansard Debates. (2nd ser. 1828) 27.

12 Holdsworth, The Movement for Reforms, p. 353.

13 William Holdsworth, *History of English Law,* Vol. 13 (1952) pp. 41-133: A. V. Dicey, *Law and Public Opinion,* p. 124 ff: ed. George Keeton and Georg Schwarzenberger, *Jeremy Bentham and the Law* (1948). H. A. Hollond, *Cambridge Law Journal,* Vol. 10 (1948) 3; cf. Julius Stone, *The Province and Function of Law,* (Associated General Publications Pty. Ltd., Sydney, 1946) Chapter 10, especially at p. 294, and *Social Dimensions of Law and Justice,* (Stevens and Sons Ltd., 1966) pp. 577-79. and note Oliver MacDonagh, *A Pattern of Government Growth* (London, 1961) and R. J. Lambert, *Sir John Simon* (London, 1963) for a theory of administrative momentum. Contr. J. Hart, 31 'Past and Present' *Journal of Historical Studies* 39 (1965).

The Court System[14]

'For the more speedy, universal and impartial administration of justice between subject and subject', wrote Blackstone, presumably in an attempt to
rationalise the chaotic court structure of his day, 'the law hath appointed a
prodigious variety of courts, some with a more limited, others with a more
extensive jurisdiction; some constituted to enquire only, others to hear and
determine: some to determine in the first instance, others upon appeal and by
way of review'. Blackstone then distinguishes between courts such as are of
public and general jurisdiction throughout the whole realm; or such as are
only of a private and special jurisdiction in some particular parts of it. Of the
former there are four sorts: the universally established courts of common law
and equity: the ecclesiastical courts: the courts military: and courts maritime.
In addition there were the courts of assize and *nisi prius* — the circuit system.
By courts of special jurisdiction Blackstone meant those courts whose jurisdiction was private and special, confined to particular spots, or instituted
only to redress particular injuries. The most important such courts were those
of the principality of Wales, of the counties palatine of Chester, Lancaster
and Durham, and the several courts which were situated within the city of
London. A number of appellate courts also existed. The discussion which
follows distinguishes between the superior, or more important, courts of
common law and equity, and the inferior courts.

Superior Courts of Common Law and Equity

Law and Equity

Equity, Maine tells us,[15] is any 'body of rules existing by the side of the
original civil law, founded on distinct principles and claiming incidentally to
supersede the civil law in virtue of a superior sanctity inherent in those
principles.' The function of the rules of equity, then, which were based
primarily on concepts of fairness or natural justice, was to supplement the
increasingly formalistic rules of the common law. The English, however,
unlike the Scots, had evolved a system under which the rules of the common
law on the one hand and the rules of equity on the other were administered in
separate courts.

Even Blackstone had conceded that there could be no 'greater solecism'.[16]

14   William Blackstone, *Commentaries on the Laws of England:* Vol. 3 (5th ed. 1773)
p. 22 ff.

15.   Henry Maine, *Ancient Law,* (ed. 1950) p. 23.

16   Blackstone, *Commentaries,* Vol. 3 (5th ed. 1773) p. 441.

In 1827 the Edinburgh Review put the same point even more bluntly: 'It is not merely that there exist two jurisdictions in this country, applying their separate rules to the intercourse and conduct of the people — but to such an extent is the absurdity carried that a suitor at common law is allowed to commence, proceed, recover, and obtain judgement, after a great expenditure of time and money — and then, at the moment when he is about to reap the fruit of the whole by an execution, the Court of Equity interposes... the Court which originally and lawfully entertained the case, managed the case, and decided upon the case, should be allowed to judge of those equitable circumstances.'[17]

Conflict might also occur between Chancery and the ecclesiastical courts. For if a will affected both real and personal property, proceedings regarding the real property would have to be taken in chancery whilst proceedings regarding the personal property would have to be taken in the ecclesiastical court. Should the decisions of the two courts conflict, great confusion would be the inevitable result.

Lord Hardwicke, a great Lord Chancellor, had commented on such inconvenience in so far as it affected Chancery and the ecclesiastical courts as early as 1742.[18] Yet with regard to the distinctive systems of law and equity, the Report of the Chancery Commission of 1826, a body whose chairman had been the highly conservative Lord Chancellor, Lord Eldon, stated quite baldly that it had not 'conceived that it came within the limits of our Commission to discuss, whether a system, so extensively established, and so intimately interwoven with the whole of our judicial policy, could be advantageously exchanged for any other'.[19] It was not a happy portent for those who argued that the divided jurisdiction was productive of great disadvantages.

It is true that the common law commissioners in 1831 did maintain that a court should be able to do complete justice. It was left, however, to a committee of the Law Amendment Society, in July 1851 not only to produce a cogent criticism of the existing divided jurisdictions but also to suggest a remedy which proved to be remarkably prophetic of the Judicature Act.[20]

Such recommendations were too radical, however, for the commissioners

17 System and Administration of English Law, *Edinburgh Review*, Vol. 45 (1827) p. 476.

18 *Montgomery* v. *Clarke* 2 Atk. 378, 379: 26 English Reports 629 (1742).

19 *Report . . . Court of Chancery* 1826 op. cit. n. 10 above at p. 6. On Lord Eldon see Llewellyn Woodward, *The Age of Reform* 1815-1870 (and ed. 1962) p. 54. and Holdsworth, *History of English Law*, Vol. 13 (1952) pp. 595-639.

20 *Copies of Reports communicated by the Law AMENDMENT SOCIETY to the Home Department, on Common Law and Equity Procedure* 1851 (223). Ordered to be printed 14th July, 1851. For the position in the new County Courts see the First Report of the Royal Commission on the Judicature 1868-69 [4130], XXV, p. 8; IUP Legal Administration 13.

of the 1850s, despite their knowing that the fusion of legal and equitable principles was apparently working quite well in New York State and despite the fact that such a dichotomy was unknown in Scotland. Instead, in essence they could really only echo the view of the common law commissioners of 1831 and recommend that jurisdiction exercised by Courts of Equity should be conferred upon Courts of Law, and jurisdiction exercised by Courts of Law should be conferred upon Courts of Equity, to such an extent as to render both courts competent to administer entire justice, without parties in the one Court being obliged to resort to the aid of the other.

The situation in the busy and vigorous County Courts which had been created only in 1846 was even more absurd. Judges of those courts were required to exercise their jurisdiction at law, in equity and at Admiralty quite separately. It was possible, therefore, that in one and the same matter three distinct suits would have to be brought in the same court and before the same judge, carried on under three different forms of procedure, and controlled by three different Courts of Appeal.

What is remarkable, then, is not that Law and Equity should finally have been united but that a commercial and vigorous country should have tolerated such a division for so long. For when reform did come with the enactment of the Judicature Acts, virtually a century had passed since Blackstone had remarked on the existence of such a 'solecism'.

Superior Courts of Common Law

There were three superior courts of common law — Common Pleas, King's Bench and Exchequer. At one time their jurisdictions had been quite distinct but by the nineteenth century their functions were largely the same.[21] This was by no means the only anomaly within the common law system upon which Brougham touched in 1828 during the course of a speech which dealt in the main with the courts, procedure, pleading, evidence and with some of the rules of the substantive law.

Some five months before delivering his speech Brougham had sought Bentham's assistance in its preparation and Bentham seems to have responded willingly to his distinguished disciple's request. 'I could this moment catch you in my arms', he wrote, 'toss you up into the air, and as you fell into them again, cover you with kisses. It shall have, aye that it shall, the dear little fellow, some nice sweet pap of my own making, three sorts of it, (1) IV, Evidence (2) Judicial Establishment (3) Codification Proposal, . . . all sent this very blessed day.'[22] Yet Brougham's speech was very much his own;

---

21 See Brougham, 18 Hansards Debates 132-133 (2nd ser. 1828).

22 Brougham Mss., 20, 24 Sept. 1827, cited by Chester New, *Life of Henry Brougham to 1830* (Oxford 1961) p. 391.

tactlessly, perhaps, he failed to offer any acknowledgement of Bentham's work. Generally speaking his speech was well received, the sharpest criticism of it coming from Bentham and his followers who felt that Brougham had betrayed a more radical vision. Brougham 'is not the Messiah of law reform', asserted the Westminster Review. 'Into the world of parliament came not he that should come: the people must look for another'.

Two commissions were issued as a result of that speech, one on the practice and procedure of the courts of common law and one on the law of real property.

The task which faced the common law commissioners was undoubtedly a huge one. Of the procedure at common law at this time a distinguished Victorian judge was to write some fifty years later: ' . . .as compared with the wants of the country, (it) had become antiquated, technical and obscure . . . . At a moment when the pecuniary enterprises of the Kingdom were covering the whole world, when railways at home and steam upon the seas were creating everywhere new centres of industrial and commercial life, the Common Law Courts of the realm seemed constantly occupied in the discussion of the merest legal conundrums, which bore no relation to the merits of any controversies except those of pedants, and in the direction of a machinery that belonged already to the past.'[23] It was a criticism which was true not only of a matter, such as the law of arrest for debt which was the subject of much public criticism but of the whole of common law procedure. And of special pleading, its absurdities, wrote a contemporary lay critic, 'are enough to make a horse laugh; a drizzling maze of empirical inventions, circuitous procedure, and unintelligible fiction, calculated for no purpose but to fortify monopoly and wrap justice in deceit and mystery'.[24] Could the commissioners possibly merely adapt, rather than refashion completely, such a system of procedure to the needs of the new age? Granted that the rules regarding pleading rested on sound foundations, could they be stripped of their superfluities and administered flexibly?

The common law commissioners issued their first four reports before the enactment of the Reform Act. On the whole they were well received and some legislation resulted so that, in Holdsworth's view,[25] these commissions effected more for law reform than any of the commissions previously appointed. For that the commissioners, all distinguished lawyers, deserve some credit. Such credit must be qualified, however, by the recognition both that

23 Charles Bowen, Progress in the Administration of Justice during the Victorian Period in *Select Essays in Anglo-American Legal History* Vol. 1. (Little, Brown & Co.: 1907) p. 519.

24 (Wade) *Black Book* (1835) p. 327. And this comment was made after the reforming Civil Procedure Act 1833 and the Hilary Rules 1834. On the membership of the Commissions, etc., see pps. 25 ff infra: The Process of Reform.

25 Holdsworth, The Movement for Reforms, p. 352.

so little had been achieved previously and by the fact that there was surely so much to do. In that light the commissioners' approach may rather be seen as essentially cautious and well in tune with the step by step approach which was to become characteristic of Brougham. Two examples illustrate this point.

Thus the Uniformity of Process Act 1832 introduced a uniform writ of summons in place of the incredible number of possible ways in which, as the commissioners report, an action could be begun before then. Certainly, that Act was a welcome step forward. On the other hand since the most common mode of beginning an action was *a capias ad respondendum,* in practice there was already a considerable degree of uniformity of process: the new Act may be seen, therefore, as a rationalization of existing practice rather than as a complete innovation. Yet there was no attempt to abolish the forms of action.[26] Secondly, the Civil Procedure Act 1833,[27] *inter alia,* required the judges to make regulations governing common law pleadings with a view to reducing delays, formalities and expense. The judges did produce such a set of regulations — yet those regulations were scarcely radical. Indeed a prac- titioners' text announced that the new Rules had 'not occasioned any material alteration either in the principles or the forms of pleading'.[28] Moreover, it was during this period that Baron Parke, who had been one of the original commissioners, was to dominate the common law Bench and to demonstrate a great love of what Lord Coleridge could later call the 'absurdities of special pleading.' Lord Coleridge had even heard him 'rejoice at non-suiting a plain- tiff in an undefended cause, saying, with a sort of triumphant air, that those who drew loose declarations brought scandal on the law'.[29] Perhaps a radical reform of pleading could scarcely have been expected, even in his younger days, from such a commissioner — or from his fellow commissioner Stephen who was also a distinguished special pleader. Baron Parke's judicial career also demonstrated that any reform would require a measure of judicial sym- pathy in its application if it were to be applied in such a way that the pleadings were no longer to be seen as an end in themselves. The policy underlying the new regulations which became known as the Hilary Rules may have been the right one: they only made the situation worse, however, because of their

---

26   2 Will. IV c. 39. *First Report of the Royal Commission on Practice and Proceed- ings of the Courts of Common Law 1829* (46) IX p. 74; Legal Administration 1: "The phrase 'forms of action' must be understood to comprehend the writs, which com- menced the proceedings and which gave names to the actions themselves, and all the proceedings leading up to judgment. It is proper even to include the forms of execution for enforcing judgment, since not all types of execution were appropriate to each action." — Potter's *Historical Introduction to English Law* (4th ed.: 1958) p. 293.

27   3 & 4 Will IV. c. 42.

28   Joseph Chitty, *A Concise View of Pleading,* (2nd ed.: 1835), Appendix.

29   Cecil Fifoot, *Judge and Jurist in the Reign of Queen Victoria* (Stevens & Sons Ltd.: 1959) pp. 13-14.

insistence on special pleading as it had been understood in the late eighteenth century.[30] It augured well for reform, therefore, when some years later Lord Campbell attacked the abuses of special pleading.[31]

What, then, would the new common law commissioners, all distinguished lawyers once again, decide? There can be little doubt but that since the creation of the new County Courts in 1846, the attitude of the profession towards the reform of the superior courts had become more progressive. No 'reform in the Procedure of the Common Law Courts would be worth any-thing', wrote the *Law Times*,[32] 'which did not so cheapen and speed justice that suitors shall give them preference over the County Courts'. The profes-sion, as a whole then, was now ready for genuine reform. What both the country and the profession got — to the disappointment of some in the profession— was simply a further ration of piecemeal reform. There was, for example, a step— but no more— to the fusion of Law and Equity: the writ of summons was not to mention the cause of action— yet the appropriate form of action had to be declared in the pleadings. One can appreciate Fifoot's point that 'just as the Reform Act of 1832 produced a temporary political equilibrium which its own implications were to upset, so the Common Law Procedure Act, by its displacement of the writ, rendered inevitable the destruction of the forms of action. The *coup de grâce* was administered by the Judicature Act, 1873':[33] and it is said that Baron Parke was so disturbed by the Acts of 1852 and of 1854 that in 1855 he resigned. Nevertheless, might not the commissioners have presented a government and a profession favourable to reform with more sweeping proposals?[34]

Chancery

Throughout the first part of the nineteenth century Taylor, Williams and, later, Parkes drew public attention to the delay and expense to which litigants in Chancery were subjected. A Select Committee had sat in 1811: a Vice Chancellor had been appointed in 1813. Finally, a Commission on Chancery reported in 1826.[35] Yet that Commission was chaired by Lord Eldon, the

30 Theodore Plucknett, *A Concise History of the Common Law* (Butterworths, 5th ed., 1956) p. 416.

31 *Law Times* Vol. 15 (1850) p. 317. Lord Campbell became Lord Chief Justice in 1850.

32 *Law Times* Vol. 18 (1852) p. 133 and at pp. 218, 225.

33 Cecil Fifoot, *English Law and its Background*, (Bell & Sons Ltd.: (1932)) p. 161.

34 *The Jurist*, Vol. 16 (1852) p. 197. For an outline of the career of James Parke, Lord Wensleydale (1782-1868) see William Holdsworth, *History of English Law*, Vol. 15 (1965) p. 486.

35 See generally William Holdsworth, *History of English Law*, Vol. 1 (Methuen 7th ed. 1956) esp. at pp. 435-445.

Lord Chancellor whom many believed to be personally responsible for much of the delay in his court, although more wide ranging critics of Eldon's conservatism would do well to bear in mind that during this period he was by no means alone in his attitudes. Not surprisingly, perhaps, that commission found little cause for concern. The remedies proposed, wrote a critic, meant that 'whereas a Chancery suit now lasts twenty years . . . and costs 50001, the alterations and amendments proposed may have the effect, perhaps, of reducing the duration to nineteen years and a half, and the cost to the sum of 47501, or thereabouts'.[36] Further evidence was not lacking of the need for reform. Bentham, for example, had sketched Chancery procedure in terms which, although harsh, were not unfair.[37] And the evidence given to the Chancery Commission of 1824 fully supports all which Dickens was to write of Chancery in his *Bleak House*.[38] There could be little doubt in the mind of any informed person that the major causes of delay and expense in Chancery before, say, 1852, were attributable to the court's procedure, mode of pleading and taking evidence, and its administration.[39] Moreover, by the late 1840s the new practice of railway and winding-up cases may have taken up so much time in the Court of Chancery and in the Master's offices that all the ordinary business of the courts was suspended.[40] Accordingly, when the Chancery Commission was appointed in 1850, few could have doubted the need of reform. And the Commission's work did result in legislation. Yet was it enough?

Ecclesiastical Courts and the Court of Admiralty

Separate ecclesiastical courts had existed in England since the time of William the Conqueror. In the nineteenth century their primary justification as ecclesiastical institutions was presumably their value to the Church as a means of enforcing church discipline. Yet figures showed that this was not the principal use of the courts: testamentary causes, for example, accounted for almost a half of the court's business. Moreover, these courts were disliked by many not only on the familiar grounds of delay and expense but because they were a part of the Established Church. And, no doubt, many lawyers wished to handle the testamentary business themselves.

36   System . . . English Law, *Edinburgh Review,* Vol. 45 (1827) p. 469.

37   Jeremy Bentham, *Introductory View of the Rationale of Evidence* Works (ed. Bowring) vi 43.

38   William Holdsworth, *Charles Dickens as a Legal Historian* (Yale University Press, 1929) pp. 79-116.

39   See generally William Holdsworth, *History of English Law*, Vol. 1 (Methuen, 7th ed. 1956) p. 443.

40   D. E. Colombine, County Court Extension, Monopoly of the Bar . . . etc., (1850); cited in *Westminster Review* Vol. 54 (1851) p. 113.

The most distinguished ecclesiastical lawyers were the handful of civilian advocates who practised at Doctors Commons near St. Paul's in London: these advocates were also the sole practitioners before the Court of Admiralty. Some critics saw the move in 1833 for a committee on Admiralty as a move inspired by the civilians in their campaign for the ecclesiastical courts to retain their jurisdiction in testamentary matters despite the recommendation contained in the Fourth Real Property Report that such business should be transferred from them. The consequence of that, the civilians argued, would be the ruin of their profession: and then how would advocates skilled in international law be available to the Admiralty Court?

In the event it was the introduction of the new divorce law and the creation of a new Court of Probate, Divorce and Admiralty in 1857 which finally stripped the civilians of their jurisdiction.[41]

Inferior Courts

Repeated demands were made over the years for local courts which might deal with small claims justly, swiftly and inexpensively. Local courts of requests were seen increasingly by some as the answer.[42] Such courts had never been popular with lawyers. Blackstone, for example, had criticised them on the ground that their lay commissioners or judges exercised tyranny.[43] A commissioner of a court of requests close to Blackstone's day, however, attributed the opposition of the lawyers to their self interest,[44] and no doubt it is possible to take such a view of the strong criticism which the distinguished common law commissioners levelled at all inferior courts in their Fifth Report of 1833. Yet there can be little doubt that much of the common law commissioners' criticism was justified.

Lord Althorp, a Whig, had taken the initiative in attempts to reform the local courts in 1821 and this initiative was eventually taken up by Peel. Peel's measure was suspended in June 1828, however, until a means of compensating the holders of certain sinecures could be devised. It was in April 1830 that Brougham made a forceful plea for a revived County Court whose jurisdiction should be extended from 40s. to £100 and whose judges should be skilled lawyers. Peel supported Brougham's proposals and all seemed set for reform.

41   Anthony Manchester, The Reform of the Ecclesiastical Courts, *American Journal of Legal History,* Vol. 10 (1966) p. 51. *Report from the Select Committee on Admiralty Courts* 1833 (670) VII: IUP Legal Administration 6:9.

42   W. H. D. Winder, The Courts of Requests, *The Law Quarterly Review,* Vol. 52. (1936) p. 369.

43   Blackstone, *Commentaries,* Vol. 3 (5th ed. 1773) p. 82.

44   William Hutton, *Courts of Requests* (1787) p. 19.

Yet the measure was held over for two years being resubmitted in March 1833. It was against this background that the commissioners issued their Fifth Report in April 1833.

Not surprisingly, perhaps, as Brougham was now Lord Chancellor, their recommendations were close to Brougham's views, although they recommended a jurisdictional limit of only £20. It was all too much, however, for the opponents of the scheme, led by Lyndhurst. At the committee stage their opposition proved successful: Brougham's bill was defeated on 9 July 1833. The grounds of opposition were varied. There was, for example, a dislike of the patronage which the Lord Chancellor would exercise in his appointments to the numerous new posts. Perhaps the key objection, however, was the view that such proposals would downgrade the metropolitan bar: local bars, it was said, would be inferior in quality — and yet judges of the superior courts were selected from the bar whose quality must, therefore, be maintained. No doubt, then, lawyers had some personal interest in putting forward such arguments: yet it is at least possible to see some elements of public interest in the arguments levelled against this measure.[45]

It was an opposition which was not to be repeated, however, when the modern County Court was formed in 1846. There is some dispute as to whether this was an entirely new court or simply the old County Court restored.[46] There can be no doubt, however, as to the modern court's popularity and its jurisdiction was soon extended. Indeed, why should many cases go before a Superior Court at all? Pitt Taylor's observations on the County Courts Report of 1855 are some evidence of this point of view. The *Westminster Review* took the point further in an article which was published in 1868. An analysis of twenty six cases tried at the spring assizes for Surrey, wrote the *Review*, had shown that 'few were fit for trial in the superior courts. They were almost all of them cases of debt or contract under 100l., or of tort under 50l., cases quite clear and easy, without any difficulty at all, events of cases turning entirely upon disputed facts, and chiefly on the credit to be given to witnesses on one side or the other on the most simple matters. Thus, for instance, the Lord Chief Justice of England was engaged for the greater part of two days in trying, with a jury, whether a stack of hay was worth 100l., or 120l., and the jury gave a verdict for 120l. It was a sort of case a farm valuer could have easily settled in an hour'.[47]

45   Arthur Lyon Cross, Old English Local Courts and the Movement for their Reform, *Michigan Law Review*, Vol. 30 (1932) p. 369.

46   W. Holdsworth, *History of English Law*, Vol. 1 at p. 191: Harold Potter, *An Historical Introduction to English Law* (4th ed. 1958) p. 238: contr. T. Plucknett, *A Concise History of the Common Law*, p. 208.

47   *Westminster Review* Vol. 34 (1868) p. 322. Cf. Harry Smith, The Resurgent County Court in Victorian Britain, *The American Journal of Legal History*, Vol. 13 (1969) p. 126.

Why, then, should cases go before a Superior Court at all? This was a question fit for the Judicature Commission.

The Judicature Acts

It was Roundell Palmer who, as Lord Selborne, the Lord Chancellor, was eventually to carry the Judicature Acts, who in 1867 sparked off the initiative which led to the appointment of the Judicature Commission on 18 September 1867. It was a large commission and for all practical purposes it was composed entirely of lawyers, for even Hunt and Ayrton had some legal background. Some effort does seem to have been made, however, to represent interest groups within the profession. Hollams and Lowndes, for example, were London solicitors: Bateson was a Liverpool solicitor. And the *Solicitors' Journal* attributed[48] the subsequent appointments of Phillimore and Bramwell to a wish to strengthen the civil and common law elements on the Commission, in the belief that the Chancery element was too strong. And it surely augured well for the success of the recommendations contained in their First Report that all the members of this large and diverse Commission felt able to sign it.

Yet Lord Hatherley, who duly founded his Judicature Bill of 1870 upon those recommendations, failed to carry his measure. In the Lords, Westbury had been highly critical and Cockburn, the Lord Chief Justice, between whom and the Lord Chancellor there had been ill feeling for some time, castigated Hatherley's proposals publicly, and was taken to reflect the views of the common law bench. Some part of the failure may be attributed also to bad management and to want of time. No further action was taken until Lord Selborne became Lord Chancellor in November 1872.

Selborne had learned a valuable lesson from his predecessors' discomfiture. As the author of one of the most important legal reforms of the century, his approach is of some interest. He wrote later: 'The Bills introduced before 1873 were too much in skeleton form, containing, upon many points which it was neither desirable nor safe to leave indefinite, mere outlines, to be filled up by judge made rules — they dealt irresolutely with the appellate jurisdiction — and counsel was not taken, before their introduction, with the leading judges and others, from whom support would be of great value, and opposition formidable. I was careful to steer clear of those errors, as far as I could; and as soon as my Bill was prepared before the meeting of Parliament, I sent copies of it to Lord Cairns, Lord Hatherley, Lord Westbury and Lord Romilly, the two Chief Justices (Cockburn and Bovill), Chief Baron Kelly, the Lords Justices (James and Mellish), and the Attorney- and Solicitor-

48 *Solicitors' Journal*, Vol. 13 (1869) p. 489.

General; giving them the opportunity of suggesting objections and amendments. The result was that when, on the 14th February 1873, I explained my scheme to the House of Lords and presented the Bill, I had received general assurances of approval from the most influential of them, and expressions of opinion, encouraging on the whole, even from those (particularly Lord Westbury and Lord Romilly) who were more disposed to be critical. As soon as it was introduced, I sent copies to every Judge, inviting from all free comment and friendly suggestion. The result was to strengthen me in many ways. From Bench and Bar of the Common Law Courts, I obtained cordial and decided support; and, if I could not say quite as much of those whose special experience was in Equity, and who were distrustful of the effect of the proposed fusion of jurisdictions upon equitable jurisprudence, I succeeded in disarming, even from that quarter, active opposition; while from Lord Cairns and Lord Hatherley, whose authority could not be gainsaid, I received powerful and consistent help.'[49]

The bill met with little opposition. Indeed it met with remarkably little comment from the profession and aroused little interest in Parliament. Yet the whole measure well nigh foundered on the question of whether the Lords should retain its appellate jurisdiction. Selborne had thought little of the recommendation of the Lords Committee of 1872; and the *Solicitors' Journal* described Charley's parliamentary amendment in favour of the Lords retaining its appellate jurisdiction as never having 'any seriousness or reality about it'.[50] Yet a change of government and political influence secured a complete reversal of policy on this point. Accordingly, Selborne's measure was suspended; finally, it fell to Cairns to set the seal on Selborne's achievement in the Appellate Jurisdiction Act, 1876, which retained the Lords' jurisdiction.[51]

The Commissioners were less successful, however, in instigating further legislation. In particular the barristers still jibbed at any possible threat to the centralized structure of the Superior Courts and so were not prepared to see the jurisdiction of the County Court increased: it was a controversy which would continue. And Ayrton could not persuade his colleagues of the merits of Tribunals of Commerce: yet in 1892 the judges were moved to establish a special commercial court in London — or rather a special list within the Queen's Bench Division. At much the same time a writer in the *Law Quarterly Review* commented that the inauguration of the City of London Chamber of Arbitration was 'a striking and significant fact. It is the outcome of a long growing dissatisfaction on the part of the commercial world with our

49   Roundell Palmer, *Memories Personal and Political* (Macmillan: 1898) Vol. 1 pp. 300-301.

50   *Solicitors' Journal*, Vol. 17 (1873) p. 628.

51   For a full account see Robert Stevens, The Final Appeal; Reform of the House of Lords and Privy Council 1867-1876. *The Law Quarterly Review*, Vol. 80 (1964) p. 343.

legal system'.[52] Admittedly, such fears among lawyers were not new. It does surely reflect upon the adequacy of the commissioners' efforts in these two fields, however, that they failed to provide an acceptable solution which might endure to the end of the century. For the only alternative was drift.

The question of a public prosecutor had been debated for some twenty years, had been the subject of five bills, and was the subject of other discussions of which the commissioners were informed. The office of Director of Public Prosecutions was formed in 1879.[53] Accordingly, too much credit for this measure should not be attributed, perhaps, to the commissioners who, incidentally, had recommended a national system under a Chief Public Prosecutor which would extend over the entire country. Indeed the lack of conviction in the Fourth and Fifth Reports show full well that by this time the commission as a whole had lost all impetus.

The Judicature Commission had acted, therefore, as a suitable vehicle for the consensual reform of the Superior Courts: it had neither the will nor the capacity, however, to achieve rather more than that, especially with regard to the inferior courts.

The Administration of the Court System

Much of the delay and expense to which litigants were subjected, during the first half of the nineteenth century in particular, can be attributed to an archaic and largely irresponsible system of court administration.

At the heart of that system lay the practice of paying court officials by fee, together with the associated practices of saleable offices and sinecures. However, as the fee system was not only rooted in long standing practice but was approved in principle by contemporary economists, it naturally appealed to Englishmen for many years despite the abuses of which it was clearly the cause. It was Adam Smith in his *Wealth of Nations* who had held that the whole expense of justice might easily be defrayed by fees of court without incurring any real hazard of corruption, provided both that the judge was the principal person to reap any benefit from them and that the fees were precisely regulated and ascertained.[54] It is a confident judgement which may have both reflected and shaped much of the responsible thinking of the period. Yet all the available evidence surely points to the existing fee system as itself being productive of both delay and expense: it could be argued, too,

52 Edward Manson, The London Chamber of Arbitration, *The Law Quarterly Review*, Vol. 9, (1893) p. 86.

53 See J. L. J. Edwards, *The Law Officers of the Crown*, (Sweet and Maxwell: 1964), Chapter 17.

54 Adam Smith, *An Inquiry into the Nature and Causes of the Wealth of Nations* (4th ed. 1850) p. 323.

that the personal interest which the judges had in the system as a whole made reform all the more difficult. It would be wrong to suggest, however, that such judicial interest had more than a marginal influence on the longevity of the system. Perhaps the most effective bar to the abolition of court offices and sinecures was the view that the official owned his office with the result that he might treat it like any other freehold interest. And a man was not to be deprived lightly of his freehold.[55] If he were so deprived, then certainly appropriate compensation must be paid to him and the sum total of such compensation might well inhibit ministers from initiating the necessary reforming legislation. Peel's measure for local courts was suspended in 1828, for example, until a means could be devised of compensating the holders of the sinecures affected: and much of reforming statutes might be taken up with the question of compensation.[56] Vested interests, it seems, were to be respected scrupulously.[57]

Yet the need for change was urgent in that the existing system encouraged a remarkable degree of administrative abuse amongst the judicial staff — scarcely surprising, perhaps, when every stage of the proceeding, every copy carried its fee to a member of the judicial staff who might be responsible directly only to a sinecurist. Complaints of abuse of procedure on the part of the judicial staff, for example, were well documented and of long standing. Thus procedure in the masters offices was described with some truth as the 'very worst part of the business of the (Chancery) court'.[58] It is surely characteristic of the slow pace of reform during this period, therefore, that although Brougham effected some minor improvements during his period as Lord Chancellor, no substantial reform of this office was achieved until 1852.[59] Other changes came equally slowly and in a similar piecemeal fashion.

Thus judges of the superior courts were paid partly by fee until 1825: yet judges of the new County Courts were paid by fee until 1850. Indeed, under the fee system some County Court judges earned considerably more than they were to be paid under the new system — and this was just as true of some of their clerks who, under the old system, had been earning rather more than the new judicial salary.[60]

55   W. Holdsworth, *History of English Law*, Vol. 1. p. 425.

56   19 Hansard Debates 876 (2nd ser. 1828): 5 & 6 Vic. c. 103 (1842) and 5 Vic. c. 5 (1841).

57   *Courts of Law, Legal Departments Commission, Administrative Departments, R. Com. 1st Report. 1874* (C. 1109) XXXI at p. 1: Legal Administration 14: 221.

58   See W. Holdsworth, *History of English Law*, Vol. 9 p. 365.

59   Court of Chancery Act, 15 & 16 Vic. c. 80. Chancery Amendment Act, 15 & 16 Vic. c. 86: Suitors Funds Act 15 & 16 Vic. c. 87.

60   13 Hansard Debates 613 (2nd ser. 1825): *Courts of Law and Equity, Fees. Sel. Ctee.* 1st Rep. 1850. (386) XIII p. 6.: IUP Legal Administration 7.

Saleable offices, sinecures, any form of patronage was reduced but slowly, then, over the years. Judicial patronage in particular lingered for some time. Judges of county courts, it was alleged, believed their sons were often well fitted for the office of registrar. Judges of superior courts, too, were unwilling to surrender all patronage. Selborne attempted to justify judicial patronage to some extent by stressing that if patronage were accumulated in one hand serious evils might result: it was an argument familiar to those who had urged without success the creation of a Ministry of Justice. It was left to Childers to point out that judicial patronage had not been responsible to Parliament, and that good results did not necessarily follow from it:[61] many responsible lawyers would have agreed.

Under Gladstone economy in government was stressed and, not surprisingly, affected the 'legal departments'. Indeed in 1873 Gladstone had even suggested that the salaries of the judges of the High Court should be reduced. It was scarcely surprising, therefore, that the Parliamentary Committee on Civil Service expenditure not only considered the question of the legal offices but concluded that there was considerable scope for economy with regard to them. One must surely sympathize with the committee's view that almost without exception the legal establishments were 'unduly expensive and it is clear that the absence of any uniform principle in their regulation must produce mischievous results'.[62] Yet lawyers suggested that the committee had concerned itself exclusively with the question of cost to the exclusion of considerations of efficiency. Selborne, the Lord Chancellor — upon the committee seeking his views — further reflected professional opinion by pointing out that the Select Committee had not had before it any witnesses who were conversant with the actual duties performed by the officers in the legal departments and welcomed the Committee's own suggestion that a separate commission should be instituted to inquire how far it might be practicable, by improved arrangements, to reduce the cost to the public without diminishing the efficiency of the several offices connected with the administration of justice.[63] That commission duly covered a great deal of ground, although it received only a muted welcome from the profession;[64]

---

61 *Courts and Law, Legal Departments Commission R. Com.* mins of ev. 1875 (C 1245) pp. 140 and 498-500: IUP Legal Administration 15: 140 and 498-500. Note that Lord Westbury, the Lord Chancellor, had been obliged to resign from office in 1865 as a result of the so called "Leeds registry scandal" which involved his son: J. B. Atlay, *The Victorian Chancellors,* Vol. 2 (Smith, Elder & Co: 1908) p. 270ff. H. C. E. Childers (1827-1896) was a former financial secretary to the Treasury (1865), a member of the Judicature Commission, a distinguished first lord of the Admiralty (1868-1871), and chancellor of the duchy of Lancaster (1872).

62 *Civil Services Expenditure. Sel Ctee. 1st Rep.* 1873 (131) VII; IUP National Finance 5: *Solicitors Journal* Vol. 17 (1873) p. 665.

63 *Solicitors Journal* Vol. 18 (1873) p. 22.

64 *Solicitors Journal* Vol. 19 (1874-5) 58.

several more years were to pass and a further Committee was to report before one of its more important recommendations — that for a central office for the Supreme Court — was to be acted upon in 1879.[65] It is only characteristic of the all-pervading piecemeal approach that only seven years later still further changes would be recommended.[66]

It can be argued that it had been the circuit system which had made our highly centralized judicial system tolerable to litigants and jurors.[67] If such a system were to work effectively, however, it would surely have to reflect the country's drastically changed patterns of population, commerce and communication. It is surely remarkable, for example, that Birmingham — a large, populous city which enjoyed good communications — did not become an assize town until 1883. Generally speaking little sustained thought was given to the matter. And on the one occasion when decisive action was taken — by the incorporation of the Welsh system into the English following upon the recommendations of the commissioners of 1829 — it could be alleged that the motives of the commissioners may not have been wholly pure. It was certain that the initial results for Wales were less than happy.

Yet proposals concerning the Court of Great Session had been in the air for some time. It had been included, for example, in Burke's comprehensive plan for economical reform of 1780 and in 1798 a Select Committee had recommended the 'gradual consolidation of the ... judicatures of Wales into one circuit — so as to have an additional number of English judges'.[68] After some intermittent consideration over the years it was the Earl Cawdor who brought the question of the Welsh Judicature to the forefront of discussion once again in 1828 — and before a commission whose members had no experience of Wales and which had declared itself not prepared to enter into a 'minute comparison' of the proceedings of the Welsh courts with those at Westminster. There may be some merit, then, in the allegation that the Welsh Judicature fell a victim, not to its own defects, which were being gradually remedied, but to the desire of English lawyers to have three more judges. And bearing in mind the existing defects in the English system one can well understand the view that for some years the Act which abolished the Welsh Judicature inflicted considerable hardship on Welsh suitors.

---

65   *Judicature Acts (Legal Offices). Ctee. rep. 1878.* (C. 2067): IUP Legal Administration 16: 417, 42, 43 Vic. C. 78.

66   *Courts of Law, Central Office of Supreme Court of Judicature. Ctee. rep.* 1887. (181) LXVII: IUP Legal Administration 16: 613.

67   W. Holdsworth, *History of English Law,* Vol. 1, p. 283.

68   W. Llewelyn Williams, 'The King's Court of Great Sessions in Wales', *Y Cymmrodor* Vol. 26. (1966) p. 1.: W. R. Williams, *The History of the Great Sessions in Wales* (1899): D. Williams, *A History of Modern Wales* (1950) p. 29 ff. *First Report of the Royal Commission on Practice and Proceedings of the Courts of Common Law* 1829 (46) IX p. 35 and esp. at p. 36: Legal Administration 1:35-36.

In view both of the lack of real consideration which had been given over the years to the question of assizes and circuits and of the fact that some of the bigger industrial cities lacked assizes, the Judicature Commission might have been expected to offer a decisive lead. This was not the case. The weak recommendations contained in its first Report were exceeded only by its disavowal of further responsibility in the fifth Report, although it is true that some useful legislation did result.[69]

Other factors also affected court administration. That court buildings should be suitable for their purpose, for example, is obvious enough: it is less obvious that the site on which they are built may affect the course of reform. Yet the new courts on the Strand, when they were opened in 1884, symbolized the achievement of the Judicature Acts and, it is interesting to note that Selborne had had to argue very strongly for that particular site in the teeth of fierce aesthetic criticism which favoured a site on the Thames Embankment. Yet such a site would have denied the new court building, in Selborne's words, 'the benefit of a situation, central between Lincoln's Inn and the Temple, and equally near to both — conditions of the scheme which were of great practical importance...'.[70]

The Legal Profession

So long as the lawyer continues to be seen as an essential part of the legal system, there will be a deep public interest in the questions of admission into the legal profession, education for the legal profession and the organization of the legal profession. All intending barristers must belong to one of the four Inns of Court. Accordingly, the Benchers of the Inns of Court exercised an all important influence on the fundamental question of potential students admission to an Inn of Court. The Common Law Commissioners, probably influenced by the unjust treatment which one Daniel Whittle Harvey had suffered in his efforts to join the Inner Temple, sought to qualify that position. The commissioners were not wholly successful in seeing their recommendations implemented. Yet it did become recognised over the years that the Benchers, since they had this privilege, had duties also. As a later commission commented, the Inns 'being entrusted with the exclusive right of conferring or withholding a position to which such privileges are incident, the community is surely entitled to require some guarantee — first, for the personal character, and next for the professional qualifications of the individuals called to the

69   Judicature Act 1873 (36 p. 37 Vic. c. 66) ss 26 and 29. Judicature Act 1875 (38 & 39 Vic. c. 77) s. 23.

70   Roundell Palmer, *Memorials*, Vol. 1. p. 24.

Bar'.[71] Success in the former role was to be balanced by relative failure in the latter.

Judicial integrity was taken for granted at the higher level, however, although over the years there was considerable public criticism of the justices of the peace.

The Scottish Reports[72]

The case for reform in Scotland was put with great vigour from the beginning of the nineteenth century. Unfortunately, although there was wide agreement on the need for change, there was no unanimity as to what those changes should be. Accordingly, reform proceeded on a basis of trial and error, the first phase lasting from 1808 to 1830 while the second phase culminated in the Court of Session Act, 1868.

To the English observer a notable feature of the Scottish system was the fact that law and equity had not been separated in Scottish practice. Indeed Lord Eldon believed that until such a division had been achieved in Scotland, the House of Lords would not be able to deal properly with Scottish appeals. Eldon did have his way, however, with the creation of a separate Jury Court for Scotland in 1815. In 1830 the powers and duties of the Jury Court were transferred to the Court of Session and the Jury Court was abolished. The Royal Commission of 1868 noted that the institution of civil jury trial had never become popular in Scotland. Nevertheless, it has survived in Scotland despite its greatly reduced use in England.

Lord Colonsay, the chairman of the 1868 Commission, had been raised to the peerage with a view to having someone in the House of Lords who knew something about Scots law, for not only were there many Scottish appeals but there had been a tendency on the part of English lawyers to anglicize Scots law. It is interesting to note, therefore, that the commissioners do not appear to consider the question of appeals to the Lords to be an issue. Indeed there is other evidence that they were well satisfied with the existing position and this may have been a factor some years later in the Lords' retention of its appellate jurisdiction.

Yet perhaps the most remarkable feature of the Scots system to the English lawyer is the important role of the local court. As Plucknett remarked:

71 *Inns of Court Inquiry Commission 1855* (1988) XVIII. 345. p. 14: *Documents relating to D. W. Harvey's application to be called to the Bar* 1834 (349) XLVIII. I.: see generally W. Holdsworth, *History of English Law*, Vol. 12, pp. 4-101.

72 See *Introduction to Scottish Legal History*, Vol. 20 (1958: The Stair Society): Thomas Smith, *British Justice: The Scottish Contribution* (Stevens & Sons Ltd.: 1961) p. 53 ff.: David M. Walker, *The Scottish Legal System* (W. Green & Son Ltd., 3rd ed. 1969).

'England had to wait until 1846 for a co-ordinated system of local courts. The crown's incurable fear of the sheriff is largely responsible for this. How great an opportunity was missed can be seen by looking at the vigorous and useful institution of the sheriff in Scotland, where the office was allowed to develop along natural lines'.[73]

In a sense, perhaps, these reports summarize some seventy years of Scots achievement in this field. That they produced no legislative reform may be because there was a wish to have more experience of the Act of 1868 before making further changes.

The Process of Reform

Maine suggested that the agencies by which Law was brought into harmony with society were three in number: Legal Fictions, Equity, and Legislation.[74] Over the years both the legal fiction and equity had played their part in the adaptation of the law and of legal institutions to contemporary needs. It was legislation, however, which was to be the means of reforming the legal institutions of the nineteenth century.

Lord Mansfield had attempted to achieve a harmonization of the rules of Law and Equity during the latter part of the eighteenth century. Yet that attempt at judicial reform had failed, a fact noted by Bentham and which may have contributed to his advocacy of legislation as the tool of reform. For to Bentham such partial amendment by judical reform was 'bought at the expense of universal certainty' and '. . .amendment from the Judgement seat is confusion'.[75] Moreover the sheer magnitude of major institutional reform surely pointed inevitably to legislation as the only available means by which such reform might be effected. Yet reforming legislation was to be preceded by due inquiry.

The inquiries themselves were of their nature conservative. There was to be no root and branch inquiry, beginning from first principles, into the overall adequacy of the existing system to meet the needs of the nation. Instead the overall framework is assumed to be right; all that was needed, the terms of reference suggested, was for adjustments to be made to bring the system up to date. Such an approach had been implicit in Brougham's speech of 1828; it was to be apparent in his gradualist approach as Lord Chancellor.

Moreover, it is not unfair to argue that the Commissioners were invariably timid in their recommendations. Whether such commissioners were selected

73   T. Plucknett, *A Concise History of the Common Law,* p. 105.

74   H. Maine, *Ancient Law,* p. 20.

75   Jeremy Bentham, *A Comment on the Commentaries* (Oxford ed: 1928) p. 214.

with a view to achieving thorough going reform is itself a moot point. One might wonder, for example, whether the presence on the Common Law Commission of 1829 of Parke and Stephen, two special pleaders, was conducive to reform — especially as Parke was known to be highly conservative in his approach to the law. Indeed, it was said of him that on one occasion he fainted in court. The restoratives applied to him had no effect. At length one of his brethren who knew his peculiar temperament 'rushed into the library, seized a large musty volume of the old statutes, came back and applied it to the nostrils of the patient. He at once opened his eyes, gave them a slight rub, and in a few seconds he was as well as ever.'[76] Even the *Law Times* criticized the composition of the 1850 Commission as there was no reformer amongst the commissioners. The *Law Times* also queried whether the choice of Walton, one of the Masters of the Court of Exchequer, was apt not expecting that 'this branch of the duties of the Commission (fees of Court) will find a very trenchant reformer in one of the officials, who must be looked upon rather as a representative and protector of the interests threatened with invasion, than as the independent reformer, regardful only of the public weal'.[77] Inquiries into Chancery had followed much the same pattern. Invariably, too, the Commissioners were lawyers although, despite the objections put forward by the Attorney-General and the Master of the Rolls, a member of parliament did secure the rather belated addition of two laymen to the Chancery Commission.[78]

Should we attribute the lawyers' domination of the membership of the Commissions to a general respect for their powers of inquiry, especially with regard to matters of which they might be supposed to have expert knowledge? To what extent, for example, were they represented on Commissions of a non legal nature? Or was it rather that the reform of legal institutions was seen primarily as a question of limited technical adjustment — a task fit only for experts? Such an attitude is reflected expressly in the Civil Procedure Act 1833 which recognizes that the special pleading system could not be amended by laymen.[79] A similar attitude can be seen also in the Master of the Rolls' attempted rejection of the proposal at a later stage to include lay members on the Chancery Commission: there were, he said, 'a great number of technicalities which the members of the Commission were intimately acquainted with, and which it was not possible for any lay member to be acquainted with, and it would necessarily take him a considerable time to understand the nature of the question, and the character of the reform that

76 Edward Manson, *Builders of Our Law* (Horace Cox, 2nd ed. 1904), p. 34.
77 *Law Times*, Vol. 15 (1850) p. 198.
78 Hansard's Debates, Vol. 117 (3rd ser.: 1851) pp. 98, 1359.
79 3 & 4 Will. IV c. 420. s. 1.

was necessary to be made in it'.[80] The inclusion, for example, of Parke and Stephen, both special pleaders, on the Common Law Commission points to the same conclusion. And whilst one notes the nice balance of legal interests in the composition of the Judicature Commission, it is remarkable that initially the lay interest was wholly unrepresented. Particular deference certainly seems to have been shown to the views of the judges on some occasions at least. Selborne especially attached great importance to securing their approval of his Judicature Bill. Able laymen on such commissions might at the very least have acted as devil's advocates by querying vigorously the assumptions of the lawyers. Yet it was not to be.

In so far as the country desired reform of its legal institutions, therefore, it looked to the lawyers to initiate such reforms. In Brougham reform appeared to have found a true champion. Yet more than twenty years after his great speech of 1828 the *Times* could comment that the 'law and its administration constitute the crying evil of the day' and could lay the blame firmly on the legal profession whose 'dogged opposition has compelled reformers to propose unconnected and often incongruous alterations .... Will they still allow blind and unreasoning prejudice to injure themselves as well as the community?'[81] Was such criticism justified? Were the evergreen allegations of the lawyers' extreme conservatism and self interest based on fact?

There can be no doubt but that reform had been, and would continue to be, slow. It would surely be wrong, however, to blame the lawyers alone for this. It has to be remembered, for example, that any reforms proposed must, if they are to be implemented, receive parliamentary approval. Thus, Brougham's proposals for local courts were similar to the recommendations contained in the Fifth Report of the Common Law Commissioners: yet parliament had rejected Brougham's proposals. It was parliament, too, which retained the appellate jurisdiction of the House of Lords rather than adopt Selborne's more sweeping proposals. Any Commission which stepped beyond the likely limits of parliamentary approval for its recommendations, therefore, was merely tilting at windmills or, at best, doing no more than educating public opinion. In this respect it was Brougham, rather than Bentham and his followers, who had a finer appreciation of political realities. One can doubt also whether any Commission, working on its own, which was composed of busy professional men, could really find the time to do more than adapt the existing machinery, no matter how much they divided the work between subcommittees. Indeed one may surely applaud the extent of

80   *Op cit.* n. 78, 1366.
81   *The Times* of December 24th, 1850 cited in Edson Sunderland, 'The English Struggle for Procedural Reform. *Harvard Law Review,* Vol. 39 (1925-1926) 725, 734. *Law Times,* Vol. 18 (1851) p. 1.

some inquiries for the industry involved, while not being surprised at the lack of any radical step forward. There was surely a need, therefore, for a continuing agency of law reform which might take an overall, rather than a piecemeal, view of legal institutions: which might not only initiate reform but which might be responsible also for taking further some of the more vague recommendations expressed by Commissions, for introducing bills into parliament and, granted parliamentary time, for doing everything possible to secure parliamentary approval of such bills. Without such a body reforms were frustrated not only by outright opposition but by sheer apathy — by what Graham called 'passive resistance',[82] by the snares of parliamentary procedure, by the lack of government interest or of parliamentary time. It was for such reasons that there was considerable pressure — including pressure from lawyers — for the creation of a Ministry of Justice.[83] Nothing came of those proposals. We continued to rely on the initiative of a Lord Chancellor burdened already with both judicial and political functions, or of a Home Secretary, or on the initiative, drive and good fortune in parliament of individuals. It was not enough. One can only speculate, of course, at the potency of other factors in delaying reforms. There is the force of sheer inertia. There is, too, the effect of the clash of personalities: might personal enmity between Hatherley and Cockburn, for example, have been a factor in the failure of Hatherley's Judicature Bill?[84]

One can assert, however, that caution was not the prerogative of lawyers alone. An outstanding feature of the whole period is surely the cautious and piecemeal character of practically all legislation. For example, no question had been discussed for so long or so thoroughly as the question of the fusion of law and equity — yet when the Judicature Bill came before the House a member in all good faith asked for, and almost succeeded in obtaining, a Select Committee. The appointment of such a Committee might well have killed the Judicature Bill.

On the other hand lawyers' motives in continuing to insist on a highly centralized system, in jibing at the new County Court and in not assisting that court to achieve its true potential may have smacked to some extent of self interest; yet even the realization of that probability should not blind us to the fact that the arguments in favour of a centralized system were substantial enough. And after, say, 1850, quite a few lawyers realized that their own self interest demanded reform of the law.

Unfortunately, perhaps, the sorry state of legal education did little to assist

---

82   Hansard Debates, Vol. 117 (3rd ser. 1851) pp. 1372-1373.

83   For example, see the evidence of Lord Langdale, Master of the Rolls, in *Courts of Law and Equity, Fees. Sel. Ctee. 1st Rep.* 159-160: Legal Administration 7:

84   *Solicitors Journal*, Vol. 17 (1873) pp. 628-629.

the lawyer to adopt a broader, more critical vision nor did his professional associations wholly remedy that failing at a later stage, although an organization such as the Law Amendment Society may have achieved some good.

Accordingly, the charges of timidity and 'vested interest'[85] which have been aimed at the lawyers may be dismissed in part as over-glib. Lawyers shared the faults of their age: the over-technical nature of their legal education, such as it was, was possibly making them less equal to the demands of a new age than their colleagues in the new professions. Yet the lawyers might also point with some pride to the distinguished reformers within their own ranks — to Brougham, to Selborne, to Field — a solicitor, pamphleteer and witness before several inquiries — and to many others. Their achievement was no mean one.

85 Llewellyn Woodward, *The Age of Reform 1815-1870*. (2nd ed. 1962 Oxford) p. 471. Cf. Harold Laski, *A Grammar of Politics*, (1925: Allen and Unwin) p. 572 ff.

Bibliography

Very little has been written solely on the legal history of the nineteenth century.

The general legal histories are of some assistance, however: T. Plucknett, *A Concise History of the Common Law,* (Butterworth's, 5th. ed, 1956); H. Potter's *Historical Introduction to English Law.* (Sweet and Maxwell, 4th ed. 1958, ed. Kiralfy). Useful briefer histories are: J. H. Baker, *An Introduction to English Legal History* (Butterworth's, 1971); Radcliffe and Cross *The English Legal System* (Butterworth's 5th ed. 1971); Alan Harding, *A Social History of English Law,* (Pelican, 1966); C. H. S. Fifoot, *English Law and its Background* (Bell and Sons: (1932); Edward Jenks, *A Short History of English Law* (Methuen, 3rd ed. 1924).

Other useful general works are: *A Century of English Law* (Macmillan, 1901 — republished by Sweet and Maxwell, 1971); C. H. S. Fifoot, *Judge and Jurist in the Reign of Queen Victoria* (Stevens and Sons, 1959).

Brian Abel-Smith and Robert Stevens, *Lawyers and the Courts – A Sociological Study of the English Legal System* 1750-1965 (Heinemann, 1967) present an interesting survey of the period. Albert Venn Dicey's *Law and Public Opinion in England during the Nineteenth Century* (Macmillan, 2nd. ed., 1963), remains the classic work on the legislative background.

However, the most valuable basic source is still William Holdsworth's Sixteen volume *History of English Law* (Methuen, Sweet and Maxwell 1903-1956). Holdsworth's, *Charles Dickens as a Legal Historian* (Yale University Press: 1929) may also be read with both pleasure and profit.

Other useful works are J. B. Atlay's *The Victorian Chancellors* (2 Vols: Smith, Elder & Co. 1908): R. F. V. Heuston, *Lives of the Lord Chancellors 1885-1940* (Oxford, 1964); Edward Foss, *A Biographical Dictionary of the Judges of England 1066-1870* (1870), Legal autobiographies and biographies are numerous.

Works of reference which may be of assistance are:

(1) P. G. Osborn, *A Concise Law Dictionary* (Sweet and Maxwell, 5th ed. 1964)

(2) Sweet & Maxwell's *Bibliography of the British Commonwealth of Nations,* Compiled by Leslie F. Maxwell.

v.1. English Law to 1800 (1956).

v.2. English Law 1801-1954 2nd ed. (1957).

(3) Institute of Advanced Legal Studies. *Union List of Legal Periodicals* 3rd ed. 1968.

(4) Leonard A. Jones. *Index to the Legal Periodicals* Vol. 1 to Dec. 1886 (Boston Book Co. 1888).

The most useful guides to professional opinion during this period are the legal magazines, citations from which are given in the notes to this essay. Item 3 above lists such periodicals and their availability in the United Kingdom: item 4 lists by subject the more important articles which appeared in the Anglo-American legal periodicals.

Quite often, however, non-legal magazines carried articles which are of considerable legal historical interest. Especially worthy of mention are the *Edinburgh Review, Westminster Review* and *Quarterly Review* — but this is a highly selective list.

For an account of the background to the legal history of Ireland see: V. T. H. Delany, *The Administration of Justice in Ireland,* (Institute of Public Administration, Dublin; 2nd ed. 1965) and F. H. Newark, Notes on Irish Legal History, *Northern Ireland Legal Quarterly, Vol. 7* (1947-1948) p. 129. And note generally P. O'Higgins, *A Bibliography of Periodical Literature relating to Irish Law,* (Northern Ireland Legal Quarterly Inc. 1966).

For some works on the legal history of Scotland see note 72 above.

The Documents
Legal Administration: General

Legal Administration: General Volume 1
FIRST REPORT OF THE ROYAL COMMISSION ON PRACTICE AND PROCEED-
INGS OF THE COURTS OF COMMON LAW WITH EVIDENCE AND APPENDICES,
1829

The commission, which was composed entirely of legal experts,
examined the proceedings of the superior courts of Common Law
with regard to civil business. The first report deals with the despatch
of business in the superior courts of Common Law at Westminster,
in the counties Palatine and in Wales. Special attention was paid to
procedure with regard to Processes Serviceable or Bailable including original writs, outlawry, arrest and bail. Evidence was collected
by means of a questionnaire on legal administration which was sent
to leading lawyers throughout England. Among the problems dealt
with by the questionnaire were the practicality of reforming the law
regulating arrest and bail and costs. The replies describe in detail
court practice and procedure and give the respondents views on the
desirability of reform. The commissioners' report agreed with the
view expressed by the majority of the respondents that while it was
desirable to reduce the cost of litigation and to speed up legal
proceedings, this should not be done at the expense of the quality of
justice dispensed by the courts.

Original reference
1829   (46) IX   Courts of Common Law, Practice and Proceedings,
                               Royal Com. 1st rep. appendices and ev.

Legal Administration: General Volume 2
SECOND AND THIRD REPORTS OF THE ROYAL COMMISSION ON PRACTICE
AND PROCEEDINGS OF THE COURTS OF COMMON LAW WITH EVIDENCE
AND APPENDICES, 1830–1831

One of the earliest tasks of the advocates for the reform of legal
administration was the simplification of procedure, the over-
elaborate and over-rigid code which was the cause of much of the
delay and costs incurred in legal proceedings. The commissioners'
second and third reports concentrate on means of reforming procedural regulations so as to bring them into line with modern requirements. The reports include short histories of the development
of law relating to such aspects of procedure as pleadings and trial

by jury as well as a detailed survey of the laws governing procedure. The commission collected evidence by means of questionnaires sent to leading lawyers, judges and court officials. Among the aspects of practice and procedure dealt with by the questionnaires were, land law, bail, judicial qualifications, pleadings, jury actions and verification of documents. The commission also received communications from judges (including Sir William Best, Lord Chief Justice and Sir James Scarlett) setting out their views on proposed changes in court procedure. The commissioners in .their reports comment both on the state of the law relating to procedure and on the views expressed by the respondents to questionnaires. An important recommendation of the commissioners was that if after twelve hours a jury failed to agree, the decision of nine of its members should be taken as the verdict.

Original references

| 1830 | (123) XI | Courts of Common Law, Practice and Proceedings, Royal Com. 2nd rep., appendices and ev. |
| 1831 | (92) X | Courts of Common Law, Practice and Proceedings, Royal Com. 3rd rep., appendices and ev. |

Legal Administration: General Volumes 3 and 4
Volume 3
FOURTH REPORT OF THE ROYAL COMMISSION ON PRACTICE AND PRO-CEEDINGS OF THE COURTS OF COMMON LAW, WITH EVIDENCE AND APPENDICES PART I, 1831–32

Volume 4
FOURTH REPORT OF THE ROYAL COMMISSION ON PRACTICE AND PRO-CEEDINGS OF THE COURTS OF COMMON LAW, APPENDICES PART II, 1831–32

The report deals primarily with imprisonment for debt. It includes a detailed survey of existing legislation governing debt collection and reasoned suggestions for improving it in the light of changing social and economic conditions. Evidence was collected principally by means of a questionnaire sent to lawyers, merchants and bankers who were asked to give their respective views on existing debt collection legislation and how it might be improved. Particular attention was paid to examining the provisions of continental law on debt collection and several respondents urged that certain of its features could advantageously be adopted in Britain. A small number of witnesses, including Joseph Hume M.P., who urged that imprisonment for debt should be abolished were orally examined. The majority of the commissioners agreed with Hume's view. They felt, however, that it should be retained for those who obtained credit by fraud. The evidence throws interesting light on the reactions of the legal profession to changes in the debt collection. Proposals by businessmen favoured a law which would encourage debtors to repay their debts rather than imprison them which usually resulted in the debt never being recovered at all.

The statistical returns relating to debt collection which were submitted to the Royal Commission are contained in Volume 4 of this set. It provides detailed information on amounts owed, number of persons in prison for debt, court procedure and details of the work of the court for the relief of insolvent debtors.

Original references
Volume 3

1831–32 (239) XXV Pt. I	Courts of Common Law, Practice and Proceedings, Royal Com. 4th rep., mins. of ev. and appendices, Part I.

Volume 4

1831–32 (239) XXV Pt. II	Courts of Common Law, Practice and Proceedings, Royal Com. 4th rep., mins. of ev. and appendices, Part II.

Legal Administration: General Volume 5

FIFTH AND SIXTH REPORTS OF THE ROYAL COMMISSION ON PRACTICE AND PROCEEDINGS OF THE COURTS OF COMMON LAW WITH MINUTES OF EVIDENCE AND APPENDICES 1833–1834

The fifth report deals with provincial courts including County Courts, Courts of Requests, Hundred or Wapentake Courts and a large number of other local courts. The history and present functions of the courts were examined and commented on. Evidence was gathered primarily by means of questionnaires sent to lawyers and businessmen who were asked to give their views on the working of the courts and to suggest possible reforms. The replies showed that reform of the system was long overdue, as it was governed by outdated and complicated procedural regulations which tended to increase costs and to delay the business of the courts. The relations between minor and superior courts including assize courts was discussed. Businessmen considered that the outdated organization of the assize courts' civil business was making them increasingly irrelevant to the needs of the community as their procedure and circuits paid no attention to changing demographic and economic circumstances. The commission fully endorsed the complaints of the business community and recommended that the county courts should be reorganized and their jurisdiction increased at the expense of the civil side of the assizes. The sixth report deals with the regulations and functions of the Inns of Court. Special attention was paid to the need to reform entry regulations which were felt to be too severe. The commission considered that because of the exceptional importance to the community of the legal profession, entry to it should not be governed by private organizations such as the Inns.

Original references

| 1833 (247) XXII | Courts of Common Law, Practice and Proceedings (Local Courts), Royal Com. 5th rep., mins. of ev. and appendix. |
| 1834 (263) XXVI | Courts of Common Law, Practice and Proceedings, Royal Com. 6th rep., mins. of ev. and appendix. |

Legal Administration: General Volume 6

REPORT OF THE ROYAL COMMISSION ON THE CIRCUITS OF THE JUDGES AND REPORTS FROM SELECT COMMITTEES ON ADMIRALTY COURTS, CHANCERY OFFICES, SUPREME COURT OF JUDICATURE (SCOTLAND), THE ADMINISTRATION OF JUSTICE AND COURTS OF LAW AND EQUITY TOGETHER WITH REPORTS ON COURT OF KING'S BENCH AND COMMON PLEAS, AND JURY COURTS (SCOTLAND) WITH MINUTES OF EVIDENCE, APPENDICES AND INDICES, 1833–1845

The Select Committee on the administration of the law in Scotland heard evidence on practice and procedure in the Court of Session and Sheriff Courts. The work of the Inner and Outer Houses was separately examined. Most witnesses were satisfied with the efficiency of the Outer House, which had been recently reorganized, but expressed dissatisfaction with procedure in the Inner House, much of whose time was taken up with useless formalities. The committee paid particular attention to the right of appeal from Inner House judgments to the House of Lords, a right which was deeply resented by many Scottish lawyers. A short report on jury law in Scotland compares English and Scottish law on the subject and suggests that England could usefully adopt some of the provisions of Scottish law in this field. Several of the reports deal with the administration of Chancery Courts and include evidence given by Chancery judges and officials who described their respective duties and in many cases put forward suggestions for the reform of outdated administrative regulations. The evidence indicated that the state had very little practical control over Chancery administration. The volume also includes reports dealing with ecclesiastical jurisdiction, assize terms and circuits and the construction of the Courts of Justice. These reports tell something of the difficulties involved in reorganizing the English legal system, which had its roots deep in antiquity, to cater for the needs of a rapidly changing society.

Original references

1833	(670)	VII	Admiralty Courts, Sel. Cttee. Rep., mins. of ev. and appendix.
1833	(685)	XIV	Chancery Offices, Sel. Cttee. Rep., mins. of ev.
1835	(314)	XLVI	Court of King's Bench and Common Pleas, Rep.
1840	(332)	XIV	Supreme Court of Judicature, Scotland, Sel. Cttee. Rep., mins. of ev., appendix and index.
1840	(500)	XV	Administration of Justice, Sel. Cttee. HL. mins. of ev. and index.
1844	(636)	XLII	Jury Court (Scotland), T. G. Wright, Rep.
1845	(608)	XII	Courts of Law and Equity, Sel. Cttee. Rep., mins. of ev. and index.
1845	[638]	XIV	Circuits of the Judges, expediency of altering, Royal Com. Rep. and appendix.

Legal Administration: General Volume 7

REPORTS FROM SELECT COMMITTEES ON FEES IN COURTS OF LAW AND EQUITY WITH MINUTES OF EVIDENCE, APPENDICES AND INDICES, 1847–1850

The reports and evidence deal not only with court fees, their regulation and mode of collection, but also with many other important aspects of legal administration such as the functions of certain courts and the duties of court officials. Much of the evidence deals with Chancery administration and was given by Chancery officials and members of the legal profession. The functions of the various Chancery offices and departments such as the Masters and Petty Bag offices and the Accountant-General's Department were examined in detail as also were the operations of the Bankruptcy and Admiralty Courts. Lord Langdale, the Master of the Rolls and a leading advocate of law reform, urged that a Ministry of Justice should be established so that court administration and finance would be administered by the state. Langdale's proposal for a Ministry of Justice drew little support from other witnesses, but many supported the idea of state control and financing of the system, especially as the evidence showed that the existing system was administered by officials subject to very little supervision and paid by litigants' fees which were not adequately regulated. Evidence was heard on the functions of Ecclesiastical and County Courts and of the High Court of Admiralty. Nearly all of the witnesses examined were court officials and their evidence presents a graphic account of the functions of these courts. Of particular interest is the evidence relating to the County Courts which though recently established were already in need of reform.

Original references

| 1847 | (643) | VIII | Fees in Courts of Law and Equity, Sel. Cttee. Rep., mins. of ev. and index. |

1847–48	(158) XV	Fees in Courts of Law and Equity, Sel. Cttee. 1st Rep., mins. of ev. and appendix.
	(307)	Fees in Courts of Law and Equity, Sel. Cttee. 2nd Rep.
	(307)	Fees in Courts of Law and Equity, Sel. Cttee. index to 1st and 2nd reps.
1849	(559) VIII	Fees in Courts of Law and Equity, Sel. Cttee. Rep., mins. of ev., appendix and index.
1850	(386) XIII	Fees in Courts of Law and Equity, Sel. Cttee. 1st Rep., mins. of ev.
	(711)	Fees in Courts of Law and Equity, Sel. Cttee. 2nd Rep. mins. of ev., appendix and index.

Legal Administration: General Volume 8

FIRST, SECOND AND THIRD REPORTS OF THE ROYAL COMMISSION ON PROCESS, PRACTICE AND SYSTEM OF PLEADING IN THE COURT OF CHANCERY WITH SUPPLEMENT TO THE FIRST REPORT AND CORRESPONDENCE WITH MINUTES OF EVIDENCE AND APPENDICES, 1852–1856

The first report of the Commission of Inquiry on the Court of Chancery contains a detailed synopsis of the functions of the court and the duties of its officers. Evidence was heard on the value of maintaining the distinction between law and equity and on the changes which would be necessary in the legal system if the distinction were to be abolished. A representative of the New York Bar was examined on the legal system of that state and the differences between New York's legal system and the English system were discussed. The observations of New York state judges on the effect of the abolition of Chancery courts in their state are given in a series of letters which accompany the report. The second report deals with the functions of Ecclesiastical Courts and with their relations to the Queen's Courts. Most of the witnesses examined were church court officials and their evidence gives an interesting account of the important functions of these courts in testamentary cases. The final report examines the functions of the Chancery examiners and as in the earlier reports—includes a summary of existing law regulating the subject and an account of the finding of previous investigations in the same field. Many of the commissioners' recommendations were implemented by subsequent legislation. Of particular importance was the establishment of the Probate Court in 1857 and the consequent reduction in the jurisdiction of the ecclesiastical courts in secular affairs. The volume includes a memorandum sent to the commission by the Incorporated Law Society urging the reform of Chancery administration.

Original references

| 1852 | (216) XLII | Practice of the Court of Chancery, Incorporated Law |

		Society Rep. and correspondence.
1852	[1437] XXI	Court of Chancery, process, practice and system of pleading, Royal Com. 1st Rep., mins. of ev. and appendix.
	[1454]	Court of Chancery, process, practice and system of pleading, Royal Com. supplement to 1st Rep.
1854	[1731] XXIV	Court of Chancery, process, practice and system of pleading, Royal Com. 2nd Rep., mins. of ev. and appendices.
1856	[2064] XXII	Court of Chancery, process, practice and system of pleading, Royal Com. 3rd Rep., mins. of ev. and appendices.

Legal Administration: General Volume 9

FIRST, SECOND AND THIRD REPORTS OF THE ROYAL COMMISSION ON PLEADING IN THE COURTS OF COMMON LAW AND REPORTS OF THE ROYAL COMMISSIONS ON COUNTY COURTS, COMMON LAW (JUDICIAL BUSINESS) AND EVIDENCE IN CHANCERY WITH MINUTES OF EVIDENCE AND APPENDICES, 1851–1860

The first report of the Royal Commission on procedure, practice and the system of pleading in the Courts of Common Law gives a detailed account of the procedures involved in the hearing of cases in these courts. Among the many aspects of legal administration examined were the duties of Court Officials, the value of the jury system, the law of evidence and conflict between the rules of common law and equity courts. The Royal Commission on County Courts reviewed the operation of these courts since their establishment in 1847 and investigated whether any changes were necessary in their organization and jurisdiction. Evidence was given mainly by court officials who described the day-to-day work of the courts. Special attention was paid to the arrangements made for financing the courts and to the value of extending their jurisdiction. The commission considered that while the courts were providing a valuable service their jurisdiction could usefully be extended and their administration reorganized. The Royal Commission on judicial business (Common Law) concentrated on examining the advisability of altering assize circuits so as to cater for the changing distribution of population. Most of the evidence was presented by deputations from towns seeking to be made assize towns. It was shown that the existing circuits did not adequately cater for the needs of rapidly growing cities such as Birmingham, which was not an assize town, while assizes were held in small villages. The commission recommended against any large-scale alterations in assize circuits.

Original references

1851	[1389] XXII	Pleading in Courts of Common Law, Royal Com. 1st Rep. and appendix.
1852–53	[1626] XL	Pleading in Courts of Common Law, Royal Com. 2nd Rep.
1860	[2614] XXXI	Pleading in the Courts of Common Law, Royal Com. 3rd Rep.
1854–55	[1914] XVIII	County Courts, Royal Com. 1st Rep. and appendix.
1857 Sess. 2	[2268] XXI	Common Law (Judicial Business), Royal Com. Rep., mins. of ev., appendix.
1860	[2698] XXXI	Evidence in Chancery, Royal Com. Rep.

Legal Administration: General Volume 10

FIRST AND SECOND REPORTS OF THE ROYAL COMMISSION ON THE SUPERIOR COURTS OF COMMON LAW AND CHANCERY OF ENGLAND AND IRELAND WITH MINORITY REPORT OF J. NAPIER AND REPORT OF THE ROYAL COMMISSION ON CHANCERY FUNDS WITH EVIDENCE AND APPENDICES, 1863–1867

The reports of the Commission of Inquiry into the superior Courts of Common Law and Chancery in England and Ireland give a detailed account of the practice and procedure in the Courts of Common Law and Equity in both England and Ireland as well as a summary of the main points of difference between the English and Irish codes. The commission collected evidence by means of a questionnaire which was sent to judges, lawyers and court officials in Ireland. Information was sought on the functions of the courts and respondents were asked to state their views on possible reforms. The second report deals mainly with costs, the official establishments of the courts and with the business of the crown side of the Court of Queen's Bench in Ireland. The commission whose distinguished membership included former English and Irish Lord Chancellors such as Lord Cairns and Sir Joseph Napier, suggested a large number of alterations in Irish procedure and practice designed to bring it more into line with English practice. Napier dissented from the majority report and issued a minority report criticizing certain aspects of the majority report. The report of the inquiry into affairs of the Accountant-General's Department gives a detailed account of the duties of this Chancery office and views of solicitors on the work of the department. There is also a short history of the department which had been formed in 1726 to administer court funds and to prevent fraud by Chancery officials.

Original references

1863	[3238] XV	Superior Courts of Common Law and Courts of Chancery of England and Ireland, Royal Com. 1st Rep., evidence and appendices.

1864	[3280] XXIX	Chancery Funds, Royal Com. Rep. and appendices.
1866	[3674] XVII	Superior Courts of Common Law and Courts of Chancery of England and Ireland, Royal Com. 2nd Rep., evidence and appendices.
1867	(285) XIX	Superior Courts of Common Law and Courts of Chancery of England and Ireland, J. Napier, separate rep.

Legal Administration: General Volumes 11 and 12
Volume 11

FIRST AND SECOND REPORTS OF THE ROYAL COMMISSION ON COURTS OF LAW IN SCOTLAND WITH MINUTES OF EVIDENCE, 1868–69

Volume 12

THIRD, FOURTH AND FIFTH REPORTS OF THE ROYAL COMMISSION ON THE COURTS OF LAW IN SCOTLAND, WITH MINUTES OF EVIDENCE, APPENDICES AND INDICES, 1870–1871

The Scottish legal system differs fundamentally from the English and is based to a large extent on continental and Roman codes. The system was first formulated in detail during the seventeenth century and was preserved by entrenched clauses of the Act of Union of 1706. Throughout the century efforts had been made by law reformers to update the system while retaining its distinctive characteristics and preserving it from the anglicizing influence of House of Lords decisions in Scottish cases. The Royal Commission which was chaired by Lord Colonsay, the first Scottish law lord, included in its membership the senior Scottish judges and law officers. It examined all aspects of Scottish legal administration. Evidence was heard from lawyers and court officials on practice and procedure in the Justice of the Peace, Sheriff and Tiend Courts and in the Inner and Outer Houses of the Court of Session. Special attention was paid to the working of the jury system in civil cases before the Outer House and criminal cases before the Court of Justiciary. The functions of Procurator Fiscals were examined. The Fiscals' duties were to some extent analogous to those of the American District Attorney. Many of the witnesses considered that procedure in the Court of Session had been greatly improved by reforms undertaken in 1868. Traders urged that procedure in the Sheriff Court should be improved. They objected especially to the right of the Sheriff Principal to upset the decisions of the Sheriff Substitute and to the exclusive right of the legal profession to audience in these courts. Because of the growing influence of English law in Scotland and its effect on Scottish law, witnesses were examined on practice and procedure in English courts and in Indian courts which, like the Scottish courts,

administered law which was a blend of English and native law. The
volume therefore, has a special interest not only for specialists in
Scottish law but for all concerned with the influence of English law
on national legal codes.

Original references
Volume 11

1868–69	[4125] XXV	Courts of Law in Scotland, Royal Com., 1st Rep., mins. of ev.
	[4188]	Courts of Law in Scotland, Royal Com., 2nd Rep., mins. of ev.

Volume 12

1870	[C.36] XVIII	Courts of Law in Scotland, Royal Com., 3rd Rep., mins. of ev. and index.
	[C.175]	Courts of Law in Scotland, Royal Com., 4th Rep. and appendix.
	[C.175–I]	Courts of Law in Scotland, Royal Com., appendix.
1871	[C.260] XX	Courts of Law in Scotland, Royal Com., 5th Rep., appendix and general index.

Legal Administration: General Volume 13

FIRST, SECOND, THIRD, FOURTH AND FIFTH REPORTS OF THE ROYAL
COMMISSION ON THE JUDICATURE WITH MINUTES OF EVIDENCE AND
APPENDICES, 1868–1874

The reform of legal administration had been undertaken largely on
a piecemeal basis. The jurisdiction of existing courts had in some
cases been extended and some new courts formed to meet the changing needs of society, but there had been no coordinated reform of
the entire system. The Royal Commission was appointed to rectify
this defect and it examined the functions of the superior assize and
county courts with a view to rationalizing the entire structure of
legal administration in the light of modern requirements. Evidence
on the working of the system was collected primarily by way of
questionnaires which were sent to leading lawyers and businessmen.
The difficulties placed in the way of litigants by the over-rigid
division between Courts of Common Law and Courts of Equity
was discussed as well as the problems created by the existence of
twelve superior courts, some with ill-defined and overlapping
jurisdiction. The commission's first report was unanimous in re-
commending the complete reorganization of the superior courts. It
recommended that the existing courts should be replaced by two
new courts, a High Court composed of five divisions, and a Court
of Appeal. This major reform was adopted in 1873 and forms the
basis for the present organization of the Supreme Court of Judicature. The commissioners could not reach unanimity on what

should be done to reform the assize system and the county courts. Barristers opposed the extension of county court jurisdiction as they feared that it would reduce the civil business of the assize courts, before which they had exclusive right of audience. Businessmen urged that the courts should adapt to the needs of the business community and recommended that litigation should be cheap and speedy. Some urged that commercial courts on the continental model should be introduced and evidence was presented on the work of such courts. The commission's final reports recommended the extension of county court jurisdiction and the alteration of assize circuits but they opposed the establishment of commercial courts.

Original references

1868–69	[4130] XXV	The Judicature, Royal Com. 1st Rep.
1872	[C.631] XX	The Judicature, Royal Com. 2nd Rep., Vol. I.
	[C.631–I]	The Judicature, Royal Com. 2nd Rep., Vol. II, Part I and Part II, mins. of ev.
1874	[C.957] XXIV	The Judicature, Royal Com. 3rd Rep.
	[C.957–I]	The Judicature, Royal Com. appendix to 3rd Rep., mins. of ev. and appendix.
	[C.984]	The Judicature, Royal Com. 3rd Rep. and appendix.
	[C.984–I]	The Judicature, Royal Com. appendix to 4th Rep. with evidence.
	[C.1090]	The Judicature, Royal Com. Vol. I, 5th and final Rep. Vol. II., 1st and 2nd appendices and mins. of ev.

Legal Administration: General Volume 14

FIRST AND SECOND REPORTS OF THE ROYAL COMMISSION ON ADMINISTRA-
TIVE DEPARTMENTS OF THE COURTS OF JUSTICE AND REPORT FROM THE
SELECT COMMITTEE OF THE HOUSE OF LORDS ON APPELLATE JURISDICTION
WITH MINUTES OF EVIDENCE, APPENDICES AND INDEX, 1872–1874

The Select Committee of the House of Lords on appellate jurisdiction examined the functions of the House of Lords as the final court of appeal from decisions of United Kingdom courts and of the Privy Council as the final court of review for the decisions of Indian and colonial courts. Much of the evidence deals with the attitude of the colonies to right of appeal from their courts to the Privy Council. The right was popular especially in India but the colonists resented the long delays involved in taking a case to the Privy Council. The question of Scottish appeals to the House of Lords was discussed. Most of the witnesses felt that they should continue but considered that the competence of the House in Scottish law cases should be increased by the appointment of additional Scottish Law Lords. The committee recommended that the Law Lords and the Judicial Committee of the Privy Council should be amalgamated. The Royal

Commission on the administrative departments of the Courts of Justice examined the offices of both Common Law and Chancery courts. The history and functions of the offices were described and commented on. The recommendations of previous inquiries and the main provisions of legislation affecting the offices were summarized. The commissioners visited many of the offices during the course of their investigations and they interviewed officials on their duties and conditions of employment. The commission recommended that Court officials should be made civil servants and that sinecure offices should be abolished.

Original references

1872	(325) VII	Appellate jurisdiction, Sel. Cttee. HL. Rep., mins. of ev., appendix and index.
1874	[C.949] XXIV	Courts of Justice, Administrative Departments, Royal Com. 1st Rep. and appendix.
	[C.1107]	Courts of Justice, Administrative Departments, Royal Com. 2nd Rep., ev., appendix.

Legal Administration: General Volume 15

ROYAL COMMISSION ON THE ADMINISTRATIVE DEPARTMENTS OF THE COURTS OF JUSTICE, MINUTES OF EVIDENCE, APPENDICES AND INDEX, 1875

The commission examined court officials, lawyers and politicians on recruitment, conditions of employment and duties of officials of Chancery, Common Law, Lunacy, Admiralty, Central Criminal and Assize Courts. The duties of Probate registrars and County Court officers were also investigated. The officials were shown to be trustworthy and well qualified for their positions, but were appointed by means of an elaborate patronage system and in some cases received excessively high salaries for short working hours. Evidence was given by solicitors that a large number of court offices were redundant and that others could easily be amalgamated. The solicitors were especially critical of the Probate and Bankruptcy Court offices. Among the politicians who gave evidence were Hugh Childers, who recommended the establishment of a department of justice, James Stansfeld, who urged that the patronage system of appointments should be abolished and Lord Selborne, who had done much to reform legal administration earlier in the century. Lord Selborne considered that the existing administrative structure of the court offices should be retained but reformed. The volume together with IUP volume Legal Administration 14 which contains the commissioners' first and second reports provides detailed and extensive information on the history, organization and functions of the various court offices.

Original reference
1875   [C.1245] XXX   Courts of Justice, Administrative Departments, Royal Com. mins. of ev., appendices and index.

Legal Administration: General Volume 16
REPORT FROM THE SELECT COMMITTEE ON COUNTY COURTS JURISDICTION (NO. 2) BILL AND OTHER REPORTS ON THE ADMINISTRATION OF JUSTICE WITH MINUTES OF EVIDENCE, APPENDICES AND INDEX, 1878–1887

The failure of the Royal Commission on the Judicature to issue an agreed report on the future development of the County Courts led to the submission to parliament of several bills aimed at increasing the jurisdiction of these courts. The Select Committee on County Courts' jurisdiction was appointed to examine the advisability of enacting such legislation. The committee examined the functions of the County Court and examined means by which they could be extended. The principle of increasing County Court jurisdiction was opposed by many members of the Bar who feared that it would endanger their livelihood since solicitors had the right of audience in county courts. Doubts were also expressed regarding the impartiality of judges who resided permanently in the areas in which their court sat. The committee recommended the extension of County Court jurisdiction in matters of common law but not in equity. The volume includes reports dealing with the re-organization of court offices consequent to the enactment of the judicature act and on the distribution of business in the Courts and Chambers of the Chancery division of the Supreme Court of Judicature. The evidence presented to these inquiries was given mainly by court officials and it provides a graphic account of court procedure and practice and of the changes in legal administration brought about by the Judicature Act.

Original references
1878   (267) XI   County Courts Jurisdiction (No. 2) Bill, Sel. Cttee. Rep., mins. of ev., appendix and index.

1878	[C.2064] XXV	Practice at the chambers of the Judges of the Queen's Bench, Common Pleas, and Exchequer Divisions, Cttee. of Judges, Rep.
	[C.2067]	Judicature Acts, effects on administrative offices of the Court of Justice, Cttee. Rep., mins. of ev.
1878	(311) LXIII	Assizes and Sessions, Rep. made by the Judges to the Lord Chancellor.
1886	(92) LIII	High Court of Justice (Chancery Division), distribution of business, Departmental Cttee. Rep., mins. of ev. and appendix.
1887	(181) LXVII	Central Office of the Supreme Court of Judicature Cttee. Rep. and mins. of ev.

Civil Disorder

J. Stevenson

Commentary

Introduction

A number of studies have shown that civil disorder was common in Britain, at least from the eighteenth century. Disturbances took place on a number of issues, including food prices, recruiting, religion, and enclosures, amongst others.[1] Food riots were the commonest form of disorder and one authority has claimed that by the latter part of the eighteenth century food riots were 'endemic', occurring at times of harvest shortage in many different parts of the country.[2] The frequency of riots in both town and country in the late eighteenth and early nineteenth centuries, suggests that riots were almost an accepted part of life in this period. In the large towns and cities, such as Edinburgh, Dublin, Birmingham, and London, the urban 'mob' seems to have made frequent interventions in both political and religious affairs.[3] The London mob in particular was notorious for its manifestations of popular feeling and the collusion which often took place between it and local politicians.[4] Its most celebrated action was in the Gordon Riots of 1780, when the mob caused extensive damage in the centre of London and defied the authorities for almost a week. Over four hundred people were either killed or executed as a result of the riots.[5] Similar instances of rioting outside London were the Porteus riots in Edinburgh in 1736 and the Priestley riots in Birmingham in 1791.[6] However, the nature of disorder was changing by the latter years of the century, for the Priestley riots themselves have been described as the 'last great action of an eighteenth century mob'.[7]

Two major developments from the end of the eighteenth century began to change the pattern of disorder and the response of government towards it. Disorder tended to become more serious with the growth of population and the development of industry and agriculture. Disorder was increasingly the outcome of economic distress, affecting large areas and considerable numbers of people. The first major disturbances of this type were the severe and

---

1 See G. Rudé, *The Crowd in History* (New York, 1964) and J. Stevenson and R. Quinault (eds.), *Popular Protest and Public Order* (London, 1975). Also E. P. Thompson, *The Making of the English Working Class* (London, 1968), pp. 64-83.

2 R. B. Rose, 'Eighteenth Century Price Riots and Public Policy in England', *International Review of Social History*, vi (1961) p. 283.

3 G. Rudé, *The Crowd in History* (New York, 1964).

4 G. Rudé, 'The London "Mob" of the Eighteenth Century', *Historical Journal*, ii (1959).

5 G. Rudé, 'The Gordon Riots', *Transactions of the Royal Historical Society*, vi (1956); J. P. de Castro, *The Gordon Riots* (Oxford, 1926).

6 See T. C. Smout, *A History of the Scottish People, 1560-1830* (London, 1969) for riots in Edinburgh; for Birmingham, see R. B. Rose, 'The Priestley Riots of 1791', *Past and Present*, xviii, (1960).

7 E. P. Thompson, *The Making of the English Working Class* (London, 1968), p. 79.

prolonged Luddite disturbances, which affected the north and midlands of England between 1810 and 1817, and required a force of 12,000 troops to contain them.[8] The post-war period also saw rioting in the agricultural districts, especially in East Anglia, as well as in several manufacturing areas. The most severe agricultural riots affected the southern counties in 1830-2. Severely repressive measures, including transportation were required to deal with them.[9]

A second factor was the growing fear on the part of the authorities that disorder could be put to political ends. From the time of Wilkes, it was apparent that the mob could be used as an instrument of political pressure and, following the French Revolution, as an instrument of revolutionary insurrection. Experience both in Ireland in 1798 and in the post-war period in Britain suggested that the fear of an insurrection was not to be neglected. Thus the government took a firm hand with any large scale assemblies or meetings, particularly when called for reform or other political purposes. The famous Peterloo 'massacre' in St. Peter's Fields in Manchester in 1819 arose out of the government's attempts to disperse a reform meeting. Increasingly, however, the authorities needed to find a more effective way of dealing with mass meetings and political demonstrations, such as took place during the reform crisis of 1831-2.[10]

In the eighteenth century the government had only the parochial authorities and the army with which to keep public order. But the need for greater flexibility and prevention turned attention towards the need for an effective police force to handle popular disorder. A nucleus of professional police was built up in London at the Bow Street office and the seven police offices set up under the Middlesex Justices' Act of 1792.[11] But in the rest of the country the army and auxiliary forces such as the Yeomanry and militia remained of importance until the introduction of professional police forces modelled on the Metropolitan Police.[12] This force was set up in 1829 and was soon copied in most other boroughs in the British Isles. Rural police forces were set up from 1840 and the armed forces were able to assume a supporting role in relation to civil disorder. Thus increasingly from this period, the government was concerned to establish and regulate the function of the police

8   See F. O. Darvell, *Popular Disturbances and Public Order in Regency England* (London, 1934).

9   E. J. Hobsbawm and G. Rudé, *Captain Swing* (London, 1969).

10 See D. Read, *Peterloo* (Manchester, 1957); G. Rudé, 'Rural and Urban Disturbances on the eve of the Great Reform Bill, 1830-31', *Past and Present*, xxxvii, (1967).

11 See L. Radzinowitz, *A History of English Criminal Law*, (London, 1956), Volume II.

12 See J. R. Western, 'The Volunteer as an Anti-Revolutionary Force', *English Historical Review*, lxxi, (1956); O. Teichman, 'The Yeomanry as an aid to the Civil Power, 1795-1867', *Journal of the Society for Army Historical Research*, xix (1940).

in relation to the various forms of civil disorder present in the nineteenth century.

The parliamentary papers illustrate the variety of the threats to public order with which the government had to deal in the nineteenth century. These ranged from the threats posed by political societies such as the Orange lodges and the International Association of Workmen, to rural disturbances in South Wales; and from political demonstrations in London to sectarian conflict in Ireland. These papers are concerned with the various responses made by the government to these events.

The 1835 Inquiry into the Orange Lodges in Britain and Ireland

According to the authoritative study by Dr. H. Senior of Orangeism in Ireland and Britain between 1795 and 1836, the Irish Orange lodges originated amongst the Ulster protestant peasantry around 1795 as a reaction to the increasing pressure from catholic political and economic movements.[13] The organisation acquired legitimacy from the support of the protestant gentry and during the rebellion of 1798 and the Act of Union came to be regarded as the principal bastion of the 'protestant interest'. Its primary political aim was to prevent Catholic Emancipation from passing through the British Parliament and in doing so it became associated with ultra-Tory opinion in Britain. The order came under scrutiny in 1825, when it was forced to dissolve because of the government's Unlawful Societies Act. Supporters of the catholic cause alleged that the Orange order was responsible for outrages in Ulster and was a dangerous secret society.

This act, however, only had force for three years, and the order was reconstituted under the threat of Catholic Emancipation becoming law. It built up its strength through Brunswick clubs, recruited from former Orangemen and with Orange peers, such as the Earl of Enniskillen, at their head. The movement was linked to the English Orange lodges by the Imperial Grand Master, the Duke of Cumberland. In spite of the passing of Catholic Emancipation in 1829, the organisation continued to flourish as an ally of ultra-Toryism in Britain and as defender of the protestant ascendancy in Ireland. Indeed the re-arming of the volunteers to deal with the tithe war in Ireland gave the order added prestige.

To Whig politicians, the Irish lodges seemed to defy the law with their processions and had irritated Whig opinion by their opposition to reform in England. It was, however, only incidental to the investigation of British Orange lodges that the whole of the movement was investigated. As Dr.

13 H. Senior, *Orangeism in Ireland and Britain, 1795-1836*, (London, 1966).

Senior has written:

> 'It is doubtful that the second Melbourne government would have taken special measures against the Irish movement had it not been for the peculiar activities of the British lodges...'[14]

It is to the history of the British lodges that we need to turn for an explanation of the investigation of the movement.

The first British Orange lodges were set up in Lancashire around 1800 as ex-soldiers' clubs. Gradually they enrolled civilian members and began to attract influential Tory support from men such as the Duke of York and the Duke of Cumberland. From an early date, their practice of administering oaths to members and their political nature led to attacks upon them from Whigs such as Whitbread on the grounds that they were rendered illegal by an act of 1799.[15] Timely revision of their rules, however, enabled the lodges to survive and, according to Dr. Senior, the movement by 1822 was established in most industrial areas and had lodges in the army. It is estimated there were three hundred lodges and about six thousand members.

In the face of Catholic Emancipation the movement embarked on an attempt to win popular support by mass meetings. Unable to prevent the passing of the Bill, the Orange order in Britain turned to a soldier and political adventurer, William Blennerhasset Fairman, to organise popular support. He set about lobbying influential men whom he thought would favour the Orange cause and made tours of the midlands, north, and Scotland. In doing so Colonel Fairman deliberately exaggerated the strength of the Orange order and presented it as an ultra-Tory ally. In his letters to his upper class friends, such as Lord Londonderry, he hinted at military action and a possible *coup d'état*. According to Dr. Senior, this was 'evidence of earnest reflections on the subject, but nothing more.'[16] However, the Whig government in 1835 was increasingly under pressure from Irish and radical members for an investigation into the activities of the British movement and Colonel Fairman. His tours through the country and his incautious language forced the government to accede to pressure and mount an investigation of the movement.

Therefore two Select Committees were set up to investigate the Orange lodges in Britain and Ireland. The committee investigating the British and colonial lodges contained representatives of the Orangemen and of their opponents, including Joseph Hume, the radical M.P. who had led the campaign for an inquiry into the movement. This committee took evidence from many prominent persons connected with the movement in Britain, including Lord Kenyon, the Deputy Grand Master of England and Wales. The commit-

---

14   H. Senior, *op. cit.*, p. 253.

15   H. Senior, *op. cit.*, pp. 169-70.

16   H. Senior, *op. cit.*, p. 272.

tee fully investigated the procedure and ritual of the movement, but concentrated upon its political objectives and its influence in the army. On the former, the committee found that the order had 'a decidedly political character' and expressed disapproval of its links with the King's brother, the Duke of Cumberland.[17] The presence of the order in the army was revealed and it was this feature which prompted the damning conclusion of the report:

'A great political body thus organised in the ranks of the army, and in every part of the British empire, is a formidable power at any time and under any circumstances; but when Your Committee look to the political tendency of the measures of the Orange Societies in England and Ireland, and particularly to the language contained in addresses to the public, and in the correspondence with the grand officers of the Institution, and consider the possible use that might be made of such an organised power, its suppression becomes, in their opinion, imperatively necessary.'[18]

Even before the committee reported on 7 September 1835, Joseph Hume and the radicals attempted to secure the suppression of the order by gathering correspondence which further prejudiced it. Hume deliberately accepted Fairman's exaggerations of the movement's strength in order to ease its suppression. In fact, Dr. Senior has concluded that the real strength of the order in the army was no more than a few hundred members scattered throughout the country and that the possibility of a rising by the Orange order in Britain was negligible.[19] But the report and Hume's pressure led the government to abolish the order. Faced with the prospect of legislation, the Duke of Cumberland dissolved the British lodges in February 1836.

The Select Committee on the Irish lodges also contained a mixture of opinions and views. Of the twenty-seven members, eight could be counted as supporters of Orangeism and twelve as opponents, including O'Connell. Evidence was taken from prominent Orangemen, such as William Venner and William Blacker, and from the catholic side with the examination of the Irish reformer William Sharman Crawford. An extensive examination of the origins, nature, and expansion of the Irish movement resulted. The evidence was submitted without a conclusion, possibly because of disagreement among the committee members. But the minutes of evidence and the appendices presented a damaging picture of the Irish situation. The appendices gave the rules and ritual of the lodges, which were important in deciding whether the movement was an unlawful society in administering oaths. Lists

17   Civil Disorder: *Report from the Select Committee on Orange Institutions in Great Britain and the Colonies with Minutes of Evidence*. H.C. 1835 (605) XVII; IUP Crime and Punishment: Civil Disorder 1, p. xxvii.

18   *Report from the Select Committee on Orange Institutions in Great Britain and the Colonies*, *op. cit.*, p. xxvii.

19   H. Senior, *op. cit.*, pp. 271-72.

of officers were drawn up and the formidable nature of the Irish movement shown. The Third Report of the committee contained a comparison of the evidence given by supporters and opponents of the order. It concentrated upon the Protestant-Catholic controversy and the outrages committed on both sides.

The picture which was presented of the Orange order in Ireland was near to the reality of the situation. It was shown that the Orange lodges controlled the Irish Yeomanry, had lodges in the army, enjoyed considerable immunity from justice, and were frequently involved in civil disorder. With the report on the British lodges, the government was compelled to act against the movement in Ireland. As Dr. Senior has concluded:

'The Orangemen represented a distinct interest of their own which made them actively oppose any government measures designed to conciliate the Catholic majority in Ireland. They were thus both a bastion to revolution and an obstacle to compromise.'[20]

Ireland was therefore included in the proposed legislation and the movement was dissolved in Ireland by the Duke of Cumberland's command as Grand Master.

The Rebecca riots and the Reports of 1839-44

Between 1839 and 1844 there were a number of disturbances in the western counties of South Wales, characterised by attacks upon turnpike toll-gates and other disorders. The riots were known as the 'Rebecca riots' from the slogan adopted from Genesis 24: 'let thy seed possess the gate of those which hate them'. The disturbances were sparked off by the imposition of heavy toll-charges on the turnpike roads in the area and the multiplication of toll-gates. Their background, as revealed by the reports, however, was one of general social and economic discontent which derived from the poverty, isolation and backwardness of the area.

That the riots took the form of attacks upon toll-gates has been described by D. Williams as 'almost accidental'. He has written that:

'The fundamental cause of the rioting was poverty, owing to the pressure of a greatly increased population on a backward economy, intensified by the industrial depression which had lowered the demand for agricultural produce.'[21]

20   H. Senior, *op. cit.*, p. 284.

21   D. Williams, 'Chartism in Wales' p. 245, in A. Briggs (ed.), *Chartist Studies* (London, 1959). On the Welsh background to the riots see D. J. V. Jones, *Before Rebecca* (London, 1973).

This poverty led to grievances about the county rate, court fees, and the operation of the new Poor Law, as well as turnpike tolls. In a heavily non-conformist area the tithe was also a considerable source of discontent. To these discontents were added a number of bad harvests which made the years 1837-9 disturbed in many parts of Britain. The riots also coincided with the first phase of the Chartist agitation in South Wales, which culminated in the Newport 'rising' on 30 April 1839.

The riots started in January 1839 when four new turnpike gates were constructed on the Carmarthen-Pembrokeshire border: almost immediately two of the gates were destroyed by a gang of men with blackened faces and wearing female clothes. They quickly acquired the name of 'Rebecca and her daughters' from the local populace, and like the names of 'Ned Ludd' and 'Captain Swing' they became the mythical authors of the disturbances. The first spate of disorders subsided only to break out anew in the winter of 1842, a period of economic depression. In this phase, more generalized attacks took place, not only on toll-gates, but upon corn-stacks, salmon weirs, and warehouses, culminating in an assault upon Carmarthen workhouse in June 1843. This phase also included attacks upon magistrates, landowners, parsons, and farmers. The disturbances spread to affect not only Carmarthenshire, Pembrokeshire, and the southern part of Cardiganshire, but Radnorshire, Brecknock, and Glamorgan. As the attacks spread eastward they began to involve industrial workmen, such as coalminers and iron-workers. Eventually the use of troops and local men as Special Constables, formed in defence associations, brought the disturbances to an end.

The government inquiry into the situation was set in motion in October 1843. Three commissioners were sent into the affected district to investigate the causes of the disturbances. They moved from county to county, collecting evidence on a wide range of subjects, such as living standards, local administration, and the state of education and religion. The inquiries were concluded in December 1843 and the report was submitted in March 1844. The commissioners' general summary of the causes of the disturbances was that they were of a general nature; they wrote:

'It is a matter of great satisfaction to state our belief that the disturbances of the country, though so widely extended, were not connected with political causes, and that nothing like a general spirit of disaffection, or organised hostility to the laws, pervaded the community. The excitement having been first stimulated by a sense of local grievances, gradually spread to other districts in which similar complaints existed, and the spirit once roused, was perverted in some instances by evil disposed persons to aggressions of a more extensive and systematic kind.'[22]

22   Civil Disorder: *Report from the Royal Commission on Turnpike roads and outrages in South Wales*. H.C. 1844 (531) XVI; IUP Civil Disorder 2, p. 1.

This was an important conclusion, for the government had suspected some link between the Chartists and the Rebecca riots. As the report showed there was virtually no direct link at all. Though modern writers have found one or two men who might have acted in both movements, they also have concluded that the only real link between the movements was that they sprang from common causes of poverty and backwardness.[23]

The report paid particular attention to the operation of the trusts in the area and the way in which the social and economic life of the area had been disrupted by the new tolls. It also raised the other social and economic grievances which the region had displayed. The final conclusions were that the backwardness of the area, its lack of English speaking people, and the weakness of the established church had contributed to the outbreak of disorder. The report hoped for some improvement in these general features of the area, but its principal recommendation was that the turnpike trusts should be consolidated and administered by county Road Boards. Parliament did act eventually to have tolls made uniform and to reduce their number.

The riots were suppressed by the action of the 'principal inhabitants' who under the aegis of the government formed themselves into 'associations for the protection of life and property'.[24] The use of self-defence associations formed of the respectable inhabitants of a disturbed town or district was a common means of suppressing disorders in the first half of the nineteenth century. In this case, the Home Office notified the Lord Lieutenants of the affected counties and urged them to form associations both to prevent and suppress disorder. Similarly, in informing magistrates of the need and the powers to suppress drilling, training, and the illegal traffic in arms, it was the Home Office which took the lead.

The Hyde Park disturbances of 1855 and the Report of 1856.

The disturbances which took place in Hyde Park in June and July 1855 had their origin in popular opposition to sabbatarian legislation, which would have prohibited Sunday trading in the capital. To protest against this legislation large crowds assembled in Hyde Park on four consecutive Sundays from 24 June 1855. The Metropolitan Police Commissioner, Sir Richard Mayne, tried to prevent these assemblies by issuing notices which declared the use of Hyde Park for popular demonstrations illegal. These were widely regarded as being of dubious legality and were ignored, so that the demonstrations also

23   D. Williams, *op. cit.*; G. Rudé, *The Crowd in History, op. cit.*, pp. 156-163; D. Williams, *The Rebecca Riots* (Cardiff, 1953).

24   *Correspondence on Disturbed Districts*, H.C. 1839 (299) XXXVIII; IUP Civil Disorder 2.

became an assertion of the right to assemble in the London parks. This confrontation led to a particularly bitter clash on the second Sunday of demonstrations, 1 July, when an estimated 150,000 people assembled in the park in defiance of Mayne's notices and began to heckle and jeer at wealthy passers-by. The police on duty endured a certain amount of provocation, but eventually they baton-charged the crowd and took 72 prisoners. Although there were further demonstrations, none provoked as fierce a reaction by the police. The press took up the issue of police brutality and the government was forced to commission an inquiry.[25]

After considerable delay, the inquiry began. A number of serious allegations were made about the administration and conduct of the police at the 1 July demonstration. The number of police assembled to deal with the demonstration seemed excessive and the absence of the police commissioner on the spot was criticised. When questioned upon this, Sir Richard Mayne admitted that he remained at Whitehall throughout the demonstration and would not expand upon his reasons for this conduct.[26] The officer on the spot, Superintendent Hughes, was accused of undue excitement, of improper language, and of ordering his men to use their staves too early.[27] The report admitted that some policemen had acted badly, but on the whole asserted its confidence in the force.[28]

Dr. B. Harrison has thrown a great deal of light upon the riots and the commission which followed. In particular he has found an explanation for the fierce reaction of the police to the demonstration and for Sir Richard's conduct on the day in question. Prior to the demonstration of 1 July, the government had received intelligence from the French police, through the British ambassador in Paris, that the demonstration might be used by a group of Chartist agitators and French refugees to initiate an insurrection. It was this intelligence which determined the disposition and action of the forces on 1 July. A large force was assembled at the park in anticipation of a serious threat to the security of the capital. Sir Richard Mayne had therefore remained in his head-quarters in Whitehall where he could direct operations more easily than from the park itself. The severity of the police response was also explained by this information. At the commission Sir Richard Mayne had been unable to reveal anything of this and the government itself had delayed the commission so as not to compromise itself or the police. In essence the

25   B. Harrison, 'The Sunday Trading Riots of 1855', *Historical Journal*, viii (1965), p. 223.

26   Civil Disorder: *Report from the Royal Commission on the alleged disturbances in Hyde Park and on the conduct of the Police*, H.C. 1856 (2016) XXIII; IUP Civil Disorder 3, pp. 239-240.

27   *Ibid.*, pp. 459-75.

28   *Ibid.*, p. xxx.

report was an embarrassment to the government and they took little action on it.[29]

On the right to assemble in the public parks in London, the commission was more forthright. It declared that Hyde Park was not an appropriate place for popular demonstrations and upheld the right of the police to disperse an assembly in the park. This ruling was not generally accepted and as a result there were a number of further challenges to it. The largest of these was at the Reform Meeting of July 1866 when a mob tore down the railings of Hyde Park in defiance of the law. Eventually legislation on the issue was passed in 1872 which granted the right to assemble in Hyde Park under certain restrictions.[30]

Disorder and Reports, 1864-95.

A miscellany of government reports on civil disorder in Britain were produced between 1864 and 1895, covering a number of aspects of the control of civil disorder. Several of these involved the relationship of the police to political or other demonstrations. The papers on the Primrose Hill meeting concerned the actions of the police at a political meeting in April 1864. This meeting followed Garibaldi's visit to London early in 1864 where he was greeted by very large and enthusiastic crowds. Fearing disorders at further meetings in the provincial towns and cities, the government had asked Garibaldi to leave the country. This provoked the protest meeting on Primrose Hill, organised by the London Workingmen's reception committee and a middle-class reception committee led by Edmund Beales. The ostensible purpose of the meeting was to celebrate the tercentenary of Shakespeare, but it was essentially a meeting to protest at Garibaldi's expulsion. As the meeting was to take place in a public park, the police mustered a force of 223 constables who violently dispersed the crowds. As a result Edmund Beales formed the Reform League who sought to ensure the right of peaceful meetings in public parks. It was this group who played an important part in securing this right through their demonstrations in London in 1866 and 1867.[31] The papers in the volume illustrate the police's determination to suppress the meetings in 1864 and 1866 which took place in public parks.[32]

Similarly, the right to demonstrate in Trafalgar Square was under attack from the government and the police. Such right as existed was customary

29 B. Harrison, *op. cit.*, pp. 234-5.

30 D. Williams, *Keeping the Peace* (London, 1967), pp. 72-3.

31 D. Williams, *op. cit.*, p. 72.

32 Civil Disorder: *Primrose Hill Meeting, police instructions*, paper, H.C. 1864 (252) XLVIII; *Police Orders for Reform League Meeting in Hyde Park, 1866*, H.C. 1888 (49) LXXXII, IUP Civil Disorder 4, pp. 9-10, 13-14, 143-44.

rather than enshrined in the statute book and the issue came to a head in the disturbances of 8 February 1886. These arose from a clash of meetings held in the square, for separate rallies had been called by the Labourers' League, by the Fair Trade League, and by Hyndman's Social Democratic Federation. The last group was particularly well attended and was addressed by speeches from leading socialists, including John Burns and Hyndman himself. Afterwards a mob moved from the square and attacked property in the prosperous streets of Pall Mall, St. James's, Piccadilly, Oxford Street, and Regent Street. The police were powerless for several hours to prevent the rioters from looting shops and smashing windows and street lamps.[33] Though the fundamental cause of the riots was distress amongst the unemployed in London, there was considerable criticism of the failure of the police to prevent the disturbances.

As a result, a Select Committee was set up by the Home Secretary, Mr. H. C. E. Childers, on 13 February. It reported on 22 February and criticised the police arrangements to deal with the demonstration. It described them as 'most unsatisfactory' and led directly to the resignation of Sir Edmund Henderson, the Metropolitan Police Commissioner.[34] He was replaced by Sir Charles Warren, a stern, military man, who took a much tougher policy with demonstrations in Trafalgar Square. He banned organised processions from approaching the square and met attempts to challenge these bans by assembling large forces of police and troops. Thus he used a force of 2,373 police to deal with a meeting of Social Democratic supporters on 29 August 1886. On 13 November 1887 he used troops to back up the police in driving back large crowds who attempted to assemble in the square.[55] This action was variously described as 'Bloody Sunday' or 'the defence of Trafalgar Square'.[36]

Eventually after considerable debate, including several court actions, a policy of non-interference in the use of Trafalgar Square for demonstrations was adopted, though the government reserved the right to prevent meetings if this was absolutely necessary.[37]

The other major disturbance which attracted attention from the government in this period was the riot at Ackton Hall Colliery, near Featherstone in Yorkshire, on 7 September 1893. A coal strike in the Yorkshire collieries from July 1893 had required policemen to remain on duty at colliery gates to prevent clashes between pickets and strike-breakers. However, the police

33 D. Williams, *Keeping the Peace*, *op. cit.*, pp. 74-5.

34 Civil Disorder: *The Origin and Character of the Disturbances which took place in the Metropolis on Monday, 8th February*, H.C. 1886 (C. 4665) XXXIV; IUP Civil Disorder 4, p. 34.

35 D. Williams, *op. cit.*, p. 45, 77-8.

36 D. Williams, *op. cit.*, pp. 74-8.

37 D. Williams, *op. cit.*, pp. 79-85.

were needed from 4 September to keep the peace at the Doncaster Races. As a result troops were drafted in to replace them. On 7 September a group of miners demonstrated at the colliery against the use of the troops and began to assault the soldiers with stones and abuse. The magistrate in charge was forced to read the Riot Act. Before the statutory hour had expired, the troops were ordered to open fire by their commander, Captain Baker, and as a result two people were killed. At the inquests which followed, one jury said that the firing was justified, whilst the other said it was not. As a result the Home Secretary set up a Special Commission, consisting of two members of parliament and a judge. The inquiry opened on 19 October and reported on 6 December.

The report criticised the removal of the West Yorkshire police and also condemned the size of the detachment of troops sent to the area. The major findings were that the circumstances justified reading the Riot Act and opening fire, even before the hour had elapsed from the reading of the Act. The report stressed in this context that the magistrate and troops in such situations must act on the principle of doing only what was 'absolutely necessary' to disperse a riot. Firearms, it was stressed, could only be used where it was necessary to protect persons and property from violent crimes. The commission made the point that the use of the Riot Act was incidental to the issue of the action taken by the troops. They could fire if it were 'absolutely necessary' without the Riot Act being read. The commission also took the view that innocent by-standers, hurt or killed in consequence of actions taken by the authorities, had no redress. The commission stressed that the troops should only be used as a last resort, as the civil power was primarily responsible for maintaining public order. These ground-rules for the activities of the army in dealing with civil disorder are substantially those which still apply today.[38]

Following this report, an interdepartmental committee deplored the use of unnecessary force in dealing with civil disorder and urged legislation to permit police and army co-operation.[39]

Two smaller issues dealt with in civil disorder reports of this period were the danger of the International Association of workmen causing disorder and legislation against Salvation Army processions on Sundays. The former was dealt with in correspondence between the Spanish and British governments on the danger to social order arising from the International Association and an

38   Civil Disorder: *Report of the Committee to inquire into the Circumstances connected with the Disturbances at Featherstone on 7th September 1893*, H.C. 1893-4 (C. 7234) XVII; IUP Civil Disorder 4, pp. 161-64.

39   Civil Disorder: *Report of the Interdepartmental Committee on riots*, H.C. 1895 (C. 7650) XXXV; IUP Civil Disorder 4, pp. 303-11.

extradition treaty between the countries to help suppress it.[40] The latter arose from a series of disturbances in the eighteen-eighties caused by Salvation Army processions and the hostility they provoked. As a result local magistrates attempted to prevent processions from taking place in their towns.[41]

The Riots in Northern Ireland, 1857-87.

The period from the eighteen fifties saw increasing sectarian violence in Northern Ireland. Where once disorders had been primarily rural in character, the growth of Belfast and Londonderry in the nineteenth century led to the development of working class areas in these cities which were sharply divided on sectarian lines and which frequently erupted into violence. The first serious riots of this nature to come to the notice of the government were the riots in July and September 1857. The report on these riots stressed the sectarian divisions within the working class areas of Belfast. There was criticism of the small number of Roman Catholic magistrates, and charges that the largely Protestant magistracy had acted slowly and with partiality.[42] Further sectarian disturbances in Belfast in 1864 promoted similar conclusions about the religious divisions in the working class areas. In this report, however, the commissioners complained of the poor representation of Roman Catholics in the police force, for only five men out of a force of one hundred and sixty were Roman Catholics.[43]

Disturbances occurred in July 1868 in Londonderry, when an aggravated election riot seems to have taken place. In the following year, the visit of Prince Arthur provoked a demonstration by the Apprentice Boys Association and rioting followed. Again the charge of partisanship was laid against the local police force. The inadequacy of the local police was roundly condemned with the words:

'The insufficiency of the local police for the suppression of riots was so clearly established by the evidence given before us, as to leave no doubt in our minds respecting it.'[44]

40 Civil Disorder: *Correspondence between the British and Spanish Governments respecting the International Society*, H.C. 1872 (C. 502) LXX; IUP Civil Disorder 4, pp. 17-22.

41 Civil Disorder: *Police and Sanitary Regulations (Torquay Harbour and District Bill, 1886)*, H.C. 1888 (215) LXXXI; IUP Civil Disorder 4, pp. 147-48.

42 Civil Disorder: *Report of the Commissioners of Inquiry into the origin and character of the Riots in Belfast*, H.C. 1857-8 (2309) XXVI; IUP Civil Disorder 7, p. 14.

43 Civil Disorder: *Report of the Commissioners of Inquiry, 1864, respecting the Magisterial and Police Jurisdiction, Arrangements and Establishment of the Borough of Belfast*, H.C. 1865 (3466) XXVIII; IUP Civil Disorder 7, p. 331.

44 Civil Disorder: *Report of the Commissioners of Inquiry, 1869, into the Riots and Disturbances in the City of Londonderry*, H.C. 1870 (C. 5) XXXII; IUP Civil Disorder 7, p. 729.

As a result of these reports the local police forces in Belfast and Londonderry were disbanded and the Royal Irish Constabulary incorporated them.

Further sectarian rioting took place in November 1883 at Londonderry. These riots arose out of a public Nationalist procession and meeting in the city, attended by the Lord Mayor of Dublin. A detachment of Apprentice Boys or sympathisers tried to force their way into Corporation Hall where the meeting was taking place. The report commented on the continued sectarian hostility in Londonderry and urged the magistrates to prevent provocative processions and meetings.[45] Serious rioting also took place in Belfast between June and September 1886, so that on one occasion firearms had to be used. The disturbances resulted from the increasing tension in Ulster following Gladstone's 'Home Rule' proposals and the encouragement given to protestant militancy by the Tory party. The commission reported that the disorders largely sprang from the degree of sectarian conflict in the Northern Irish cities and the organisation of both sides into militant political organisations. The continuance of the disorders was blamed upon 'certain serious defects in the magisterial and police arrangements of the town.'[46] As a solution the majority report recommended the establishment of a single police authority under one man, answerable to the Irish Executive and to the Inspector General of the Royal Irish Constabulary. One commissioner disagreed with this recommendation and urged the setting up of a special constabulary.

The reports of this period from 1857 to 1887 illustrate the growing sectarian violence in the northern cities and the growth of militant protestant opposition to 'Home Rule'. The reports also dealt with the condition of the police forces in Belfast and Londonderry. A common theme in them was the partiality and inefficiency of the local forces. The reports therefore urged the elimination of local forces and the development of a strong centralised command structure which could deal effectively with disorder.

Conclusion

Though the parliamentary papers on civil disorder cover a wide range of issues, certain conclusions can be deduced from them about the nature of civil disorder in the nineteenth century and the problems facing the authorities in controlling it. The various papers and reports make clear two important features in the pattern of disorder. In the first place, serious

45 Civil Disorder: *Report of a Commission appointed to enquire into Certain Disturbances which took place in the City of Londonderry on 1st November 1883*, H.C. 1884, (C. 3954) XXXVIII; IUP Civil Disorder 8, p. 19.

46 Civil Disorder: *Report of the Belfast Riots Commissioners*, H.C. (C. 4925) XVIII, IUP Civil Disorder 8, p. 157.

disorder was increasingly an urban phenomenon, for after the rural disorders in South Wales in 1839-44, most of the serious disorders took place either in London or the manufacturing areas. Even in Northern Ireland the emphasis of sectarian conflict had moved from the rural areas, as shown in the reports on the Irish Orange order in 1835, to the expanding industrial centres, such as Belfast and Londonderry, as shown in the later reports. Such a development was a natural consequence of rapid population growth and urbanisation, so that popular protest and disorder became increasingly centred on the towns and cities of Britain and Ireland.

The nature and purpose of disorder was changing too, and this pattern is also revealed in the reports. The disturbances which took place in South Wales in 1839-44 were very similar in character to the riots of the eighteenth and early nineteenth centuries. They were disorders which were seen, initially at least, as acts of 'popular justice' in the same way as the classic food riots of the earlier period. They took place in an isolated and poor rural environment, similar to that in which rural outrages took place in Ireland. The later reports, however, show different patterns of disorder emerging, which were increasingly associated with political or industrial issues. Thus the commonest cause of the disorders covered in the later reports were popular demonstrations or political meetings. On the other hand, disorder frequently arose from industrial disputes, such as strikes, as shown in the disorder at Ackton Hall colliery. These two elements were to dominate the pattern of disorder in the twentieth century.

In the concerns of the authorities, there are also significant common factors. There was a constant concern with groups which might present a threat to the order or security of the country. Thus the Orange lodges were examined and dissolved in 1835 and similar organisations were examined in the reports on Irish disorders in the middle of the nineteenth century. Similarly, the government sought to suppress extreme socialist groups, such as the International Association of Working Men. But the most consistent theme of these reports and papers was the need to improve and define the relationship between the police and popular assemblies. In these papers and reports the regulation of processions, the right to demonstrate in public places, and the administration and conduct of police and army in relation to civil disorder were regulated and defined. Though the precise legal boundaries were not always fixed, at least working arrangements were made to accommodate public order and popular protest and assembly. Some of the decisions, such as on the role of the military in civil disturbances, were to provide the basis for operations up to the middle of the next century.

Thus both in the development of the nature of disorder and in the authorities' response to it, these papers reveal the emerging pattern of twentieth-century developments.

Bibliography

There is no satisfactory standard work which covers the subject of civil disorder in the nineteenth century. Introductions to the study of disorder can be found in G. Rudé, *The Crowd in History* (New York, 1964) and in his collection of essays *London and Paris in the Eighteenth Century* (London, 1971). Two articles on riots in the late eighteenth and early nineteenth centuries are useful; R. B. Rose, 'Eighteenth Century Price Riots and Public Policy in England', *International Review of Social History*, vi (1961); E. P. Thompson, 'The Moral Economy of the English Crowd in the Eighteenth Century', *Past and Present*, 1 (1971). E. P. Thompson *The Making of the English Working Class* (London, 1963) puts the pattern of disorder into a broader social and political context. Attempts to relate disorder with economic fluctuations have been made in W. W. Rostow, *British Economy of the Nineteenth Century* (Oxford, 1948) and 'Economic Fluctuations and Some Social Movements since 1800' in E. J. Hobsbawm, *Labouring Men* (London, 1964). An important attempt to put changes in the nature of disorder into a European context is C. Tilly 'Collective Violence in European Perspective' in H. D. Graham and T. R. Gurr (eds.), *The History of Violence in America* (New York, 1969). An interpretation of the development of English protest is contained in the same volume of essays, B. C. Roberts 'On the Origins and Resolution of English Working Class Protest'.

Specific episodes of disorder are dealt with in F. O. Darvall, *Public Order in Regency England* (Oxford, 1934); M. Thomis, *The Luddites* (London, 1971); and G. Rudé and E. J. Hobsbawm, *Captain Swing* (London, 1969). The Chartist period is best studied from this respect in F. C. Mather, *Public Order in the Age of the Chartists* (Oxford, 1959). There are no satisfactory treatments of disorder in the middle or late Victorian periods.

Secondary works which are essential for the disturbances dealt with in the IUP volumes are: on Orangeism, H. Senior, *Orangeism in Ireland and Britain, 1795-1836* (London, 1966); on the Rebecca riots, the standard work is D. Williams, *The Rebecca Riots* (Cardiff, 1953); for the Hyde Park disturbances in 1855, see B. Harrison, 'The Sunday Trading Riots of 1855', *Historical Journal*, viii (1965). Some aspects of later disturbances in London are touched upon in F. Sheppard, *London 1808-1870: The Infernal Wen* (London, 1948). For the Irish background, see F. S. L. Lyons, *Ireland Since the Famine* (London, 1971) and references, especially J. C. Beckett and R. E. Glassock (ed.), *Belfast: The Origin and Growth of an Industrial City* (Belfast, 1967) and E. Jones, *A Social Geography of Belfast* (London, 1960).

The administration of the authorities in relation to civil disorder is covered in D. Williams, *Keeping the Peace* (London, 1967) and L. Radzinowitz, *A History of English Criminal Law* (London, 1956).

The Documents
Civil Disorder

Civil Disorder Volume 1

REPORT FROM THE SELECT COMMITTEE ON ORANGE INSTITUTIONS IN GREAT· BRITAIN AND THE COLONIES WITH MINUTES OF EVIDENCE, APPENDIX AND INDEX, 1835

This Select Committee was established to examine the origin, nature, extent and tendency of British and Colonial Orange Institutions. The evidence collected, the committee reported, 'is amply sufficient to prove the existence of an organized institution, pervading Great Britain and her Colonies to an extent never contemplated as possible; and which your Committee considers highly injurious to the discipline of His Majesty's Army, and dangerous to the peace of Her Majesty's subjects.' The constitution, working procedures, ritual of introduction and objects of the institution are delineated in the report. In spite of their professed non-political character, the committee reported that the Orange Institution had 'a decidedly political character' and that all their proceedings had had some political object in view.

Evidence was received from Lord Kenyon, the Deputy Grand Master of England and Wales, Mr. Nucella, Commissioner for the Continent and many other persons connected with the British Orange Institution. The committee expressed strong disapproval of the high-ranking members of the institution which included the Duke of Cumberland (brother of the King), the Duke of Gordon and several members of the Houses of Lords and Commons, and made an unqualified recommendation for suppression of Orange societies.

Original reference
1835   (605) XVII   Orange institutions in Great Britain and the Colonies, Sel. Cttee. Rep., mins. of ev., appendices, index.

Civil Disorder Volume 2

REPORT FROM THE ROYAL COMMISSION ON TURNPIKE ROADS AND OUTRAGES IN SOUTH WALES AND CORRESPONDENCE ON DISTURBED DISTRICTS, PROTECTION ASSOCIATIONS AND ON ARMY AND TRAINING, 1839-1844

The heavy charges at toll-gates in South Wales acted as a catalyst for more general social and economic unrest in the area resulting in riots in 1839 and 1843. These riots were known as the 'Rebecca riots' from the slogan adopted from Genesis 24 referring to Rebecca, 'let thy seed possess the gate of those which hate them'. The commissioners visited many parts of South Wales in the course of their investigations into the causes of the riots and collected valuable sociological information on living standards, local administration, the management of the turnpike trusts and the state of education and religion. The report includes a history of the course of the riots. Two further papers in this volume deal with the formation of local self-protection associations during this period when the Chartist Movement was strong and antagonistic. In these papers the government indicated its willingness to supply arms to the 'principal inhabitants' if they formed protection associations. The remaining paper in the volume deals with the suppression of illegal sale of arms.

Original references

1839	(299) XXXVIII	Disturbed districts, formation of associations for the protection of life and property, correspondence.
	(559)	Disturbed districts, formation of associations for the protection of life and property, numbers formed, returns.
	(179)	Army and training, letters.
1844	[531] XVI	South Wales, Turnpike roads and outrages, R. Com. Rep.

Civil Disorder Volume 3

REPORT FROM THE ROYAL COMMISSION ON THE ALLEGED DISTURBANCES IN HYDE PARK AND ON THE CONDUCT OF THE POLICE WITH MINUTES OF EVIDENCE, APPENDIX AND INDEX, 1856

The disturbances in Hyde Park in July 1855 had their origin chiefly in popular opposition to a proposed bill to prevent Sunday trading. The crowds which had assembled were baton charged by the police and numbers were arrested. As a result of complaints that police had 'exceeded their duty, and used unnecessary force and violence' the commission of 1856 was set up. Its purpose was to examine the causes of the disturbances and to investigate the complaints. Nearly two hundred witnesses gave evidence on the events, including police officers and people who had been arrested during the riots. A detailed account of the actions of the crowd and of the police was given and the treatment of prisoners was condemned (in one instance forty-three persons were kept overnight in a badly ventilated cell, twenty four feet long, eight feet wide, eight feet high). Although satisfied that a number of policemen were guilty of misconduct, the report concluded that their confidence in the police force remained firm.

Original reference

| 1856 | [2016] XXIII | Disturbance in Hyde Park, Com. Rep., mins. of ev., appendix, index. |

Civil Disorder Volume 4

REPORTS AND PAPERS RELATING TO PUBLIC MEETINGS, DISTURBANCES
AND RIOTS IN ENGLAND AND WALES AND CORRESPONDENCE ON THE
INTERNATIONAL SOCIETY, 1864–1895

The papers in this volume deal with the control of public meetings by police and the causes for particular disturbances. Among the disturbances reported on were the Trafalgar Square riots of 1886 which resulted from an attempt by the Social Democratic Federation to turn a large Fair Trade meeting into an unemployment demonstration; the Primrose Hill meeting held to commemorate the tercentenary of Shakespeare; and the serious rioting at Featherstone over a colliery dispute. Among the problems raised by such riots was the use of military force to assist or replace the civil police. In 1895 an interdepartmental committee deplored the use of unnecessary force and urged legislation to permit police and army co-operation. Also included in this volume is correspondence between the Spanish and British governments on the danger to social order arising from the activities of the International Association of workmen and on an extradition treaty between these countries to help suppress the organization.

Original references

1864	(252) XLVIII	Primrose Hill meeting, police instructions, paper.
	(272)	Suppression of meetings for public discussion in parks, paper.
1872	[C.502] LXX	International Society, correspondence.
1875	(115) LXI	Mertyr Tydfil (Preservation of the Peace), correspondence.
1886	[C.4665] XXXIV	Origin and character of the disturbances (Metropolis), Com. Rep.
1886 Sess 1	(26) LIII	Origin and character of the disturbances (Metropolis), Com. Rep., memorandum.
1888	(49) LXXXII	Proclamation of Reform League meeting, Hyde Park, paper.
1888	(215) LXXXI	Torquay Bill 1886 (Public Procession, Sunday), paper.
1893–94	[C.7234] XVII	Disturbances at Featherstone, Dept. Cttee. Rep.
	[C.7234–I]	Disturbances at Featherstone, Dept. Cttee., mins. of ev.
1895	[C.7650] XXXV	Riots, Inter-dept. Cttee. Rep.

Civil Disorder Volume 5

FIRST AND SECOND REPORTS FROM THE SELECT COMMITTEE ON ORANGE
LODGES IN IRELAND, WITH MINUTES OF EVIDENCE AND APPENDICES, 1835

This volume contains the findings of two of the three reports on Orangism in Ireland. A fourth report dealt with British and military lodges (IUP volume Civil Disorder 1). The commissioners did not

submit a conclusion on the Irish situation, possibly because—
according to the recent work on Orangism by Dr. H. Senior—of
differences of opinion among committee members. Evidence was
taken from prominent Orangemen such as William Verner and
William Blacker, and from the Irish reformer William Sharman
Crawford. The Select Committee, which included Daniel O'Connell,
made a penetrating and comprehensive examination of Orangism.
The origins, the nature, the expansion and the activities of the
movement are documented in detail in the evidence. The appendices
include, the rules and ritual for Orange Lodges revised by the
central committee between 1799 and 1835; lists of officers of the
1,827 lodges; extracts from proceedings and correspondence of the
Grand Orange Lodges of Ireland. This volume is an essential
source for the early history of Orangism; it also contains valuable
material on other Irish secret societies, and for social and political
history—particularly of the north of Ireland.

Original references

1835	(377) XV	Orange Lodges in Ireland, Sel. Cttee. 1st rep., mins. of ev., appendices.
	(475)	Orange Lodges in Ireland, Sel. Cttee. 2nd rep.

Civil Disorder Volume 6

THIRD REPORT FROM THE SELECT COMMITTEE ON ORANGE LODGES IN
IRELAND, WITH MINUTES OF EVIDENCE, APPENDICES AND INDEX, 1835

This volume continues the investigations of the Select Committee
on 'the nature, character, extent and tendency of Orange lodges,
associations or societies in Ireland' (see IUP volume Civil Disorder 5).
It contains the evidence of witnesses, drawn from various professions,
most of whom were opposed to Orangism. The leading apologists of
the Orange Lodges were called before the committee again and their
contradictions and equivocations became more pronounced. Items
of discussion included the relations between lodges in Ireland,
England, the United States and Canada. Both the commissioners and
the witnesses revealed a near obsession with the Protestant-Catholic
controversy, underlining the unhappy relations between planter
and native in Ulster. Much of the reports were concerned with
terrorist and counter-terror activities attributed to Orangemen. The
appendices to this volume include documents on the lodges, on the
army, yeomanry, militia and police and on Orange processions. The
index covers the three reports (IUP volumes Civil Disorder 5 and 6)

and provides useful cross-references. These three Select Committee reports with the report in volume 1 of this set on the Orange Lodges form the most important single source for the history of the Orange movement up to 1836.

Original reference
1835   (476) XVI   Orange Lodges in Ireland, Sel. Cttee. 3rd rep., mins. of ev., appendices and index.

Civil Disorder Volume 7

REPORTS FROM COMMISSIONS OF INQUIRY ON RIOTS IN BELFAST AND DERRY WITH MINUTES OF EVIDENCE AND APPENDICES, 1857–1870

Three commissions were set up following outbreaks of violence in 1857 and 1864 in Belfast and 1869 in Derry. Their reports underlined the growing confrontation that was taking place between Protestant and Roman Catholic in Ulster towns. The origins of the politico-religious dissensions were discussed; the nature of Orangism and of the Apprentice Boys Association was investigated. In the reports, minutes of evidence and appendices, the commissioners collected a large volume of material on the two cities, on the circumstances of the riots and on the attitudes of a wide range of opinion. The commissioners were confined chiefly to making recommendations on the reorganization of the civil authorities. The character of the police force in northern cities came under close scrutiny and in the second report on the 1857 riots allegations of partiality on the part of the constabulary were investigated. Following on these inquiries the local police forces in Belfast and Derry were disbanded and incorporated into the Royal Irish Constabulary. The commissioners considered the peculiar nature of processions in Ulster. They re-opened the debate on the wisdom of allowing the Orange Lodges to flourish. The contents of this volume provide valuable insight on the evolution of Irish nationalism and of Ulster unionism.

Original references
1857–58 [2309] XXVI   Riots in Belfast, Com. of Inquiry Rep., mins. of ev. and appendices.
1857-58 (333) XLVII   Riots in Belfast, conduct of the constabulary, Rep., mins. of ev.
1865   [3466] XXVIII   Belfast inquiry, Com. of Inquiry Rep.
          [3466–I]   Belfast inquiry, Com., mins. of ev. and appendices.
1870   [C.5*] XXXII   City of Londonderry riots, Com. of Inquiry Rep., mins. of ev. and appendices.

Civil Disorder Volume 8

REPORTS FROM COMMISSIONS OF INQUIRY ON RIOTS IN BELFAST AND

DERRY WITH MINUTES OF EVIDENCE, APPENDICES AND CORRESPONDENCE 1884–1887

This volume includes the findings of the commission set up to investigate the Derry disturbances of 1883, and correspondence between local magistrates and the executive in Dublin.

The commissioners appointed following the riots which convulsed Belfast between June and September 1886 were instructed to examine all matters relating to the disturbances, and the possible reorganization of the civil authorities. The background to the riots was the violent reaction of Irish Protestants to Gladstone's home rule proposals, the intensive political activity and, according to the *Annual Register*, the rise in temperature caused by Randolph Churchill's 'Ulster will fight' speech. The majority report recommended the establishment of a police authority, under one man—answerable to the Irish Executive and to the Inspector General of the Royal Irish Constabulary—who would be responsible for the preservation of order in Belfast. One of the commissioners disagreed, and in his more comprehensive report he advocated such changes as the setting up of a special constabulary. The contents of this volume are of major significance in explaining the attitudes of an influential section of opinion at an important turning point in Irish history. The depths of sectarian animosity and the basis of Northern Irish intransigence to a self-governing Ireland are documented in the findings of these commissions.

Original references

1884	[C.3954] XXXVIII	Londonderry disturbances, Com. of Inquiry Rep., mins. of ev.
1884	[C.4010] LXIII	Correspondence with magistrates on Londonderry disturbances.
	[C.4057]	Londonderry counter-demonstration, correspondence.
1887	[C.4925] XVIII	Belfast riots, Com. of Inquiry Rep.
	[C.4925–I]	Belfast riots, Com., mins. of ev. and appendices.
	[C.5029]	Riots in Belfast in June, July, August and September 1886, a commissioner's rep. and supplements.

Police

Jenifer Hart

Commentary

Introduction

For many years those who have written about the history of the police in England have approached the question within a traditional frame of reference, making certain assumptions — namely that the forces of 'law and order' needed strengthening in the late eighteenth and early nineteenth centuries in the 'public interest', that the creation of paid, professional, full-time police forces was clearly the correct policy, and that those who opposed such action were shortsighted, obscurantist and misguided. The development of 'the police idea' is thus seen to have been the only rational, enlightened course.

Recently however the subject has been approached from new angles, in particular by socially radical historians and sociologists, with the incidental result that police history has been promoted from its previous low status as a dim, unimportant aspect of administrative or technical history of only peripheral interest at the most, into occupying if not the centre of the stage at least a more respectable position having links with other recognized, acceptable historical issues.[1]

What new notions and analyses have been introduced? What new answers given? The reform of the police in England is seen as the outcome of a classic confrontation between an agrarian military tradition and a pacific commercial and industrial one; in other words the urban and industrial propertied classes were, it is alleged, less willing to take on the tasks of defending property and maintaining order than had been the agrarian men of property who had served in the yeomanry. The social rationale underlying the yeomanry was that the people would be less violent when confronted with their masters whom they respected, than if confronted with professional soldiers. But the yeomanry was becoming less effective and was exposed to attack once an emergency had passed; the manufacturing classes saw that the use of social and economic superiors as a police force exacerbated rather than mollified class violence. So that those who sprang from newer sources of wealth abandoned the traditional means of self-defence against violent uprisings, and turned towards a bureaucratic professional police system that would, they hoped, insulate them from popular violence; it would draw attack and animosity upon itself and would separate the assertion of constitutional authority from

---

1   See for instance: (a) Allan Silver, 'the demand for order in civil society: a review of some themes in the history of urban crime, police and riot', in *The Police; Six sociological essays* ed. by David J. Bordua (New York 1967). pp. 1-24. (b) Frank J. Remington, 'The role of the police in a democratic society', *Journal of Criminal Law, Criminology and Police Science*, Vol. 56, 1965. pp. 361-5. (c) James Q. Wilson, 'The police and their problems: a theory', in *Public Policy*, Vol. 12. ed. by C. J. Friedrich and S. E. Harris (Cambridge, Mass. 1963) pp. 189-216. (d) R. B. Rose, 'Eighteenth century price riots and public policy in England', in *International Review of Social History*, Vol. VI. 1961. pp. 277-292. (e) E. P. Thompson, *The Making of the English Working Class* (London 1963).

that of social and economic dominance. In an unpoliced society such as eighteenth- and early nineteenth-century England, ordinary people could gather in alarming mobs and express their will through riots; the elites, being frightened, since they were not anonymous or physically inaccessible, learned to listen and to respond to some of the demands made. But the privileged classes attempted to define popular protest as criminal and illegitimate, and once the State had made its presence felt in the form of police, it could enforce its demand for 'law and order'. Some of the 'new look' writers also see the desire of the new manufacturing classes to impose work discipline in factory towns as an important element in the reform of the police: they wanted, it is emphasized, more effective methods of social control over the lives and traditional amusements of the working classes in order to get them to work harder. However it was realised from the start that coercion alone would not be effective and that the police required the moral assent and cooperation of the general population; therefore the earliest policemen were instructed how to evoke that assent. The bureacratic police organization could thus supervise daily life more closely and continuously than ever before, not just through coercion but because of an extensive form of moral consensus.

But there was a snag: the very success of the police raised absurd expectations and exposed them to pressures engendered by the idea of a uniformly peaceful society. Could they not 'clean up' crime and control violence, it was asked, just as other bureaucracies had eliminated such things as plagues? From here the 'new' writers are drawn on to considering the effect of these demands on the policeman himself; they look at the role of the police as experienced by policemen, bearing in mind also the status of the profession. They are struck by the fact that the individual and the occupation were and are usually given a low esteem, an esteem much lower than the ostensible importance of the goals policemen are expected to serve. They emphasize that the police are faced with a very complex task; their goals are difficult to define and to achieve, much more difficult than are those of for instance firemen. In particular they must exercise discretion in enforcing laws, because their resources are not adequate to enforce all laws and because the law is often too general or too ambitious: it may reflect the aspirations of the community rather than achievable goals. The police have therefore a policy-making responsibility. But they are often denied the status, training and resources necessary for their work because the difficulty of their task is not appreciated. To make matters worse, the individual policeman was expected to behave in an exemplary fashion; but there was little possibility in fact of his being able to live up to the standard set by the authorities. The result in the nineteenth century was that hordes of policemen were dismissed from their forces. The result later on was a feeling of alienation from the rest of the community.

The question how far this new approach is acceptable is a large and complicated one. As a small and tentative step towards testing its validity, it is proposed here to examine the contemporary evidence as revealed mainly in parliamentary papers. This will throw some light on the main persons or centres from which pressure for a more efficient and professional police came, on the main arguments which were used by them and against them, and on the tensions which developed amongst the police themselves.

London. Pre-1829

There are many descriptions, both contemporary and later, of the policing of London prior to the formation of the Metropolitan Police Force in 1829. From these we can build up a picture of the numerous authorities who were concerned with some particular area or aspect of this task, and of how the various persons involved saw and performed their duties. Looking back on this complex administrative structure and on the various practices (such as the reward system) which were current at that time, it is easy to be supercilious and to criticise contemporaries for clinging to outmoded arrangements and for glossing over or defending what seem to us corrupt and dubious practices; but there are (and were) various things which one can legitimately advance in favour of the 'system' as it then was (both in London and indeed in the rest of the country), in particular that its direct cost to the public (i.e. to the ratepayer and taxpayer) was small, and that because of its very inefficiency it involved relatively little interference with the freedom of at any rate many persons to live as they wished. Moreover not all the existing police officers were inefficient or corrupt. Also it may be that some historians have misinterpreted the meaning of the evidence by ignoring a sense of the word 'police' now obsolete. Thus when contemporaries said 'the general state of the police' was bad, they were often referring to the *mores* of the people, i.e. drunkenness, the profanation of the sabbath, or the alleged increase in crime, and not to police officers or even to the system under which they worked. Indeed, we should perhaps rather be astonished that the arrangements were so drastically changed in 1829 than that they lasted so long.

It is true however that some contemporaries were critical of at any rate some aspects of the policing of the capital. Indeed this had been the concern of a number of different people for many years, that is throughout the greater part of the eighteenth century and in the early nineteenth. The need for an improvement in the arrangements for preventing and detecting crime was the theme of books, pamphlets, petitions to parliament, enquiries, debates and the subject of some practical experiment. But no major changes were made until the Metropolitan Police Act was passed in 1829. How does one explain why many people objected to the various changes which were proposed? First is the fact that the very word 'police' when it was introduced into England in the early part of the eighteenth century was regarded with great suspicion as a portent of a sinister force which held France in its grip. The point was not just a linguistic one. Everyone who thought about the subject was well aware that in France there was less liberty than in England: for instance the French police could arrest on suspicion, and had greater powers of *surveillance* over the people. Some foreign visitors to England described the arbitrariness and ruthlessness of the French police and expressed an understanding of the English attitude. Others pointed out that there were many more policemen in Paris than in London; some that the French system was more centralized. It would in fact be difficult to put too much emphasis on the English fear and dislike of the French model during the eighteenth century and for a considerable part of the nineteenth. The nation in whose history the operations of the police was most conspicuous was France, particularly France of the Ancien Régime and Napoleonic France, but under other régimes too. It did not therefore assist Patrick Colquhoun to get his proposals adopted to eulogize as he did the French police; and the instances he recounted of French police methods did not reassure the British.

Secondly, many of the people who proposed changes in the organization · and working of the police were not concerned only with the prevention or detection of physical evils, i.e. of crimes against the person or property. They were concerned with what they saw as moral and social evils, e.g. drunkenness, prostitution, vagrancy, sabbath breaking, gambling, cruel sports, etc. They wanted the existing laws concerned with these matters to be much more strictly enforced by the police and magistrates; this required an improved machinery of enforcement. They also wanted the enactment of far more stringent laws in these areas.

To give but a few examples of the many which could be produced from the late eighteenth and early nineteenth century: Colquhoun recommended that all lodging houses should be registered and that they should give the police an account of their visitors; that it should be possible to apprehend women known to be prostitutes, make them disclose their addresses, and get the names of the other lodgers in their dwellings; that magistrates should have the power to send prostitutes to an asylum where they would be given religious and moral instruction, or to return them to their parishes if they came from outside London. Colquhoun also thought adultery should be a criminal offence, and he wanted to give the police powers to prevent people remaining in pubs and inns, etc., for longer than was necessary for refreshment. Another magistrate recommended the control of coffee houses, and yet another the appointment of a superintending constable who would clear the streets of nuisances such as beggars. A Bow Street police officer said the hiring of boats on Sundays should be stopped as it was the ruin of many young men. The founder of the Society for the Suppression of Vice was against allowing cricket on Sundays.

Many of these people saw a close connection between what one might call ordinary crimes and all these other issues: thus they constantly stressed that many pubs were places in which thieves congregated and planned their crimes. Similarly they thought there would be less crime if one cut down prostitution, if one prevented youths congregating in fields near towns on Sundays and made them go to church, if one stopped Sunday morning trading, and controlled fairs far more stringently. And no doubt there was *some* justification for such a view: e.g. the existence of enormous numbers of public houses in London at this time helped the criminal element in the population. But these reformers also had the cleaning up of the Metropolis, and indeed of the whole country, as a separate objective; they wanted to raise the moral and social behaviour of the people for its own sake, and not merely because of the close connection they saw between ordinary crimes and the general laxity of manners. This comes out in the many writings of Colquhoun, and again and again in the evidence given to the various parliamentary committees of enquiry. Moreover, the order of priorities of some witnesses was strange: thus one magistrate considered that the allegedly obscene devices made by certain prisoners of war which were on sale to all and sundry were worse than murder, because they involved a mischief to the community with no bounds, whereas a murder was one limited event.

But not everyone at the time accepted what one can call the 'Evangelical' standpoint. Thus William Fielding, a Westminster magistrate, stressed that the people must have their amusements and holidays, and the select committee of 1817 in its first report protested against a wanton and meddling interference with the wants and pleasures of the poor. Some stimulants, it remarked, were necessary for the support and relief of human toil. Many people, including magistrates, their clerks, and police officers who gave evidence before the various committees thought the way to improve the morals of the lower classes was not through stricter laws enforced by an improved police, but through such things as extended education, a reduction in distress and unemployment, and even political reforms.

Thirdly, many of those who were anxious to see a decrease in crime and debauchery thought the price they were being asked to pay for it was too high. They had rather that some criminals escaped detection than that, for instance, certain traders and all dealers in second-hand goods and pawnbrokers should be licensed and regulated; or that the police should be given wide powers to search suspects, and to arrest on suspicion; or that restrictions should be placed on certain categories of persons such as Jews and gypsies; or that the whole country should be covered by confidential informants; or that all schoolmasters and teachers of youth should be licensed by the clergy.

It is important to realize that those who were unenthusiastic about the establishment of a preventive police were not objecting to the idea that it would be good if there were less crime. But a preventive police in the contemporary terminology meant a police which prevented crimes by interfering with all sorts of people, like itinerant dealers in old clothes, or persons with stamping machines; a police which could arrest reputed thieves and vagrants, and clear the streets of beggars and prostitutes. These were the kinds of power possessed by the French police and current experience of the exercise of discretionary powers by the London magistrates gave ground for legitimate apprehension; for instance, it was found that persons of good character were sometimes driven out of the drink trade by the arbitrary or biased acts of justices. Such action might well be based on information supplied by a corrupt, dishonest and unreliable high constable, whose statements concerning the character and conduct of the victuallers carried much weight with the bench. And even a man such as Henry Grey Bennet, M.P., who was keen to improve policing arrangements, considered that it was dangerous to give constables the power of apprehending reputed thieves in public places: the great sufferers would be Irish labourers, and, like the apprehension of vagrants, it would be another easy way of earning five shillings.[2]

Fourthly, some of the people who wished to reform the police were partly, or indeed at times mainly, motivated by a desire to contain political radicalism. This was a quite important factor in Colquhoun's mind in the 1790's; he was a strong patriot and loyalist, and anxious to get the licensing law used to prevent combinations of workmen, or meetings of allegedly seditious clubs in pubs. The police were also to try to ensure that tea gardens and places of public entertainment should be made to foster loyalty to the sovereign. love of their country, and respect for the laws. And such considerations undoubtedly encouraged the support for his police scheme which was offered by the Committee of 1798 and by the Government which in 1799 toyed with the idea of a bill to implement his proposals.[3] Some of the people who were advocating the control of coffee houses, which sprang up in large numbers in the second decade of the nineteenth century, were undoubtedly thinking of them as centres of political radicalism. The result of this was that some of those who wanted better defences against ordinary crime did not see how this could be done without putting greater powers in the hands of the Government, which they were reluctant to do. Thus if something like a central record of criminals were built up for London or the whole country it could be used, they feared, for political purposes.

2   Hansard 2 May 1821, cols. 494-495, on second reading of the Metropolis Police Bill.

3   Extracts from Colquhoun's evidence to the 1798 committee on Finance and the committee's report were reproduced as Appendix 4 by the Select Committee of 1834. See IUP Police 6, pp. 404-433.

There were various other factors in the minds of contemporaries. For instance the police officers attached to the magistrates' courts since 1792 had not got a good reputation in many circles: they were often thought to be spies and were particularly disliked by the parish constables. The system of paying them salaries but allowing them also extra remuneration at the discretion of the magistrates came in for much criticism, and the Bow Street Runners were notoriously corrupt. But to cut down on the reward system would, it was felt, involve a greater expense falling on the public — although in fact most rewards were paid from public funds and not by private individuals. The main argument in favour of the reward system was that police officers on a fixed salary would not be motivated to do their job. This was widely believed. Further some of the suggestions which were made to reform the system looked like an extension of the existing Police Offices structure and were therefore not well received: for the very close relationship which existed between the Home Office and the Police Magistrates was viewed, understandably, with great suspicion by many people. Moreover the cost of the reforms which had been made during the last decades was considered prodigious by some contemporaries who were alarmed at its continuing rise.

Given all these factors (and many others could be cited) to account for the opposition to reforms, one may ask how they were ever brought about. The answer is the traditional one viz: largely by the efforts of Robert Peel. He did not share the Evangelicals' outlook, and saw clearly that one should disentangle the subject of crimes against property and person from debauchery and moral depravity. He was not concerned to strengthen or widen the laws in these spheres. Nor did he wish to forge a better tool against political radicalism — much though he disliked it; the way to head it off, in his view, lay mainly through economic improvement. What worried him was the increase in crime that had taken place in recent years; he had in mind mainly crimes against property. He also wished to mitigate the severity of the criminal laws, and he thought it would be easier to get agreement on this if fewer offenders escaped detection. Hence the need to improve drastically the efficiency of the police. He could also, and this is very important, see his way through the administrative maze. Even though many people considered the existing arrangements defective and deplored in general terms the lack of unity of control, etc., they had not, with one or two exceptions (e.g. Colquhoun and Bentham) given much thought to what new structure was desirable in the Metropolis. This is true even of Edwin Chadwick: the memorandum he submitted to the 1828 select committee was little concerned with the organization of the police, and in so far as his article on Preventive Police in the *London Review* of 1829 recommends the unification of the police of the Metropolis, he seems to have taken the idea from the recommendations of the 1828 committee whose report, among others, he was reviewing. Peel's considerable experience in office since 1810 had ingrained in him an administrative outlook and caused him to think a lot about the policing of London. Moreover, according to the Commons Journal, but not to Hansard, he was on the 1812 Select Committee on the Police. But above all he was able to succeed because he was in office. This is an obvious, but nonetheless crucial point. Since about 1800 the main foci of concern had been outside governmental circles: namely Colquhoun, Bentham and their followers, the evangelically inspired reformers, and various backbench M.P.s and other public spirited persons who were concerned mainly with the severities of the criminal law, the state of the prisons and the increase in crime.

Earlier, viz. in 1785, and again from about 1797 to 1800, the government or some members of it had tried or at least wished to do something. But there was little sign of further governmental concern until about 1820. Thus in the debate in parliament on 18 January 1812 on the setting up of a Select Committee on the Nightly Watch and Police of the Metropolis, Richard Ryder, the Home Secretary, said complacently that in other countries atrocities such as those they had recently witnessed, occurred almost nightly[4] although those countries had an armed police furnished with many powers; and that in his view the statute of 1774 and various local acts regarding the nightly watch were probably sufficient if acted on. Spencer Perceval, the Prime Minister, was also generally sceptical in the same debate about the possibility of improving the situation. Nor was the next spokesman for the Home Office, J. H. Addington, any more concerned in 1816. He said that until he had heard Bennet's speech in favour of setting up another Committee of enquiry, he was at a loss to conceive on what ground the motion would be made, for the magistrates had recently 'all declared, with the greatest satisfaction, that they had never known the Metropolis more tranquil than at present.'[5]

After Peel became Home Secretary in 1822, the contrast is great. Thus it was he who moved in 1822 for a Select Committee, emphasising 'the paramount importance of the subject' and he who became its chairman. The chairman in 1816, 1817 and 1818 had been Bennet.[6] From 1822 to 1826 Peel did what he could by administrative action to improve the existing system,

---

4 Presumably an exaggeration, since the atrocities he was referring to involved the elimination of two whole families.

5 Hansard 3 April 1816, col. 892.

6 For some information about Henry Grey Bennet (1777-1836) see L. Radzinowicz, *History of English Criminal Law* (London 1956) Vol. 2, p. 74, and Austin Mitchell, *The Whigs in Opposition 1815-30* (Oxford 1967). Bennet was an aristocrat, being the son of the Earl of Tankerville, but a radical. Thus in 1819 he presented a petition for the Manchester radicals pressing for an enquiry into Peterloo, and asked for a committee to enquire into the state of the manufacturing districts. He stressed that poverty was produced by unemployment and falling wages.

but these changes did not compensate in his view for fundamental defects in organization, and by 1826 he had determined on a fresh effort to bring about an organic reform of the London police. From the end of that year onwards (apart from a gap between April 1827 and January 1828, when he was out of office), until he had secured the passing of the Metropolitan Police Act in 1829, he was extremely active, collecting information, formulating a plan, getting it through the Select Committee of 1828, which was set up at his instigation and of which he was a member but not chairman, and finally getting a bill through parliament. The absence of difficulty and opposition in parliament which was very marked considering the previous history of the matter can be accounted for partly by the absorption of public and parliamentary interest at this time in the Catholic Emancipation crisis.

No less than six Select Committees of the House of Commons sat between 1812 and 1828 to consider the policing of the Metropolis and related problems, and much can be learned from their reports and the evidence they accumulated[7] both about the 'police' itself and about many other matters, including the magistrates and the administration of justice, the habits of the poorer people, and the attitudes of the reformers. The 1812 Committee is the least useful as it did not publish the evidence it received, nor even the names of the witnesses it heard, and its report is only eight pages long. The reports of the other five Committees are fairly short too, amounting altogether to only about 100 pages, but the evidence they heard covers a great deal more space, 1200 pages of small print plus extensive appendices, and is detailed and revealing. With the exception of the 1828 Committee, the reports themselves do not usually refer specifically to the evidence they took.

The membership of the Committees ranged from twenty-one to thirty-eight persons, but five was always the quorum. The names of members can be found in the Commons Journals, but one cannot unfortunately tell how many members attended at any session, or who asked the questions. As to continuity in membership, the 1816-18 Committees consisted mainly of the same persons, but only six of these had been on the 1812 Committee; over half the members of the 1822 and 1828 Committees were new, being no doubt carefully selected by Peel.

London. 1829-39

There was naturally much opposition to the Metropolitan Police during its first years. Many of the parochial authorities complained of the expense they had to bear;[8] they also wished to reassert their authority and to have some say

7   See IUP Police 1-4.

8   For a good example of such complaints, see the report of a committee of the Marylebone Vestry of 27 March 1834 printed in IUP Police 8, p. 241.

in particular on appointments and on the disposition of the men. Members of the public complained that the police were insolent and high-handed, too hasty and inconsiderate in the performance of their duties. This is not astonishing considering the numbers of persons the new police took into custody, viz. 73,000 in 1831 and 77,500 in 1832. Comparable figures for pre-1829 apparently do not exist, but they are certain to have been very much smaller. There were also difficulties and jealousies due to the continuance of the Police Offices with constables under the sole control of the Police magistrates.

Complaints were most carefully investigated personally by the two Commissioners, but it soon became politically necessary to institute parliamentary enquiries. The first of these was a Select Committee appointed on 22 April 1833 to inquire into the state of the police of the Metropolis and the state of crime in the Metropolitan district. The occasion of the appointment was a request made by Benjamin Hawes (Radical, Lambeth) on 15 April 1833 on the second reading of the Metropolis Police Offices bill. The Committee was clearly meant to treat the subject widely and to look very thoroughly at the working óf the police since 1829. The Committee which had thirty-two members was a strong one. The chairman was T. G. B. Escourt (Cons., Oxford University), who had chaired the 1828 Committee. They set about their work at once and heard many witnesses between April and the middle of July 1833, but they got delayed for various reasons, one of which was the appointment of two other Select Committees, one on 1 July 1833 to enquire urgently into the Popay case, and one on 11 July 1833 to enquire, also urgently, into the conduct of the police at the Coldbathfields meeting. There was a certain amount of interlocking membership among these Committees. Peel was on all of them.

The Popay Committee reported on 6 August 1833. Its report (IUP Police 5) is very brief, amounting to only one page, though it had taken a lot of evidence, the witnesses being asked over 4,000 questions. Alderman Matthew Wood (Radical, City of London)[9] was chairman most of the time. The Committee censured the behaviour of Sergeant Popay very severely, regarding it as highly reprehensible. They considered that those in authority over him had been lax, and they laid down some general principles regarding the employment of policemen in plain clothes.

The next report to come out — on 16 August 1833 — was a short interim report of the first Select Committee (IUP Police 5). They did not at this

---

9 For Matthew Wood (1768-1843) see Donald Rumbelow, *I Spy Blue* (London 1971) which is a history of police and crime in the City of London from Elizabeth I to Victoria. Wood is an interesting character. He was an M.P. for the City from 1817 to 1843. He fought for twenty-five years to reform the City's police and watch, but not by consolidation with the Metropolitan Police. He was on all the select committees on the police from 1818 to 1838 except Coldbathfields.

juncture publish the evidence they had heard; this came out with the final report of the Committee in 1834 (IUP Police 6). The Select Committee was in the summer of 1833 clearly very anxious to do what it could to restore confidence in the Metropolitan police force, whose continuance was in doubt. The interim report stated that it was economically run, that very great and increasing care was taken in the selection of the individuals employed, and that 'on the whole, the conduct of the men has been very creditable to them.' They also praised the Commissioners for the way in which they had discharged their duties.

The next report to emerge — on 23 August 1833 — was the one on the Coldbathfields meeting (IUP Police 5). This Committee was chaired partly by the Rt. Hon. James Abercromby (Whig, Edinburgh) and partly by Sir George Grey (Whig, Devonport). It too heard a great deal of evidence — involving over 5,000 questions — but reported very briefly, largely exonerating the police of improper behaviour at the meeting, but issuing a warning against the use of unnecessary violence on such occasions.

The first Select Committee was reappointed on 10 March 1834, a month after parliament had reassembled. Its membership included most of the people who were on the Committee appointed on 22 April 1833, and a few people who were on one or both of the Popay and Coldbathfields Committees. This was important because the reports of these Committees were referred to the 1834 Committee. The following were on all four committees: Sir Thomas Fremantle (Cons., Buckingham), Sir R. Peel, William Clay (Radical, Tower Hamlets) and Benjamin Hawes. The current Parliamentary Under-Secretary at the Home Office was also a member of all these committees, as was the custom at the time. We still do not know which members attended each session, apart from the chairman, who in the case of the 1834 Committee was mainly John Bonham Carter (Whig, Portsmouth). This Committee did not take much new evidence: it asked just over 1,000 questions, not 2,000, as a mistake in their numbering (on p. 370) might suggest. However, there was a lot of material for it to work on, and when it finally issued its report on 13 April 1834, it was aware of the importance of the occasion, considering that its report would probably be the last of a series on this subject. So it reviewed briefly, with some telling examples and statistics, the situation before 1829, showing again 'the imperious necessity that existed for an alteration in our Police system'. It is pertinent to observe here that the 1833-34 (main) Committee included ten M.P.s who had been members of the 1828 Committee, so that their assessment of the work of the 1828 Committee could not have been wholly detached. But this is not to suggest that they do not make out a convincing case in answer to many of the complaints which had been made, especially in connection with the expense and financial management of the force, these having been by far the most numerous of the complaints brought against the new system. They also pointed out appositely enough that most of the witnesses examined appeared more desirous to improve than to oppose an efficient system of Police. But the tone of the report is rather smug and complacent. Thus they dismiss as absurd the previous fears which had been voiced about the liberty of the subject (though rather inconsistently they say they concur with the Popay report), and they see the Metropolitan Police force as 'one of the most valuable of modern institutions' as respects its influence in repressing crime. This tremendous 'write up' may well have been justified in the circumstances of the time: the new force was on their criteria undoubtedly a vast improvement on what had gone before. But reports such as this probably encouraged complacency in some quarters — though admittedly ossification did not set in until later. It is also interesting to note that the two Commissioners were treated differently from other witnesses in that they were allowed to see the evidence taken by the Committee and to comment on it, though they were questioned searchingly and in considerable detail on a great many matters — a salutary practice which, it seems, did not continue. Indeed later on the Commissioner was actually a member of a committee of enquiry into the administration and organization of the force.

The Committee recommended that the horse patrol should be amalgamated with the Metropolitan Police force; that the constables allocated to the Police Magistrates' offices should be incorporated into the force (a delicate issue); and that some provision for pensions for policemen should be instituted. The Committe also made certain recommendations to improve the administration of justice. It concluded its report with a declaration of the then standard view about how to diminish crime — namely that this depended also on an enlightened system of prison discipline and secondary punishments, and 'the still wider diffusion of moral and religious education, which are the great and only means of permanently advancing the moral and social condition of the People.'

Only one of the recommendations of the Committee of 1834 was acted upon — namely the transfer of the horse patrol to the Metropolitan Police force. So yet another Select Committee was appointed on 14 April 1837 to enquire into the provisions of the Metropolis Police Offices Act, 1833. Of its fifteen members, nine had been on the 1834 Committee, and four on the 1828 Committee as well. These were Sir Robert Peel, T. G. B. Escourt, Alderman Wood and Charles Ross (Cons., Northampton). Its chairman was Benjamin Hawes. The Committee heard a number of witnesses, but its work was interrupted by the termination of the parliamentary session due to the death of William IV. It therefore issued an interim report on 29 June 1837 with the evidence taken so far. It was reappointed on 24 November 1837 (the reference to 24 November *1838* on p. 238 of I.U.P. Police 7 is clearly an error), with five new members *vice* five old ones. It heard a lot more evidence and reported on 11 July 1838. The Committee did not confine itself to investigating the Metropolis Police Offices Act, 1833, which dealt with the administration of justice in the Police Offices and the prevention of crimes on the river — indeed it is not clear why its terms of reference were confined to enquiring into the provisions of this Act. It saw its task to be the completion of the work started by the Committee of 1828 on which it lavished great praise, and it therefore recommended, *inter alia*, (a) the union and consolidation of all Police Establishments in the Metropolis: these were the constables under the control of the Police Office Magistrates, the River Police, and the City of London Police, and (b) that police magistrates should execute only duties of a judicial character, duties of an executive character being committed to the charge of the Metropolitan Police. It also proposed that the police should be given certain extra powers: e.g. the power to arrest without warrant offenders duly charged by the aggrieved party; and that the law concerned with certain nuisances in the streets (e.g. obscene books in shop windows, and mendicants) should be tightened up. The police had taken 4,300 beggars before the Magistrates in 1837; but 2,500 of these had been immediately discharged. This worried the Committee who commented that 'all the magistrates are not governed by the same views of the pernicious tendency and inexcusable character of this vice of mendicancy.'

For the first time in the history of Select Committees on the police, this Committee recorded which of its members attended each session. Out of a total of thirty sessions when evidence was taken, Peel only attended one, namely the occasion when the secretaries of the societies for the Suppression of Vice and of Juvenile Prostitution were heard. However he attended four out of the eleven meetings when the Committee met for purposes other than the hearing of evidence. J. A. Roebuck attended no meetings at all. The most assiduous attenders were Hawes (all meetings), Lord Hotham (Cons., Leominster), Escourt and Charles Lushington (Radical, Westminster). This Committee was also unusual in that a long gap occurred between the hearing of evidence, which ended on 4 April, 1838, and the issue of the report in July. During this period the Committee met nine times, which suggests that it gave a great deal of thought to what should go into its report.

With one very important exception — namely the extension of the Metropolitan police area to include the City of London — the 1837-38 Committee's main recommendations were implemented in the Metropolitan Police Act, 1839; but this act contained much else as well. It is, with 80 sections, a long act; and it is important because it gave the police extensive powers. Some of the act consolidated the existing law, but it also created new offences. It regulated *inter alia* public houses, refreshment houses, unlicensed theatres, gaming houses, prostitutes, obscene books, and playing games in the street. Its most notorious section is probably sec. 54(13) which, going considerably further than section 7 of the Metropolitan Police Act, 1829, authorises the police to arrest without warrant any person using 'any threatening, abusive, or insulting words or behaviour with intent to provoke a breach of the peace, or whereby a breach of the peace may be occasioned', such activities being declared offences. Before, the police had been instructed by the Commissioners that they were not justified in depriving anyone of his liberty for words only.[10] This provision has in effect given the police tremendous powers arbitrarily to arrest *inter alia* political or other demonstrators. It is still on the statute book and has been much used over the years. Another important provision of the 1839 act was section 66 which gave the police power to stop, search and detain without warrant any person reasonably suspected of having or conveying anything stolen or unlawfully obtained. This too is still on the statute book. Other sections of the act also have lasted a long time; some of those most restrictive of the public's behaviour were only repealed in the 1960s. These examples show the tenacity of legislation, at least when it is of convenience to the police, and suggest that those who warned that a reformed police might endanger liberty were in the long run not as wide of the mark as is often said.[11]

How did such a law come to be passed? Little research appears to have been done on the genesis of the act. Indeed it is not even mentioned in the standard works on the political or social history of this period, including biographies of Lord John Russell who was Home Secretary at the time. Many of the suggestions for tightening up or extending the law came from the Metropolitan magistrates who were consulted by the 1837-38 committee. Their answers are printed in Appendices Nos. 1-8 to the Committee's report.[12] Otherwise it seems probable that the main pressure came from the Metropolitan Police Commissioners, who had for years asked the Home Office for the removal of the many legal difficulties which they felt impaired their efficiency; indeed the act embodied in important respects a victory for their conception of their roles and of the role of the police. It seems possible that Chadwick may also have had some influence over parts of the 1839 Act; he was after all working with one of the Metropolitan Police Commissioners (Rowan) on the Constabulary Commission from 1836 to 1839. Certainly the idea of involving the police in the enforcement of sanitary and other similar laws which was embodied in the act was one on which Chadwick had for long been keen partly because it would be economical.

10   P.P. 1830, XXIII. Return made in June 1830 of all the orders issued by the Commissioners since 1829.

11   For a good summary of the special powers of arrest conferred upon the Metropolitan Police by this act, see Thomas W. Haycraft, *Executive Powers in relation to Crime and Disorder, or, Powers of Police in England* (London 1897), pp. 38-42.

12   IUP Police 7, pp. 473-489.

It may be thought strange that such an act as the Metropolitan Police Act, 1839, was passed under the auspices of a Whig government, for the Home Office under the Whigs in the 1830s was very equivocal, often hostile, to the Metropolitan police. Thus the Home Secretary issued some formal rebukes to them and resisted increases in police powers and in the numbers of the force until about the end of 1838.[13] But the Commissioners of Police had strong Tory support in parliament, and one can only surmise that when they asked that more extensive powers should be given to the police, the weakness of the Government in 1839 was such that it was possible for Tories rather than Whigs to shape police legislation — as they did on the Birmingham and Manchester Police bills. However the whole issue of party alignments on police questions could well be investigated further; the position is probably more complicated than is suggested by some writers, e.g. Charles Reith.

Several M.P.s tried hard to delete what they considered the more obnoxious and oppressive clauses from the bill during its arduous passage through parliament which lasted from February to August 1839. They succeeded on a few points, e.g. they prevented the police having new powers to stop gambling in the street, but generally they did not make much impact on the bill. During the debates Peel emitted his usual complacent and self-congratulatory remarks about the act of 1829. Thus he said the act had given 'the greatest satisfaction. Indeed the only persons who had cause to be dissatisfied with it were the thieves and rogues.' The act had been 'universally approved of' (an obvious exaggeration) and 'found so efficient'.[14] The debates bring out clearly that he is thinking far more of the interests of the 'respectable part of the community' and 'the thinking part of the public' than of the poor or underprivileged who enjoyed going to penny theatres, or sitting about with persons even of notoriously bad character in refreshment houses both of which activities were made offences. It is clear that the activities of the new police impinged far more on socially deprived persons than on the educated classes: for instance in 1848 only 8% of those taken into custody by the Metropolitan police could read or write well.[15]

Outside London

Before 1839
The policing of provincial England whether of urban or rural areas attracted much less attention in the late eighteenth and early nineteenth centuries than

---

13   For this subject generally see Charles Reith, *British Police and the Democratic Ideal* (Oxford 1943), Part two.

14   Hansard 11 Feb. 1839, col. 247.

15   See official figures quoted by Joseph Fletcher in his paper 'Statistical Account of the Police of the Metropolis', *Journal of the Statistical Society*, Vol. 13, 1850, p. 261.

did the policing of the Metropolis. This has also affected its coverage by historians, for they have not had to hand the same plentiful supply of material in parliamentary papers as they have had for London. Moreover the policing of London has also been extensively written about at various levels of usefulness by officers of Scotland Yard on their retirement; and one can easily see how their professional careers gave greater scope for such reminiscences than did those of provincial policemen.

When the Royal Commission on a County Constabulary was set up in October 1836, the first step had already been taken to improve the policing of provincial towns. This was the inclusion in the Municipal Corporations Act, 1835, of a requirement that the council of every borough to which the act applied should immediately after their first election appoint a Watch Committee, who were in turn required to appoint a sufficent number of constables to police the town. Many history books wrongly state that the police sections of this act were permissive. There does not exist a comprehensive survey of the organization and state of the police in boroughs on the eve of the changes made by the act of 1835, but a detailed picture of the policing of individual towns can be obtained from the reports of the Commissioners who investigated the Municipal Corporations, for they enquired in each case into the management and usually into the efficiency of the police in every town which they surveyed. These reports can be studied in Volumes 3, 4 and 5 of the I.U.P. volumes on Municipal Corporations (1835). They make varied and interesting reading. It should be remembered however when they are being used to assess the state of the police proper, that the word 'police' at that date was still often used to mean not only watching and 'police' in the modern sense, but also the general management of such things as paving, lighting, cleaning and water supply. Thus the interesting article on 'Police' in the Encyclopaedia Brittanica of 1842 says the word has two meanings: (1) the internal polity, or protection of society against moral and physical evils, the science of regulating whatever belongs to the economy of a state; and (2) the system of preventive justice.[16] The reports of the Assistant Poor Law Commissioners who were at work from 1832 to 1833 are also of some use, particularly for rural areas, for these Commissioners were directed to enquire into the means possessed by the parishes to enforce public order. They are to be found in volume 8, 9, and 17 of the I.U.P. volumes on the Poor Law (1834).

Who at the time had expressed concern about the policing of the country outside London? The problem of public order was of course constantly to the fore in the early decades of the nineteenth century, but the organization and efficent working of policing arrangements in connection with 'ordinary' crime outside the Metropolis were, it seems, not much discussed. Typically

16   This article was written by John Ward, who also wrote a piece on 'Police of Metropolis' in the *Edinburgh Review*, Jan. 1838. For some facts about him, see the D.N.B.

Peel saw the necessity for some action: he mentioned it publicly on a number of occasions between 1829 and 1832; and Chadwick in his thinking about crime, poverty, dissipation and disease had seen the problems as national and not just metropolitan. Already in the early thirties, if not before, he was urging the need for a municipal and a rural police.

The extent to which and pace at which the police provisions of the act of 1835 were implemented have been the subject of some debate. My article on 'Reform of the Borough Police, 1835-1856' (*English Historical Review,* 1955) put forward certain theses, some of which have been questioned. Thus Mr J. J. Tobias in his book *Crime and Industrial Society in the nineteenth century* (1967) criticises me on pp. 233-6 for allegedly maintaining that criminals did not migrate to less well policed areas as a result of police improvements. I am sure that they did, though to what extent has not in my view been established. Nor was I in my article meaning to deny that this took place, though I can see how this impression was given. I was merely exploring the question whether the reform of the borough police in 1835 and of the rural police in 1839 was a response to the migration of criminals, or whether it was done for other reasons. Recent detailed and useful work by Mr Midwinter on the police in Lancashire has shown conclusively how the period 1835-56 constitutes no watershed, at any rate in Lancashire. 'It is not a tale of black suddenly becoming white. It is a tale of cautious, often ramshackle, adjustment to an ever-changing problem of crime and disorder.'[17] We could well do with similar studies for other areas.

What events led up to the appointment of three commissioners on 20 October 1836 to inquire as to the best means of establishing an efficient constabulary force in the counties of England and Wales? Already in the summer of 1836 if not earlier the Home Secretary was hoping to bring in a bill in the next session to establish a rural police generally, but before he had done so he succumbed to the suggestion of Chadwick that a small commission of inquiry should be appointed. Chadwick had been interested in improving the police since at least 1828 when he submitted a short memorandum of his views on the subject to the Select Committee of that year, and elaborated them further in a long article (56 pages) published in the *London Review* in February 1829. He saw an improved rural police as a necessary adjunct to Poor Law reform and it was this primarily which led him to recommend a commission in 1836. It consisted of Chadwick himself, Col. Charles Rowan, who was one of the two Metropolitan Police Commissioners, and Charles Shaw-Lefevre, who was meant to represent the views of country gentlemen,

---

17   Eric C. Midwinter, *Social Administration in Lancashire* (Manchester 1969), p. 174. The section of this book on the police follows very closely Mr Midwinter's article on 'Law and Order in early Victorian Lancashire' published in 1968 as *Borthwick Papers no. 34,* University of York, Borthwick Institute of Historical Research.

for, residing principally in Hampshire since 1823, he had interested himself in county business for some years. Chadwick had intended that the two other commissioners should be cyphers, and that he himself having studied the subject very thoroughly would do all the work; but it seems that Rowan played an important part: his experience of the Metropolitan police was obviously relevant to the commission's constructive proposals and he took a considerable interest in their fate. Shaw-Lefevre had been a Whig M.P. since 1830, and in 1835 was chairman of the committee on agricultural distress. It is commonly said that he played little if any part in the work of the commission; this is most probably true as he was chairman of a number of parliamentary committees at the same time and attended closely to their work. However he signed the report along with his two colleagues. Chadwick later said Shaw-Lefevre 'left us when he became Speaker',[18] but he was not in fact elected Speaker until 27 May 1839, after the report was published. There are a number of other errors in Chadwick's later accounts of what happened.

The Commission issued questionnaires to magistrates throughout England and Wales and to Watch Committees, though it is not clear from the report whether they circulated all Watch Committees. They also collected evidence from Boards of Guardians of the New Unions and they examined 'numerous witnesses of every rank and class in society down to the confessions of criminals', who must incidentally have found answering the seventy-one questions they were asked rather taxing. There are extensive quotations from many of these witnesses in the Commission's report, but it seems that the raw material from which the report was compiled has not been thoroughly worked over since Chadwick's day. It might be worth doing this, particularly to test the reliability of the report: it has been constantly used by social historians, who have not perhaps been sceptical enough about its value. For it is clear that Chadwick sought to present so alarming a picture that the public would stampede in the direction he pointed out. So the report conveyed the impression that the life and goods of every section of the community were in imminent danger, and it highlighted things like labour disputes in a way which was clearly designed to appeal to the currents of opinion and prejudices dominant at that time. The value of the report as evidence about the state of crime should therefore be tested if possible against independent testimony.

Work on the report took longer than Chadwick had intended partly because he became ill and partly because he was hard pressed with other things. After the First Constabulary Report finally came out on 27 March 1839, it secured a wide distribution: by November 1839 about 5,000 copies had been sold and over 3,000 had been distributed free. But in spite of all the Commissioners' work and effort, the report's recommendations were not acted upon. At least their specific plan for the creation and deployment of a paid police force,

18   Benjamin Ward Richardson, *The Health of Nations*, 2 Vols. (1887). Vol. II, p. 392.

ingenious though it was in many ways, was not implemented. It was extremely unpopular in virtually all quarters, and it would have been impossible for the Government to have embodied the proposals in legislation even if it had wanted to, of which there is no evidence. However the report probably had some effect. The horrifying picture it drew of the level of crime and vagrancy must have alarmed many people at any rate for a time and made them more willing to accept the need for more effective policing. But it would be difficult to estimate how influential it was, and it was the threat to public order created by the Chartists which induced the government to take action in the summer of 1839.

1839-1856

The question whether the County Police Act, 1839, should be adopted by a county or part of one was much debated in Quarter Sessions during the next few years. The easiest way to get an overall picture of what was happening is to look at the reports in the *Times* newspaper which, since it was passionately hostile to the County Police Acts of 1839 and 1840, reported fully, if perhaps with a certain partisan bias, events from the localities. The main arguments used against the implementation of the 1839 act were that it would be a great burden on the rates and thus on the landed classes, that the existing system was perfectly adequate and that the act gave too much control to the Home Secretary. (It did on paper, but with no exchequer grant and no inspection, it did not in practice.) Hostility to the act merged imperceptibly into and was reinforced (unjustly) by hostility to Chadwick and all he stood for. This lively interest in the policing of rural areas was reflected in Parliament. Thus returns were asked for almost every year from 1840 to 1853 showing what areas had adopted the act, how many police had been appointed, and above all their cost in great detail. These were all published as parliamentary papers. M.P.s took much less interest in the police of boroughs, about whom only a few returns were asked for and made. This contrast illustrates once again the well known predominance of the landed interest in the House of Commons.

By 1853 when a Select Committee was appointed 'to consider the expediency of adopting a more uniform system of police in England and Wales, and Scotland', the position in England and Wales appears to have been as follows: twenty-five counties had adopted the act for the whole of their area, four for part of it, and twenty-seven had taken no action. At this date 'a more uniform system' normally meant a system under which there would be police in all parts of the country, not more uniformity in the administration of such police forces as existed. Who was the moving spirit behind the appointment of the committee? The actual movers of the motion in parliament on 26 April

1853 were E. R. Rice (Liberal, Dover) and Joseph Hume (Radical, Montrose), but the committee was so warmly welcomed by Palmerston who was then the Home Secretary that it has been suggested perhaps with justification that its appointment was the direct outcome of his concern with the deficiencies of the situation. He had certainly been interested in police matters for some time before he became Home Secretary in December 1852. He thought the matter fell within the legitimate range of the Government's duty; they would be prepared to take an active and decisive part; and the committee would by collecting information prepare the way for beneficial legislation.[19] The M.P.s who supported the appointment of a select committee appear to have had in mind primarily the policing of rural areas, but one M.P. commented that the police in some towns were wretched beyond description and that the evils were so notorious, a committee was hardly necessary; and Palmerston referred to the jealousies of small municipalities which caused inconvenience and injury to the public.

The committee had fifteen members: eight conservatives and seven liberals or reformers. Rice took the chair. One member, Sotheron (Cons., Wilts. N.), seems to have inherited his father's interest in the police, for he was the son of T. G. B. Escourt who had been on most of the committees concerned with policing the Metropolis between 1828 and 1838. (Sotheron took his name on marrying an heiress). It met on nine occasions to hear witnesses who were asked 4,300 questions, and twice to draw up its report. Attendance of members was quite high: five attended all sessions. These were E. R. Rice, H. N. Burroughs (Cons., Norfolk East), J. Mackie (Liberal, Kirkcudbrightshire), Sir John Trollope (Liberal, Lincolnshire South), and Sir James Anderson (Liberal, Stirling district). Two members, Trollope and C. A. Moody (Cons., Somerset West), voted against the committee's recommendation that the maintenance of an efficent police force should be mandatory in all areas, and two, H. Rich (Richmond) and Anderson, both Liberals, fearing for the independence of the police, voted against the recommendation for some financial aid from the government.

The committee devoted more time to the rural areas than to the boroughs: thus more than two-thirds of the fifty seven witnesses came from country districts. The witnesses included twenty magistrates (four from boroughs), seven county chief constables, four borough chief constables, eight other police officers mostly from rural areas, eight landowners or farmers, two prison governors, two solicitors, one mayor, sheriff, doctor, clerk to borough magistrates, poor law inspector, and Chadwick. The committee also received

19 Hansard 26 April 1853, col. 550. For some information about Palmerston's concern to improve the provincial police, see David Roberts, 'Lord Palmerston at the Home Office', *The Historian*, Vol. XXI, No. 1, Nov. 1958; and for Palmerston's continuing interest, see Charles Reith, *A New Study of Police History* (Edinburgh 1956), pp. 259-260.

certain written evidence, about three-quarters of which was from the chief constable of Essex, Captain J. B. B. McHardy, who was then probably the leading chief officer of police in the country, having held that post for thirteen years. No Home Office witness appeared before the committee and no information was supplied by the Department in writing. Each witness was asked to say how many police there were in his locality, but the total picture given is incomplete. However the evidence throws much light on the state of policing in the mid-nineteenth century. The greatest defect in the system which seems to have struck contemporaries was the lack of cooperation and indeed often hostility between the separate forces. No witness claimed that there was adequate cooperation between the boroughs and other forces, and several stressed that it was singularly lacking. It is true that these witnesses came mainly from rural areas and their evidence must therefore be treated with some caution: a chief constable of a county had an obvious interest in enlarging his area of jurisdiction; but they include, besides five county chief constables and two magistrates who acted mainly in rural areas, two borough chief officers (Bath and Manchester) and one ex-Superintendent from Liverpool. Moreover the county chief constables concerned were mostly in charge of large and important counties (Essex, Hants, Lancashire, Durham and Wilts) and seem to have spoken with some authority. One can therefore attach a good deal of weight to the consensus of opinion which was that the various police forces knew little of what each other was doing and seldom cooperated in the day-to-day work of preventing and detecting crime. The situation was so bad that most witnesses recommended some degree of compulsory amalgamation: not all went so far as the magistrate from Gloucestershire who advocated one police force for the whole country, but the following variants were suggested: four regional forces, the abolition of all borough forces, the amalgamation with the county of all borough forces where the population did not exceed 100,000 inhabitants (which would have left only about six boroughs with their own forces), or the abolition of the forces of all 'small' boroughs. It is interesting to see that many people in the middle of the nineteenth century did not regard the pattern of police organization which then obtained as by any means the best, but it survived nevertheless not radically changed for many years. It was later defended with all the arguments which are used to uphold local self-government, but it was clear even in 1853 that the chief reasons why the borough authorities clung so assiduously to the right to police themselves were because they valued the patronage which the control of a force enabled them to dispense, and because they did not wish to see certain laws too meticulously enforced. The committee's report consists merely of eight resolutions, four of which are conclusions regarding the state and cost of the rural police, and four of which are recommendations, some of which are rather ambiguous.

The County and Borough Police Act, 1856, and the machinery of an inspectorate it set up imposed a few common conditions on the provincial police, but did not alter the general structure of policing in England and Wales. The differences between county and borough forces which had been established at an early date therefore continued, as did also their separation from the Metropolitan police both at the operational and administrative level. Indeed there have been few radical changes in the police service since 1856 until recently.

The Policeman's lot

As early as 1829 Chadwick had the vision of the police as a profession. He recommended that in order to secure the new, better organized police which he thought eminently desirable it was 'expedient to place them on a more respectable footing; to give them adequate remuneration for valuable and responsible service — cheap service being in a police, as in most things where talent is required, uniformly bad service'. Their appointments should be for life with pensions on superannuation as in the army; their promotion should be determinable by the amount and value of service, and only cet. par. by seniority. The cost of the police would be amply offset by the reduction in the social costs of crime.[20] He made this point again in the Constabulary Commission report.[21]

But this wise advice was not acted on, largely because the simple and understandable aim of all the authorities (viz. Home Secretary, Watch Committees and Justices) was to keep expenditure on the police as low as possible, with the result that the police can hardly be said to have offered a professional career to the mass of its members during the nineteenth century. This can be illustrated by looking at four things: insecurity of tenure and turnover in membership, numbers in the various ranks and chances of promotion, pay, and pensions.

Insecurity and turnover. Policemen could be dismissed arbitrarily without reason given by the Commissioners in London, the Watch Committee in boroughs, and the chief constable in counties, and a great many were. Thus in the first thirty years of the Metropolitan police, nearly one-third were dismissed.[22] The proportion dismissed (down to 1874) in boroughs was about the

---

20 Preventive Police. *London Review,* 1829 No. 1. pp. 288-9.
21 §IX, 4, of Conclusions. IUP Police 8, p. 184.

22 See extract from Dr Farr's report of 1862, printed with the papers considered by the Departmental Committee upon Metropolitan Police Superannuation, 1889. IUP Police 10, p. 463. There is a lot of information on the matters discussed here in the papers handed in to this committee. IUP Police 10, pp. 417-474.

same, in counties a little less, nearer one-quarter than one-third.[23] Lesser punishments could also be inflicted at the complete discretion of the relevant authorities without right of appeal to any body. In the Metropolitan police (and maybe elsewhere) constables were very much at the mercy of Sergeants whose duty it was to become well acquainted with the men under them and to keep a journal recording misconduct or faults. They certainly seem to have compiled assiduously with this instruction, for often as many as half the constables serving were reported by sergeants in one year.[24] The numbers reported as resigning voluntarily (though no doubt in fact under pressures of various sorts) without pension or gratuity were also very high, namely half of the Metropolitan police between 1829 and 1860, and over half in the provinces (down to 1874), viz. 56 out of every hundred men who joined. The result was that the mean term of service at this time was only five years in London and in borough forces, and six in counties.

Ranks and promotion. The vast majority of policemen were at any one time in the lowest rank, that of constable. Thus in London in 1874 87% were constables, and as many as 97% were in the two lowest ranks, that of sergeant or constable. The proportions in county forces were rather lower: 78% were constables, and 93% were sergeants or constables. Comparable figures do not appear to be easily available for boroughs, but they would no doubt be roughly similar. The Commissioners' early orders stated encouragingly that 'every police constable . . . may hope to rise by activity, intelligence and good conduct to the superior stations' and that they all had a right to look forward to promotion.[25] But in fact most policemen never got promoted; and even if one did rise, the process was very slow: thus in county forces those who ultimately became superintendents had on average spent eighteen years as constables to start with.[26]

The relatively small number of superior and well paid posts was one factor in discouraging the more educated classes from wishing to join the police, except in the top ranks. This was in fact not fortuitous in the case of the Metropolitan police, but the result of a definite policy. It is well known that Peel thought it important from the start to guard against the new system becoming 'a job'; so that when in September 1829 Croker had pressed that the police should be paid more, Peel replied 'I have refused to employ gentlemen — commissioned officers, for instance — as superintendents and inspectors,

23   See section III of Dr Farr's memorandum of 5 Feb. 1877, printed as appendix to the report of the Select Committee on Police Superannuation Funds, 1877. IUP Police 10, p. 67.

24   P.P. 1860 XL. Returns relating to the Metropolitan Police.

25   P.P. 1830 XXIII.

26   See § (9) (k) of Dr Farr's memo. of 5 Feb. 1877. IUP Police 10, pp. 61-2.

because I am certain they would be above their work'.[27] This attitude is understandable given the workings of the patronage system at the time, and it prevented the police becoming a class-ridden establishment like the army. On the other hand not enough effort was put into training the men and so arranging things that the more intelligent amongst them could rise with reasonable speed and take the posts of responsibility. Croker's advice on this was sensible and far-sighted, but was disregarded by Peel, with the result that no Commissioner of Police in London was chosen from the force until the 1950s, twenty years after the Hendon Police College had been operating. Another result of this policy was that the sort of independence of mind which is fostered by higher education has never been at a premium in the police. This tendency was strengthened by the habit of appointing men with military backgrounds as Chief Constables of many county forces. Chadwick typically saw this weakness in the Metropolitan police long before it was generally perceived. Thus in his evidence to the Select Committee of 1853 he recommended that there should be more men of education as officers in the Metropolitan police; he agreed it had been impossible to get any other service when the force was established but he considered the activities of the force would be improved if it comprised more educated superior officers.[28] Some years later it began to be realised more generally that all was not well with the organization of the Metropolitan police, and various committees of enquiry were set up. Those of 1868 and 1879 wanted greater decentralization and made various proposals to implement this; but very little was done. The 1886 Committee on the Disturbances of February 1886 (in I.U.P. Civil Disorder 4) considered that there were probably insufficient officers of superior rank and education. The second 1886 Committee (I.U.P. Police 10) agreed and recommended the creation of chief constables. But whilst it made the very sensible comment that 'the real efficiency of a force greatly depends on the way in which promotion is administered', it also inconsistently considered that chief constables should be 'gentlemen of good social standing, and, as a general rule, officers who have seen service in the Army or Navy. We believe [they added] that such men would be treated with respect and regarded with confidence by the force.'[29] This committee was appointed in February 1886 to enquire into the administration and organization of the Metropolitan police force with the view of making such changes as might be necessary to remedy the defects pointed out by the Disturbances committee, but its report which did not come out until 19 July 1886 is an unimpressive document, only four pages long.

27   Croker Papers (London 1885). Vol. II p. 19.
28   17 June 1853, in answer to question 3662.
29   p. 186.

Pay. When the Metropolitan police was set up, constables were all paid 19s. a week. In due course classes of constable were created with different rates of pay. By 1842 about a quarter of the constables were receiving only 17s. a week, but another quarter, the top class, was getting 21s. These rates did not rise much until 1872, when the lowest class of constable got £1 a week and a first class constable got 30s. In addition they got allowances for clothing and coal, but they had to pay for their housing. The highest ranking Metropolitan police officer, a superintendent, in 1829 got £200; by 1872 this had risen to £350-£400, with higher rates for certain categories. In counties the Home Secretary's Rules of 1839 fixed the pay of constables at 15s.-21s. per week. By 1870 actual pay was usually at the top of this scale, but even a first class constable still got only about 24s. in 1872. Superintendents in counties received on average only £140 a year in 1872. In boroughs there was considerable variation in pay as it was not regulated by the Home Secretary.

By the 1890s there had been some improvement in police pay although this was slow and irregular; so that although it still varied greatly between different parts of the country, by the end of the century the average constable was approximating to the level of a skilled worker, whereas in the 1850s he was probably paid in effect about the same as an agricultural worker.[30]

Pensions. Before 1890 only a small proportion of policemen received pensions on retirement. For example between the years 1829 and 1860, out of every 100 Metropolitan men who left the force, only 14 were pensioned. The figures for counties and boroughs in the mid-seventies and probably until after 1890 were 12 and 8 respectively. Those retiring from the higher ranks were far more likely to get pensions than those retiring from the lower ranks: thus in 1874 in the provinces, about one-quarter of those on pension were of the rank of Inspector or above, although they constituted only about 7% of the forces, and more than one-third of the pension money went to them. The statutory provisions regulating the granting of pensions were extremely complicated and diverse; they are set out as far as English counties and boroughs are concerned in the report of the Select Committee on Police Superannuation Funds of 1877[31] and for the Metropolitan police in Paper II submitted to the Departmental Committee on Metropolitan Police Superannuation of 1889.[32] But diverse though the provisions were, there was one basic universal fact governing all forces, namely that although most policemen (except chief constables at least in counties) had to contribute 2½% of their pay throughout their service to the pension fund, all pensions were entirely at the discretion of the police authorities, who could grant or withhold them at pleasure, and

30   For some useful figures about police pay from 1860 onwards, see J. P. Martin and Gail Wilson, *The Police: A study in Manpower* (London 1969), pp. 14-21.

31   IUP Police 10, pp. 11-13.

32   IUP Police 10, pp. 460-1.

who in the provinces had not in general bound themselves to any fixed rate of pension.[33] Nor did most of the men who left without pension even get their contributions returned to them: the figures of those who did were 3% in London, and just over 1% in the provinces. Even so the pension funds of many authorities were in an extremely precarious state, being built up from a hotch-potch of sources such as stoppages from police pay, fines on the police, and fines imposed on the public by courts for certain offences e.g. drunkenness. But even where the pension funds were solvent, it was quite often the practice not to grant any pensions. Thus in 1884 sixty-one forces had pension funds but no pensioners. The pensions of Chief Constables at any rate in counties were however safe enough, as they were paid from the police rate, not from the superannuation fund. In Scotland there was virtually no possibility of paying pensions at all, though policemen aged sixty, if infirm, could be granted gratuities.[34]

This being the position it is not astonishing that there was considerable discontent amongst policemen particularly about pensions from at least the early 1860s onwards until the Police Act of 1890 was passed. Evidence of the continuing discontent can be found in much of the evidence given to the 1875 Select Committee on Police Superannuation Funds, in this committee's report of 1877, and in the evidence given to the 1889 Departmental Committee on Metropolitan Police Superannuation. All the policemen who appeared before these committees, except some of the provincial Chief Constables, represented in no uncertain terms the dissatisfaction which existed amongst all ranks on this issue. The 1875 committee considered that the complaints made by the men especially regarding the uncertainty of pension were on the whole reasonable. Moreover they also recommended that if a new scheme was introduced it should apply to chief constables of counties on the same conditions as to other members of the force, thus ending their exemption from deductions. The committee was presumably not impressed by the plea of the chief constable of Hampshire that the terms for chief constables should be superior: he had suggested that their pensions should be calculated on their allowances and free accommodation if any, as well as on their pay. The report of the Departmental Committee on Metropolitan Police Superannuation was, it seems, not published, but, judging by the fierce and hostile way in which the chairman Godfrey Lushington (Permanent Under-Secretary at the Home Office) grilled witnesses, and by his extremely sceptical approach to the validity of their complaints, he at least was not convinced that better con-

33   See Memorandum in explanation of Police Bill 1890, in IUP Police 10, p. 296.

34   See report of Select Committee on the County and Burgh Police Systems of Scotland, 1868. IUP Police 9, p. 11, and the examination of Dr Farr, questions 2451-2456.

ditions should be granted. The terms of reference of the 1875 committee incidentally included the Metropolitan and City of London police forces as well as the counties and boroughs of England and Wales, but the committee did not in its report refer to either of the two London forces. No representatives of the Home Office came before the 1875 committee or submitted evidence.

The proceedings of both committees bring out the absence of any recognized machinery or methods by which members of police forces could make representations about their pay or conditions or service, and also suggest that those who did speak out were running considerable risks, since to complain was often thought improper and since the security of their jobs and the chance of getting a pension rested, anyway in the provinces, so very much on the discretion of the chief constable and/or police authority. Consider for instance the following exchange between a member of the 1875 committee and the chief constable of Leeds, one of whose Superintendents, Gibson, had come before the committee and given evidence of great dissatisfaction in many forces. He appears to have been well qualified to speak on this matter, as he had previously been a Superintendent in the Hampshire force and had given evidence to a committee of enquiry there; he had also received many letters from a great variety of police officers as a result of his communications to the *Police Guardian*.

Q.4405. (Col. Dyott) I should like to know how this man Gibson came to be called as a witness. You are at the head of the force, are you not? — I am.

Q.4406. Were you consulted at all about his coming? — I was not consulted at all. I knew nothing at all about his coming here until he showed me the order for his attendance before you. Mr. Gibson has always, even before he joined our service, been a man taking an interest in the matter, and writing to the newspapers, and generally making a public question of the matter.

Q.4407. A species of agitator, I suppose? — Just so.

Col. Dyott incidentally might well have been a little more sympathetic to the case for better police pensions, since he had himself retired from the army on half pay at the age of thirty-four after only fifteen years' service.

Similarly a member of the Birmingham Watch Committee (Manton) saw in the press a report of the evidence given by a constable (Green) from Birmingham who told the committee that it was the practice in Birmingham when a man applied for his pension for the defaulters' book to be brought out and his pension reduced even after twenty-five years' service on account of disciplinary offences for which he had already been punished. In one such case the pensioner was granted only one shilling a day. Manton demanded to

come before the Select Committee, said he had never heard there was dis-
dissatisfaction among the force, and denied that the practice of the Watch
Committee was as reported by Green, though he admitted that the general
character of a man was taken into consideration when his pension was being
determined.

One reason for the extreme reluctance of the authorities to improve the
position in spite of the threat of trouble was that many people felt that some of
the arrangements had in the past been too generous, at least in the Metropolitan police. When their practice was investigated by Dr. Farr of the
Registrar General's Office in 1862, he had found a curious state of affairs. In
his view it had originally been intended that pensions should only excep-
tionally and under special circumstances be granted to policemen aged less
than sixty, but what had been intended as the exception became the rule.
Thus of 1,957 men pensioned, all except 37 had left the force before age 60. He
considered it very suspicious that, as was the case, so many policemen
suddenly became incapable of work exactly when they were entitled to ask
for pensions on medical grounds, and that their expectation of life was
thereafter better than that of the rest of the population. In effect he alleged
that there was much malingering which the system of administration did not
manage to prevent, the arts of obtaining a pension being known as 'schem-
ing'. As a result of these revelations, the pension arrangements were altered
adversely for those joining after 1862, which naturally caused discontent; but
some of the people in authority, being well grounded in Farr's memorandum
of 1862, seem to have been determined not to make any concession, in spite of
the strong case made out by the police, because they wanted at all costs to
prevent a return to the lax position of earlier years.[35] The mistake had of
course been to grant medical pensions so easily at first, rather than developing a system of smaller long service pensions, payable as of right at certain
ages as to the armed forces.

There was also disagreement between the police and some officials as to
how harsh were the conditions of employment, and how they compared with
those of other workers. The representatives of the Metropolitan police
argued before the 1889 committee that their duties were becoming heavier
and that the strain on them was greater, whilst their pension position
deteriorated, as was shown by the decrease in the percentage of men eligible
for pensions who actually received them — from 12.5% to 7.3% between 1879
and 1889.

35   For this see the attitudes shown by Lushington and others on the 1889 Departmental Committee. Apart from the Home Office, the departments represented on this
committee were the War Office, the Treasury and the Metropolitan Police (Commissioner and Receiver).

No action was taken by the Conservative Government on the Select Committee's report of April 1877, although the chairman of the committee (Sir H. Selwin-Ibbetson) was the Parliamentary Under-Secretary of State at the Home Office until 1878. It would in fact have been difficult for them to have gone ahead with the committee's scheme as it involved making pensions a direct charge on the rates. Indeed it is strange that a committee containing a majority of Conservatives should have made this recommendation in the climate of opinion at the time. This committee like so many other select committees did a good job in hearing witnesses (though they failed to hear any representatives of the county ratepayers), and in amassing factual evidence: over fifty witnesses came before them, including nine policemen from the two lowest ranks and the editor of the *Police Guardian*, a journal which had existed for seven years and acted as a focus of discontent. But the committee was weak when it came to constructive proposals: these only occupied a few pages of an already short report.

The Liberal Government of 1880-5 made various attempts to legislate on this issue. It introduced bills in 1882, 1883 and 1884, but they all foundered quite quickly because they were fiercely resisted by the advocates of relief to local taxation. On the other hand the Treasury refused to agree that Exchequer grants should be paid on pensions as it was on police pay and clothing, although one could well argue that pensions were deferred pay; and the Government was too weak here, as on so many other issues, to get its proposals through in the face of opposition and threats of obstruction. Some opponents also argued that local authorities should retain the discretion to grant or not to grant pensions which was allegedly a valuable sanction on good behaviour, and they taunted the Home Secretary for being inconsistent since on other occasions he had propounded the virtue of decentralization. The failure of the Liberals to legislate was particularly unfortunate because Sir William Harcourt, the Home Secretary, was considered to have made a promise of action in public to the police in June 1881. H. H. Fowler who had been Parliamentary Under-Secretary at the Home Office from December 1884 to June 1885 made a further attempt to get legislation on this subject when he was in opposition in July 1885, and Selwin-Ibbetson also introduced private bills in 1886 and 1887, but all with no success. The matter was not settled until the Conservatives had got the Local Government Act of 1888 through and managed to persuade the Treasury to agree to contribute from central funds. In the view of some M.P.s, for example R. G. B. Cunninghame Graham, the Government was only legislating then because, alarmed at the spread of socialist doctrines, they wanted a contented police force to suppress the meetings and other constitutional rights of the working classes, instead of using the military. However he was pleased to see proposals which would raise the social condition, remuneration and condition of life of the

police. Harcourt generously enough acknowledged in 1890 that the chief
credit on this issue should go not to him, but to Fowler, and to J. T. Hibbert
who had held office at the Local Government Board, Home Office and
Treasury in various Liberal Governments since 1872.

The parliamentary papers proffer less evidence about the state of feeling
amongst the Scottish police. The lack of pensions was certainly seen by the
authorities and by the Select Committee of 1868 on the County and Burgh
Police Systems of Scotland as a weakness, because it led to considerable
wastage and to a drift of Scots policemen into English forces. The Scottish
police system suffered too, as did the English only to an even greater extent,
from the large number of separate and often small police forces which
existed. There were other specifically Scots problems also: namely the
respective functions of Procurators Fiscal and Chief Constables in connection with the detection of crime, and the use of the police to suppress
salmon poaching. Incidentally some information about the English police can
be found in the evidence given to the Scottish committee of 1868, as they
heard some witnesses from England, and as some of the Scots Chief Constables had served previously in the English police.

The following tentative conclusions are offered as a result of this survey of the
parliamentary papers on the Police in the nineteenth century. The 'new look'
analysis of the forces making for change in the organization of the police and
of the opposition they encountered is useful and valid as a partial explanation
of the motives and desires of some of the participants; but it is not adequate as
a total explanation, for there were many more strands of opinion amongst the
reformers and their opponents and many more considerations and arguments
than the new writers postulate. For instance whilst it can be plausibly argued
that the immediate stimulus which led to the passing of the County Police Act,
1839, and the consequent setting up of county police forces in some areas was
the preservation of public order in the face of the threat of Chartism, this must
be seen against a background in which many people were also concerned with
ordinary crime and its alleged increase in rural areas. Moreover concern with
crime against persons and property was a more important factor in the events
leading up to the formation of the Metropolitan police force than was the
desire to control mob violence or riots; and in the case of the boroughs, the
impetus to improvement came from the desire to improve the general quality
of life in towns by e.g. better paving, lighting, cleaning and policing.

However the new writers' contribution to what could be called 'the police
problem' is greater, for here the analysis fits much better. It enables us to see
more clearly than we did before the absurdity of the demands which were
made on these earlier policemen, who were after all only ordinary working

class men with no training, dressed up in uniform. For instance the first Metropolitan regulations stipulated that police officers were to be so vigilant and active that it should be extremely difficult for anyone to commit a crime within the area of their charge. They were to have a perfect command of their tempers. While on duty they must not enter into conversation with anyone, except on matters relating to their duty; in particular they were not to talk to servant girls. They must not even stop and talk to other police officers whom they met on their beats, but only exchange a word and pass on. Given that policemen were on duty for very long hours, their life would have been intolerably isolated if they had complied strictly with these regulations. There was clearly an enormous gap between what was expected of policemen by the authorities (and later by the public) and what it was realistic to expect of them given the field of recruitment, which was in turn circumscribed by the level of pay offered. Some people even thought that the police could have a direct moral influence on the mass of the population,[36] but it is difficult to see how this could have occurred given that police forces were hardly more than bodies of barely literate and often drunken ex-labourers with a rapidly changing membership. Indeed one result of the gap was the high level of dismissals which obtained throughout all forces for a long time. Probably many of the men who were sacked early in their careers would have made good policemen if such high standards of behaviour had not been demanded of them. As one chief constable put it in 1875, not only was a policeman not to be drunk on duty: he must not get drunk off duty either.

Moreover there was a certain incompatibility between on the one hand the level of skills they were expected to possess and the degree of stability in character which it was assumed they would display, and on the other hand the poor material rewards they were offered (in terms of pay, promotion prospects, insecurity and pensions) and the low esteem in which both they and their occupation were held. Many policemen came to realise this from the middle of the nineteenth century onwards.

Finally there was an incompatibility between the idea of the constable as an independent arm of the law, an intelligent being who would think and act for himself, and the respectful underling of Police Regulations who would always strictly obey the commands of his superiors, and who had to submit himself to endless drills and soldierly parades to the neglect of his more important duties.

36 See for instance the remarks of J. Fletcher, an Inspector of Schools, on pp. 264-5 of his paper referred to in note 15 above.

Bibliography

No professional historian has written a comprehensive and authoritative account of the British police in the nineteenth century. The most illuminating of the older books is F. W. Maitland, *Justice and Police* (London 1885), the chapter on the Constabulary being a model of succinct and vivid writing. It is also still worth reading Captain W. L. Melville Lee, *A History of Police in England* (London 1901).

A great deal has been written about the state of policing in London before 1829 and about the history of the Metropolitan Police. The best books on this subject are J. F. Moylan, *Scotland Yard and the Metropolitan Police* (London 1929), and George Dilnot, *Scotland Yard: its history and organisation 1829-1929* (London 1929). There is also a short and well written piece by J. F. Moylan on 'Police Reform before Peel: the Fieldings and the Bow Street Police' in the *Police Journal*, Vol. II 1929, pp. 150-164. A much fuller account of the problems of London before 1829 and of the early years of the Metropolitan Police will be found in Leon Radzinowicz, *A History of Criminal Law*, Vols. 2 and 3 (London 1956), and Vol. 4 (1968). Vol. 4 also covers, though much more briefly, developments outside London down to 1856. There are also things of interest in the writings of Charles Reith, in particular in (1) *The Police Idea: its history and evolution in England in the eighteenth century and after* (London 1938). The book ends in 1829. (2) *British Police and the Democratic Ideal* (London 1943). This is largely concerned with the Metropolitan Police between 1829 and 1840. (3) *A New Study of Police History* (Edinburgh 1956). This also deals with the Metropolitan Police from 1829 to the mid-century focussing much on Col. Rowan. It repeats the contents of (2) above to some extent, but also contains much new material. For Peel's part in the story, Norman Gash, *Mr Secretary Peel* (London 1961) and the same author's *Sir Robert Peel* (London 1972) are authoritative and essential. The relations between the Commissioners, the Home Office and Parliament are interestingly discussed on pp. 405-413 of the unpublished Oxford D.Phil. thesis of A. P. Donajgrodzki on *The Home Office, 1822-48* (1973).

For the City of London, see Donald Rumbelow, *I Spy Blue* (London 1971). The popular title is misleading.

There is a little sketchy history in J. M. Hart, *The British Police* (London 1951). The fullest general account of the police in the nineteenth century is in chapters 2 to 5 of T. A. Critchley, *A History of Police in England and Wales 900-1966* (London 1967). For Chadwick, by far the best thing is S. E. Finer, *The Life and Times of Sir Edwin Chadwick* (London 1952). F. C. Mather, *Public Order in the age of the Chartists* (Manchester 1959) is a useful book. Certain aspects of provincial police development are dealt with in the following articles: Jenifer Hart, (1) 'Reform of the Borough Police 1835-1856', *English Historical Review* 1955; (2) 'The County and Borough Police Act 1856', *Public Administration* 1956; and Henry Parris, 'The Home Office and the Provincial Police in England and Wales 1856-1870', *Public Law* 1961.

Valuable information about police pay, conditions of service, rates of separation from the forces, etc., will be found in chapter 2 of J. P. Martin and Gail Wilson, *The Police: A Study in Manpower* (London 1969). Those interested in the working conditions of policemen should also study the evidence given to the Select Committee on a Police Weekly Rest Day, P.P.1908, IX, and to the Desborough Committee of 1919-1920 on the Police Service. There is also much information to be culled from various parliamentary papers not directly concerned with the police to throw light on how they saw their role and did their work, e.g. those dealing with the Poor Law, Public Houses, Drunkenness, and the Game Laws.

The Documents

Police

Police Volume 1

REPORTS FROM SELECT COMMITTEES ON THE POLICE OF THE METROPOLIS
WITH APPENDICES AND EXTRACTS FROM THE EVIDENCE OF REV. THOMAS
THIRLWALL, 1812–1817

Two Select Committee reports which examined the effectiveness of
London's law enforcement agencies are included in this volume. The
1812 committee investigated the efficiency of the night watch. On
finding that it was reasonably effective and that many of its
defects were being remedied, they turned their attention to law
enforcement in the metropolis. The appendices contain a comprehensive list of the statutes governing the duties, jurisdiction and financing
of the several London police forces, dating back to the Statutum
Civitatis of Edward I in 1285. The committees considered that the
existing legal framework within which the police operated was
outdated and should be reformed. They strongly urged that a single
police force should be formed under government control. They
recommended that efforts should be made to improve the quality of
recruits, and that an efficient system of police records be introduced.
The 1817 committee heard evidence on many aspects of law enforcement, particularly on the magistrates courts, from magistrates and
civic officials. Particular attention was paid to the causes of crime
and the effectiveness of the police in preventing it, to corruption and
bribery in the police and to the extent to which poverty and drink
could be blamed as causes of crime.

Original references

1812	(127) II	The nightly watch and police of the metropolis, Sel. Cttee. Rep.
1816	(510) V	The state of the police of the metropolis, Sel. Cttee. Rep.
1817	(231) XVII	Police of the metropolis, Rev. Thomas Thirlwall, Sel. Cttee. extracts of ev.

Police Volume 2

REPORTS FROM SELECT COMMITTEES RELATING TO THE STATE OF THE
POLICE IN LONDON AND THE OPERATION OF THE LICENSING LAWS
WITH MINUTES OF EVIDENCE AND APPENDICES, 1817

The first report of the Select Committee on the state of the police in
the metropolis deals mainly with licensing problems and contains a
history of the development of licensing laws. The committee noted

the difficulties involved in carrying out the provisions of the licensing laws relating to publicans found guilty of breaches of the regulations. Evidence was given on the growing tendency of brewers to monopolize the trade by means of tied houses, a practice the committee deplored. The second report deals with two main subject areas, the bounty system of parliamentary rewards for the capture of criminals and juvenile offenders. The committee examined the advantages and disadvantages of the bounty system and highlighted its drawbacks. It received extensive evidence on the evils of placing juvenile offenders in adult prisons which was the common practice of the period. Witnesses told of the desirability of establishing separate juvenile prisons or reformatories with the aim of reforming young delinquents. In connection with this report, a significant development later in the century was the appearance of industrial schools or 'houses of refuge' for juvenile offenders.

Original references

1817	(233) VII	The state of the police in London, Sel. Cttee. Rep., mins. of ev., appendix.
	(484)	The state of the police in London, Sel. Cttee. Rep., mins. of ev., appendix.

Police Volume 3

THIRD REPORT FROM THE SELECT COMMITTEE ON THE POLICE OF THE METROPOLIS WITH AN ADDITIONAL REPORT, MINUTES OF EVIDENCE AND APPENDICES, 1818–1822

These reports deal with three principal subjects, the state of the police establishments in the metropolis, the conditions in the city's prisons and the state of public morality. The volume contains information on many aspects of law enforcement. The committee paid special attention to examining the organization of the police officers and magistrates. The committee found that the London police forces were efficient but that there should be a better system of communication between the several police offices. The report is critical of the prison system which it considers to be a nursery of further crime. Details are given of prison discipline and administration, both of which were considered lax. In its examination of the state of public morals the committee heard evidence on the operation of the licensing laws, female prostitution and on the state of public morals generally. Of special interest are extensive tables giving statistics of police and prison expenditure.

Original references

1818	(423) VIII	State of the police and prisons in the metropolis,

Police Volume 4

REPORT FROM THE SELECT COMMITTEE ON THE POLICE OF THE
METROPOLIS WITH MINUTES OF EVIDENCE AND APPENDIX, 1828

Public concern over the rapid increase in London's crime rate led
to the appointment of the Select Committee which examined the
causes of crime in the metropolis and investigated means of reducing
the crime rate. The committee noted that the population of the
capital had risen by nineteen per cent between 1801 and 1821 while
the crime rate had risen by fifty per cent. The report summarizes the
findings of previous committees and contains extensive evidence on
the causes of crime, the organization of the police officers and the city
prisons. Evidence presented to the committee led it to attribute the
rise in crime to the existence of commercial distress, neglect of
children and the cheap price of spirits. The committee considered
that the granting of free pardons to bank robbers who returned
stolen property should be ended and that in future no rewards
should be given for the recovery of stolen property. They felt that a
juvenile prison should be established and greater efforts should be
made to prevent children turning to crime. Of special interest are an
appendix which explains the duties of the Bow Street police office
and evidence describing the functions of the several other police
forces in London.

Original reference

Police Volume 5

REPORTS RELATING TO THE ADMINISTRATION OF THE POLICE WITH
MINUTES OF EVIDENCE, 1833

The reports in this volume deal with policing the metropolis and with
relations between the police and public. The Select Committee of
1833 examined the results of the partial adoption of a plan recommended in 1828 (see IUP volume Police 4) for the reorganization of
the several London police forces. Evidence was given on many
aspects of law enforcement in London. The committee suggested
that modifications in the plan would be necessary in view of the

lapse of time since it was first proposed. Of special importance are the two reports which deal with relations between the police and the emerging working-class political association and acted as an *agent provocateur*. The Select Committee which examined his conduct censured his activities but considered that the employment of plain-clothes policemen was justifiable in certain cases. The Select Committee investigating the conduct of the police in dispersing a meeting of the National Union of the working classes at Cold Bath Fields heard evidence on the working of the union. They considered that the police had acted correctly, and they regarded the union as an undesirable association.

Original references

1833	(675) XIII	Metropolis Police, Sel. Cttee. Rep.
	(627)	Plain-clothes police, Sel. Cttee. Rep., mins. of ev.
	(718)	Coldbath Fields meeting, Sel. Cttee. Rep., mins. of ev.

Police Volume 6

REPORT FROM THE SELECT COMMITTEE ON THE STATE OF THE POLICE OF THE METROPOLIS, WITH MINUTES OF EVIDENCE, APPENDIX AND INDEX, 1834

The 1834 committee was established to continue the investigations into the policing of the metropolis which had been commenced by the 1833 committee (see IUP volume Police 5). The committee examined three main topics: the management and conduct of the metropolitan police; the strength of the force and the efficiency of the existing provisions for law enforcement in London. Much of the evidence dealt with the work of the metropolitan police. Details were given of recruitment methods and the general organization of and methods employed by the force. The committee paid particular attention to the financial administration of the police force in London and to the means employed in compiling statistics of crimes committed in the metropolitan area. The committee's recommendations stressed the benefits which the provision of an efficient and well-paid police force would bring to all sections of the community. They urged in addition that the force be well paid in order to keep members of the force free from corruption in carrying out their duties.

Original reference

1834	(600) XVI	Police of the Metropolis, Sel. Cttee. Rep., mins. of ev., appendix and index.

Police Volume 7

REPORTS FROM SELECT COMMITTEES ON THE POLICING OF THE METRO-
POLIS WITH MINUTES OF EVIDENCE, APPENDICES AND INDICES, 1837–1838

The advisability of introducing a unified police force into the
metropolis in place of the five distinct forces then engaged in law
enforcement in the capital was one of the major areas investigated
by these Select Committees. The committees, whose membership
included Sir Robert Peel, also heard evidence from aldermen and
police magistrates on their functions as law enforcement officers and
witnesses told of the success of the Bow Street runners in combating
crime in the London area. Of special interest is the evidence given by
Edward Gibbon Wakefield in which he put forward the views that
the primary duty of a police force was to prevent crime and that
separate prisons should be provided for juvenile delinquents.
Wakefield strongly urged that juvenile delinquents should be
reformed and educated while in prison rather than punished. The
committees' recommendations closely followed the advice they had
received in evidence from police magistrates. They recommended the
formation of a unified police force for the metropolis, and proposed
that police magistrates should be called on only to perform duties of
a judicial character, while duties of an executive nature should be
reserved to the metropolitan police force which should be placed
under the control of the Home Secretary.

Original references

| 1837 | (451) XII | Metropolis police office, Sel. Cttee. Rep., mins of ev., appendix and index. |
| 1837–38 | (578) XV | Metropolis police office, Sel. Cttee. Rep., mins. of ev., appendix and index. |

Police Volume 8

REPORTS RELATING TO POLICE WITH MINUTES OF EVIDENCE, APPENDICES
AND INDICES, 1839–1853

A major problem involved in the efficient enforcement of law and
order in England and Scotland was the existence of numerous
police forces. The reports deal with the desirability of amalgamating
the smaller forces. The Royal Commission on the establishment of
county police forces which presented its report in 1839 examined all
facets of the causes of crime and the best means to prevent it. The
commission, whose membership included Edwin Chadwick, paid
particular attention to the causes of crime and they considered that
poverty was not a major cause. The commission's report contains

many statistical returns relating to crime in rural areas. The commissioners recommended that separate police forces should be established in each county. The Select Committee on the expediency of adopting a uniform police system examined the disadvantages of separate county and town police forces. In its report it proposed that the smaller forces should be subject to inspection by the Home Office. The volume contains a short report which gives details of the organization of police forces in continental Europe and in the United States of America.

Original references

1839	[169] XIX	The establishment of a constabulary force in the counties of England and Wales, R. Com. 1st rep.
1843	(248) XLII	Mary-le-bone Vestry expenses for metropolitan police, Cttee. Rep.
1845	[658] XXVII	Petition from Eliza Price on ill-treatment by two constables of Stafford, N. Rodgers, Com. Rep., etc.
1852–53	(603) XXXVI	Expediency of adopting a more uniform system of police in England, Wales and Scotland, Sel. Cttee. 1st rep., mins. of ev., appendix and index.
	(715)	Expediency of adopting a more uniform system of police in England, Wales and Scotland, Sel. Cttee. 2nd rep., mins. of ev., appendix and index.
	(715–I)	Expediency of adopting a more uniform system of police in England, Wales and Scotland, Sel. Cttee., index and analysis of evidence.

Police Volume 9

REPORTS RELATING TO THE POLICE SYSTEM IN SCOTLAND AND POLICE SUPERANNUATION FUNDS IN ENGLAND AND WALES, 1867–1875

The Select Committee of the House of Lords which examined the police system in Scotland heard evidence from Chief Constables and Justices of the Peace on all aspects of law enforcement. Three main problems were considered by the committee: how many police forces should Scotland have; who was to control the police forces; and how were adequate pensions for retired constables to be financed. The evidence presented to the committee supported the view that the smaller forces should be amalgamated. There was general support for the introduction of a police superannuation fund which would be a charge on public funds. The committee recommended that control of police forces should be vested in Police Committees instead of Justices of the Peace. They suggested that the duties of Procurators Fiscal and Chief Constables should be carefully defined in order to prevent any overlap of duties.

The Select Committee of the House of Commons on police superannuation funds heard evidence on police duties from all grades of
police officers. Witnesses stressed that good pay and conditions were
necessary to induce men to join the force. Details of the unsatisfactory state of the existing pension scheme was given. This scheme
was financed by deductions from constables' pay, by fines, and by
the sale of discarded uniforms. It provided an inadequate fund and
pensions were very low as a result.

Original references

1867–68	(486) IX	County and burgh police systems of Scotland, Sel. Cttee. HL. Rep., mins. of ev., appendix.
	(486–I)	County and burgh police systems of Scotland, Sel. Cttee. HL. Rep., index.
1875	(352) XIII	Police Superannuation Funds, Sel. Cttee. Rep., mins. of ev., appendix and index.

Police Volume 10

REPORTS RELATING TO POLICE WITH MINUTES OF EVIDENCE,
APPENDICES AND INDICES, 1877–1892

The reports deal with many aspects of the administration of British
police forces in the last quarter of the nineteenth century. Several
committees examined proposals to improve the police pension
scheme. Evidence was given by chief constables on the increasing
need to recruit well-educated entrants due to the growing complexity
of police work. They felt that only by the provision of secure pension-
able employment could such men be recruited. Details of police
training and methods of working were provided in evidence. Of
special interest are descriptions of methods employed by the police
to prevent road accidents. The evidence tells of the growing involve-
ment of the police in work unconnected with crime, such as accident
prevention and of the improved status of the police officer who was
now regarded as a friend of the people rather than as a government
spy. The committee's recommendations stressed the desirability of
providing reasonable pensions financed by rates and government
contributions. They urged that the smaller forces should be amalgamated to form forces of a more efficient size. The volume includes
reports from British representatives abroad dealing with the control
and organization of police forces in Europe and in the United
States of America.

Original references

1877	(158) XV	Police Superannuation Fund, Sel. Cttee. Rep., mins. of ev., appendix and index.

1886	[C.4894] XXXIV	Administration and organization of the metropolitan police force, Cttee. Rep.
1889	(264) IX	City of London Police Bill (pensions), Sel. Cttee. Rep., mins of ev., appendix and index.
1890	(324) XVII	Police (Scotland) (Pensions, etc.) Bill, Sel. Cttee. Rep., mins. of ev., appendix and index.
1890	[C.6065] LIX	Police Bill, 1890, Explanatory Memorandum.
	[C.6075]	Metropolitan Police Superannuation, papers and notes of ev.
1892	[C.6749] LXXIX	Control and organization of the Police (Foreign Countries). H.M. Representatives abroad, Reps.

Index